A SEARCH FOR FAIRNESS

Volume II

A SEARCH FOR FAIRNESS
IN FINANCIAL
REPORTING
TO THE PUBLIC
Volume II

Selected addresses and articles by

LEONARD SPACEK

1969-1973

This book contains addresses and articles by one of the leaders of the firm of Arthur Andersen & Co. A list of the volumes prepared in this manner follows:

Title	Author
Behind the Figures	Arthur Andersen
A Search for Fairness in Financial Reporting to the Public (Volume I)	Leonard Spacek
Footsteps Toward Professionalism	Joseph S. Glickauf
In Pursuit of Professional Goals	George R. Catlett and Norman O. Olson
A Search for Fairness in Financial Reporting to the Public (Volume II)	Leonard Spacek

Foreword

I N 1969 when we published Leonard Spacek's book, *A Search for Fairness in Financial Reporting to the Public,* it was inconceivable to most of us that Leonard would actually be leaving the firm four years later at age 65. But that is his decision, and the parting date is July 1, 1973.

As a farewell gesture of appreciation of his tremendous service to the firm, we are publishing some of his more important speeches and articles of the last four years in this, the second and his last, volume in the series of *A Search for Fairness.*

PAUL D. WILLIAMS

LEONARD SPACEK

About Leonard Spacek

Leonard Spacek will retire as an active partner on July 1, 1973. As he approaches a transition in his life from active participation in our firm, it is time for reflection by his associates, who have known him not only in a business capacity but also as a friend. The words, search for fairness, were selected by Leonard as a title for both this book and his previous book, and these words put his life in perspective better than any others that could be chosen.

This search has had a great impact on all who have been fortunate enough to have been associated with him. If he is given good health in the years ahead, we all know that his search is not over. Although this search has resulted in the development of our organization, it was never planned to achieve size or prestige, but resulted from an abiding dedication to the idea of fairness: fairness to all of his associates, from office boys to senior partners; fairness in speaking out on what was right in his chosen profession, even when under heavy criticism by his contemporaries; fairness in all his advice, counsel and relationships with clients; and, most important, fairness in all of his human relationships.

Leonard was born in 1907 in Cedar Rapids, Iowa; shortly thereafter his mother became seriously ill and was hospitalized for many years. His father and two brothers lived on a farm until the family income became insufficient to maintain the home, and from the time Leonard was eight years old until he was thirteen he lived with farm families in the neighborhood, working for his board doing farm chores mornings and evenings and going to school during the day. About the time he entered high school, his father moved into Cedar Rapids. At various times Leonard had paper routes, worked in a garage as a tool boy, and operated a bicycle shop.

In 1924, at the age of seventeen, he went to work for Iowa Electric Light and Power Company in their accounting department. By 1925 he had completed his evening high school courses and started on some evening courses at Coe College in Cedar Rapids. The experiences of his early years undoubtedly formed a basic personal dedication and understanding of life from which to start a professional career and "a search for fairness."

On December 1, 1928, the fifteenth anniversary of our firm, he joined the staff of the Chicago office of Arthur Andersen & Co. He was admitted to partnership in 1940, and demonstrated unusual competence, integrity and overall concern for fairness as partner in charge of our utility practice and later in charge of the Chicago office.

With Arthur Andersen's death in 1947 a serious question mark hung over the firm; could it survive without its founder, could it maintain its reputation, and especially could it continue to grow? Many partners were involved in bringing the firm through this period of crisis, but Leonard was the leader and prime mover. His foresight and courage as the new managing partner not only brought the firm through this difficult period but carried it to a level even he could not have anticipated. Many of the fundamental concepts of the firm were Arthur Andersen's, but

Leonard added many of his own and put them into a framework that provided the firm with a sound philosophical basis. But always as he developed these concepts, worked with the younger people, worked with clients, or spoke out for improvement in the accounting profession, out in front was the ideal of fairness.

Many of the ideas which he has put forward, although not immediately accepted, have stood the test of fairness, with his partners, his supporters and even his critics. These ideas were the result of hours of thinking, discussion and argument with his partners, who had great confidence in his leadership. All of us have been proud of his forward thinking, his willingness to break with the crowd when he thought he was right and his ability to stand alone without arrogance or reliance on position when he concluded that his answer to the issue was fair to all involved.

His pattern for the accounting profession and accounting principles and his leadership in changing the course of the profession can be evaluated only by future generations. I am confident that the ideas, thoughts and suggestions contained in these two volumes will stand the test of time. Hopefully, the search for fairness will never end. New approaches, new concerns for financial reporting will be required and others will take up the search. Leonard's greatest contribution to his firm, his partners and his profession may well be in developing a philosophy that there is a never-ending search for fairness.

HARVEY KAPNICK

April 3, 1973

Contents

Selected Addresses and Articles by Leonard Spacek, 1969-1973

The merger accounting dilemma— proposed solutions

Before the American Bar Association
National Institute, New York,
October 23, 1969

The problem of accounting for business combinations involves more basic concepts than any other problem which has ever faced the business community and the accounting profession. It highlights in an embarrassing way the current deficiencies in accounting.

What is a conglomerate?

As NEARLY AS I CAN determine, a conglomerate is any company that one might choose to single out and label "conglomerate." More precisely, the current press identifies as a conglomerate any company which has made several acquisitions in recent years.

Actually, almost every one of today's corporate giants is the product of one or more mergers. Without these mergers, our nation's capacity to produce goods and services would very likely be only a fraction of today's production. That limited capacity would be divided among many weak corporations. To have effective competition we must match the competitors. Our present Justice Department policy does not result in this kind of competition. Companies that became giants in the past are allowed to remain giants, but mergers that would create a fair competitive matching with those giants are not allowed.

Mergers are like fires; they furnish the power for progress, but they also possess the power to destroy. Our society needs proper guidance for mergers, not a quenching of them, if we are to achieve sound economic progress.

Conglomerates and the status quo

We might define a conglomerate as a multimarket company that operates through many individual entities. Chart A, on the following page, shows the multimarkets and operating entities of *Fortune's* list of the 500 largest manufacturing companies.

Only the starred companies have been classified by *Fortune* as "conglomerates." Conglomerate connotation ordinarily starts with companies serving three markets or more. If this is a fair demarcation we must

CHART A

PRODUCT MARKETS/OPERATING ENTITIES FOR *FORTUNE'S* 500 INDUSTRIALS
AND CERTAIN CONGLOMERATES

4/16	3/27*	1/15	4/20	3/29	4/35	2/22	4/8	4/15	1/54
9/13*	4/30	7/73	2/33	1/4	2/14	3/60	2/12	1/74	2/4
4/135	5/130	1/73	1/11	2/9	2/49	4/66	3/4	2/11	1/17
2/18	2/10	3/8	2/7	2/54	12/8*	3/16	1/3	4/8	1/49
2/50	4/7	8/9*	1/23	1/14	4/6	11/40*	6/126	4/24	2/8
3/31	4/34	6/69	3/29	1/21	2/8	1/4	4/9	3/19	4/46
4/13	3/3	5/28	4/6	1/36	3/39	1/12	3/7	2/16	5/5
2/15	1/61	2/13	2/3	3/46	4/10	1/2	3/18	2/14	3/19
2/6	5/19	2/52	4/19	3/17	3/5	1/18	3/11	2/23	4/15
1/22	5/62*	3/17	6/44	5/24	3/8	7/28	2/13	3/58	3/53
4/5	2/10	10/16	3/31	2/13	5/10	4/28	3/78	4/13	5/54
4/31	4/14	5/160	2/23	3/42	4/15	8/53	4/28	2/20	3/18
4/13	5/17	4/19	2/1	2/9	2/9	2/7	1/40	2/48	5/4*
6/14	3/42	1/3	6/59	4/42	6/30	4/13	3/28	6/6*	3/13
2/75	2/48	6/49	3/15	3/21	1/25	2/7	4/6	3/18	4/24
6/51	2/20	6/9	1/9	2/5	1/3	2/5	1/9	2/9	2/9
6/46	4/13	3/52	2/24	3/8	1/12	3/29	6/8	6/13	1/15
5/18	5/172	1/67	2/19	1/22	3/29	8/10*	4/27	3/20	2/180
3/40	2/7	1/34	2/84	6/30*	5/37	2/97	4/102	2/5	1/3
1/5	1/22	2/17	2/5	4/152	7/39*	2/3	2/12	2/24	1/13
2/10	5/11	1/73	2/3	1/18	6/49	3/12	2/16	2/4	3/22
5/14	1/6	3/29	3/9	1/3	4/6	3/11	3/19	1/12	2/8
2/8	3/12	1/58	4/8	2/22	4/13	3/35	3/26	3/4	3/31
1/13	2/52	2/96	5/13	11/285*	1/3	4/6	4/44	2/45	1/14
1/10	4/24	1/19	5/16	1/4	1/5	1/8	1/12	2/12	2/5
5/13	2/44	3/12	4/6	3/70*	3/35	1/8	4/31	6/37	2/10
4/14	1/40	4/21	4/35*	3/17	1/37	3/5	4/10	1/22	2/18
3/18	4/6	1/4	1/3	3/11	10/19	2/24	1/1	4/29	4/45
7/5	4/36	10/73	2/127	6/13	6/34	6/35	2/19	3/26	3/3
3/65	6/44	2/6	8/102	2/24	3/10	1/2	2/5	4/13	10/1
12/44*	8/14	4/25	3/74	7/20	6/46	4/29	6/11	6/14	4/35
1/1	1/9	3/9	4/45	5/110	4/9	5/15	3/53	6/9	8/97
4/2	5/14	3/10	6/30	3/17	12/14	3/16	4/22	6/22	9/41
4/22	9/9	7/6	2/1	10/15	3/15	6/24	5/9	3/22	2/10
3/66	6/11	7/29	4/18	3/6	4/34	3/5	4/7	6/46	3/14
6/21	9/26*	4/1	1/5	8/40	7/42	4/6	2/30	4/49	2/10
5/13	7/39	2/18	3/10	1/15	17/82	8/14	7/27	5/131	6/8
6/37	3/5	5/12	2/5	5/7	6/44	5/15	7/55	5/46	5/41
7/24	9/1	3/15	5/17	4/30	5/24	4/10	7/6	3/10	10/54*
9/98	3/35	5/43	5/16	7/55	5/10	10/179	9/25	5/134	8/6
1/13	5/38	5/32	4/26	6/52	5/22	2/15	7/21	4/42	6/55
5/2	3/53*	8/26	5/48	2/13	4/33	4/14	5/8	2/24	4/20
3/9	6/2	3/9	5/5	6/21	5/38	3/5	8/12	4/13	3/3
5/12	5/6	4/91	9/30	2/21	4/7	4/41	6/19	4/27	9/15*
1/21	3/7	4/17	3/11	5/9	4/23	3/17	6/12*	9/36	5/15*
13/20	5/18	4/12	5/15	10/13	5/13	3/6	2/14	7/18	5/7
3/8	5/8	3/6	1/13	2/5	4/10	1/16	1/1	2/11	5/4
1/20	1/2	3/6	2/9	1/2	2/1	1/4	1/24	3/14	6/29
1/22	3/8	1/7	5/64	4/22	6/10	4/11	5/23*	4/15	3/25
2/4	3/8	7/11*	2/7	4/13	7/7	8/15*	4/44	3/2	5/9
4/7	3/16	2/36	1/5	5/31	4/27	3/7	2/8	3/80	5/25
4/7	5/8	6/27	2/3	4/36	8/10				

*Conglomerates, including those in *Fortune* 500.

2

conclude that two thirds of the entire list are actually conglomerates.

The label "conglomerate" is used by some as a derogatory term to apply to a company whose acquisitions have interfered with our status quo. What we today call conglomerates have essentially the same nature as most other large companies insofar as their historical formation and financial problems are concerned.

Accounting options available to conglomerates are also available to others

Contrary to widespread impressions, the accounting options available to conglomerates are no different from those available to other companies. Criticism of conglomerates for electing to follow undesirable accounting alternatives is not fair, when such alternatives are equally available to, and have been utilized by, other companies.

The financial press has stated that the accountants are going to tighten their accounting rules to make mergers more difficult. Here we need to make one point crystal clear—an absolute prerequisite to the existence of the public accounting profession is that no accounting principle should possess a bias for or against any business transaction, any industry, or any legal corporate activity. Any other position eliminates the objectivity of the opinions of the public accountant. Accounting principles must have only one objective, and that is to communicate to the reader of a financial report the economic facts surrounding transactions that occur. That objective does not include passing judgment on whether the transaction should have occurred.

Why is conglomerate accounting criticized more than the accounting for other companies?

Conglomerates have been subject to severe criticism for the manner in which they have accounted for mergers. The true basis for this criticism lies in merger accounting

deficiencies, and these are often compounded for conglomerates simply because of the greater number of their acquisitions. If a company makes five acquisitions, the deficiencies in merger accounting occur five times. The effect is bound to be more visible and thus more subject to criticism. However, the deficiencies in merger accounting have had equal or even more pronounced effects on investors in companies not ordinarily classified as conglomerates.

Criticisms of merger accounting

Two basic options are available in accounting for a merger; these are pooling-of-interests accounting and purchase accounting. The major criticisms of merger accounting, most of which stem from the pooling concept, are as follows:

First, the differences between pooling and purchase accounting are not and cannot be understood by the public. To the public an acquired company is generally being taken over by the acquiring company, whether the merger is called a pooling or a purchase. The stockholders of the acquiring company now own another type of business, and a purchase and sale have taken place regardless of what we call the transaction or how we choose to account for it.

Second, an option is available to account for a stock-for-stock merger either as a purchase or as a pooling. This option enables companies to avoid the unfavorable consequences of either method, thereby compounding misunderstanding. For example, when the book value of the acquired company exceeds the value of stock consideration given, a choice may be made to account for the merger either as a purchase or as a pooling. Many times purchase accounting is elected, since that method gives rise to a credit referred to as "negative" goodwill. Under purchase accounting this credit is often amortized to income over a short period, thereby creating instant earnings. The result is the same as amortizing some of the equity of the acquired company into income.

Third, the option to account for a stock-for-stock combination as a pooling results in a number of abuses. Some of these are:

a. Instant profits are created on a retroactive basis by pretending that the two merged companies have always been one company. Stockholders ask why historical earnings of the acquirer are different after a stock-for-stock merger from those previously reported. No such difference arises when a company is acquired from the proceeds of a sale of stock. Why must the acquirer bury its own earnings performance and pad its earnings with those of the acquired company, one with which there had been no connection prior to the acquisition?

b. Since pooling assumes the two companies have always been together, acquisitions made subsequent to the annual report date are included in reported earnings for the prior reporting period. This result is contrary to the facts. In this way the record of how the acquirer performed alone is buried even deeper.

c. Pooling accounting carries forward the book values of the acquired company's assets into the accounts of the acquiring company. In recent times the current values of many assets have been much greater than their book values. If such assets are sold after the merger, huge profits are recorded, when such profits actually were paid for by the acquirer in the consideration given in stock. Is this not reporting the proceeds of the issuance of capital stock as income?

d. To compound the readers' confusion, in some mergers both cash and stock are given as consideration, and these are accounted for as part pooling and part purchase. It is impossible to apply the marriage philosophy to explain this procedure. The accounting results yielded by this approach must be virtually incomprehensible to everyone.

Fourth, and a final criticism made of merger accounting, is that in a purchase recognition is given to the total value of the acquired enterprise, including its goodwill. The difference between the fair value of the separable resources and property rights of the company and total value of consideration given in exchange is labeled purchased goodwill and recorded as an asset. The goodwill may remain on the balance sheet forever or by option be written off over some arbitrary period. What is the meaning of such an item on the balance sheet? What current useful information does it convey? What is the nature of charges to income for its amortization? Knowledgeable investors and analysts remove this item from financial statements. The accounting profession has been justly criticized for its bookkeeping approach to this item. Incidentally, the goodwill problem can be evaded completely by merging the acquiring company into the acquired company following a cash acquisition. The goodwill disappears under the guise of being part of the cost of the acquired company in buying up its own stock.

Each of the above criticisms is valid, and present merger accounting needs to be changed in order to eliminate such criticisms and restore stockholder confidence in the reported results.

What were objectives of pooling?

The pooling concept was officially authorized in 1950. Prior to that date, mergers were made in such a way that no goodwill arose, or if it did arise, existing accounting principles permitted a write-off of goodwill to surplus. Goodwill was properly evaluated then as being a function of stock market valuation and not a matter for financial statement presentation. Goodwill was written off, not because it had lost its value, but because the amount on the balance sheet was not a fair representation of the goodwill value of any company.

Likewise, in 1945, because of the various arbitrary write-ups during the pre-1933 period, the distinction between "earned surplus" and capital was very jealously guarded. On January 20, 1945, the SEC issued its Accounting Series Release No. 50 which said that henceforth no goodwill could be written off to capital surplus. This was a declaratory requirement without reason or support.

At that time the term "economic merger" or "pooling of interests" was invented. The purpose of the invention was two-fold: first, to avoid recording goodwill and, second, to carry forward earned surplus.

We should note here a condition present in 1945 which is vastly different today. The probability of fair values of assets being different from their costs in 1945 was practically nil. The Consumer's Price Index in 1944 was 60.9 as compared to 61.9 in 1921 —twenty years before. The American Appraisal Construction Cost Index in 1944 was 38.6 and in 1921, 31.7. The absence of revaluation of physical assets was of practically no concern when the pooling-of-interests concept originated. The accounting profession and the SEC accepted the concept in order to carry through historical costs and earned surplus and thereby to avoid the recognition of goodwill on the balance sheet.

Criteria of pooling

To establish "pooling," four criteria were more or less contrived to represent the intellectual support for such accounting. They were continuity of substantially the same proportionate equity interests, relative size, continuity of management, and similar or complementary activities.

The primary objectives of pooling were not supported by the criteria devised. These four criteria were arbitrary, and were not relevant to the accounting for mergers or to the objectives of the pooling concept. Such criteria were bound to deteriorate. Account-

ing for mergers resulted in financial statements not at all representative of the merger transaction.

The retroactive marriage illusion and the continuity of ownership criterion

Under the continuity of ownership concept, all the conditions of each corporate partner that existed before the marriage were carried forward into the resulting unit. From this concept it was reasoned that the marriage was consummated as of the original date of each corporation's existence. The marriage once made was retroactive to date of birth. This concept is responsible for many of the criticisms and errors of pooling. It justified—even demanded—a retroactive combination of earnings as though the companies had always been together. The concept is simply contrary to all the facts.

The retroactive combination of financial statements severed the continuity of accountability between management and the stockholders of the continuing enterprise. The means of measurement of management's achievements through business acquisitions was destroyed. Stockholders cannot and could not understand assumptions which they knew to be contrary to facts.

The SEC bolstered the illusion of continuity by requiring the major stockholders of one of the companies merged to remain as stockholders for two years. No similar requirement was imposed on the major stockholders of the other member of the merger. This contrived ownership criterion was an interpretation of the concept which stated: "In a pooling of interests, all or substantially all of the equity interest in predecessor corporations continue. . . ."

If the SEC's rule of continued ownership for two years was meaningful for one of the predecessor corporations, it was equally as meaningful for both. If applicable to both members of the merger then major stockholders of both had to be locked in, and the

major ownership of either member could
not materially change for two years. Also, if
this applied forward why would not it apply
backward?

Thus, one artificial assumption or rule
followed another until their compound effect
was to bring all poolings into disrepute.

Relative-size criterion

The relative-size criterion reflected the
original concept that only corporations of
comparable size would qualify as merger
candidates. This concept overlooked the
fact that the 1934 tax law, which gave birth
to stock-for-stock, tax-free mergers, made
no distinction between corporations on the
basis of their relative size. It was this tax
law that encouraged mergers accounted for
as "poolings of interests."

The size of a corporation should not
affect the accounting principle applicable to
the facts of any transaction. The economics
of a transaction are not changed by reason
of corporate size. This size criterion never
did and never could support an accounting
principle and never should have been listed
as a prerequisite to pooling accounting; consequently its deterioration was inevitable. In
accounting, equity cannot tolerate a different applicability for a small company
than for a large company or for any combination of sizes.

Deterioration of the size criterion helped
bring poolings into disrepute.

Management-continuity criterion

Fundamental to all accounting principles
is the underlying requirement that proper
reporting must ignore "who" the personality
is behind any transaction. If ever the
accounting profession erected a false god it
was in adopting the management continuity
criterion.

This criterion states, "Similarly, the continuity of management or the power to
control management is involved. Thus, if

management of one of the constituents is
eliminated or its influence upon overall
management of the enterprise is very small,
a purchase may be indicated."

This was pure rhetoric. It must have been
plain to see that no one could apply that
criterion in any meaningful way with any
basis for reliable checking. Furthermore,
corporate operations are perpetual, assuming conditions permit. Management's life is
related to human life that ends or changes
without notice over a very limited span of
years. Management's life cannot be controlled by any merger agreement. Even
management contracts do not assure management; they assure employment and sal-
ary. This criterion was, and is, pure window
dressing.

Complementary-activities criterion

The complementary-activities criterion
attempted to deny pooling accounting for a
merger transaction if the combined companies would involve several market products. It implied that if one side of a merger
involved a restaurant and the other a steel
mill, a particular accounting principle could
not be applied in the same way that it would
if the transaction occurred between two
restaurants or two steel mills. This is obviously absurd.

This criterion had no effect, and could
have none, on accounting for mergers. It
soon disappeared as an applicable criterion
for pooling accounting.

What went wrong?

Any chance that pooling might have had
of evolving as a useful accounting concept
was eliminated by the deterioration of the
contrived criteria that fronted for the objectives of such accounting. Since the genuine
objectives of pooling were never honestly
put forward, it was natural for everyone to
take the stage backdrops—the criteria—at
face value. We were all led into the never,
never land of preposterous assumptions. To
stockholders these assumptions were contra-

dictory to facts, could not be understood in their theoretical framework, and thus were not accepted.

Acquiring a "going concern"
is not the same as acquiring
individual assets

When first adopted, pooling provided an accounting procedure to combine "going-concern organizations" composed of "established working units" dedicated as a whole to specific business or production functions. A contrast to pooling would be the accounting for building a similar organization by buying or selling individual machines, securing customers, obtaining financing, getting officers and employees, and obtaining all of the elements of a viable organization working in coordination.

Pooling provided an accounting procedure for the second step of growth in our economic system, growth through the combination of unit enterprises into organizations with greater productive capacity. These enterprises contained elements of value that could not be identified with and were not applicable to the individual properties of which they were comprised. Those values related to going organizations.

Thus, the value of a combination of corporate entities already established is not the same as the value of the aggregate of the individual items necessary to build those entities. A different accounting was devised to communicate these economic facts to public stockholders. The stockholders of each member were involved and each had to see how the operating units went together if they were to have the knowledge to vote on the combination under the stock-for-stock, tax-free exchanges that came into being in 1934.

In the final analysis, an accurate conveyance of economic facts to stockholders in financial reporting is the one and only objective of public accounting reports. Such reporting must reflect the substance of the economic facts in a manner that stock-

holders can readily understand, whether they be sophisticated or unsophisticated. The unsophisticated stockholder should have the same chance at understanding as the sophisticated. Therefore, communication must be made as clear and as simple as possible. In the final analysis, the public stockholder is entitled to a statement of principles that applies to all corporate combinations, whether we technicians call them pooling, purchase, or acquisition.

When pooling came on the scene in 1945, price levels had been constant for twenty years. Asset book values and fair values were not significantly different for many companies, and pooling accounting attained the communication objectives to a reasonable degree. Assets other than goodwill could be accepted at book amounts in combination, harm no one, and be understandable to the public.

Accountability of "going organizations" is different from the accountability for a lathe in a workshop. The accounting for a combination of going organizations must transfer the going value of any eliminated corporation into the acquiring corporation on a basis consistent with the way going value is always determined by the stockholder, that is, at the market value of his stock. A going, viable corporate organization may not be accounted for simply as individual pieces of property, liabilities, and personnel. These items are to the going organization value what a grocery list is to a final delectable meal. Going value is what happened in putting the pieces together—and that value is based on opinion of value, and not on any mathematical calculation. Thus, a living corporate organization cannot be valued as the sum total of the physical parts that comprise it.

What causes our major accounting
problem in corporation combinations?

While we strive to make truth and usefulness of accounting statements the underlying foundations of financial reports, we have had and still have accounting concepts which "grew up" from proprietary ownership and which are not properly related to accountability of assets to absentee owners. These erroneously based concepts of accounting for both assets and liabilities result in major errors in the balance sheet, including the carrying amounts for assets. Because of conservatism and other factors which may have been desirable at one time but are now no longer defensible, the increases in value of assets are not recognized by capitalizing the costs which create such values.

Higher asset values are created in corporations than the amounts at which assets are carried in the balance sheet, primarily because of improper cost accounting; and these deficiencies have not been given sufficient recognition. However, these deficiencies become obvious when a business combination occurs. The owners of the acquired corporation demand recognition of full value whether or not the cost of assets has been properly capitalized.

The accounting principles that result in understating the carrying value of assets are largely responsible for the variations in value that arise in combinations of corporations. If all costs incurred in the acquisition and development of assets were capitalized on a reasonably accurate basis and if price-level accounting were applied to those costs, balance sheets would contain amounts for assets much closer to the value of the assets. In many cases, these amounts would be the best evidence of value that could be established for those assets.

The assets that cause the great difficulty in business combinations are those which have been arbitrarily understated by cost accounting practices (not principles) that have been accepted because they are conservative and produce offsets within the income account that can be tolerated. However, the error accumulating in the balance sheet becomes evident when a combination occurs. This understatement arises from

noncapitalization of proper costs in many areas, such as (a) indirect items relating to construction of plant, (b) discoveries, development and growth of all natural resources, (c) product development, and (d) LIFO inventory. If these items were properly accounted for, the adjustments needed at the time of business combinations would be much less significant and would not occur very frequently.

Since 1945, when pooling was first undertaken, price levels have soared, while prior to that date they had not changed materially for 20 years. Every year since 1945 has produced a substantial increase in all price levels which in turn reflects itself in current values. This is shown by the following changes since 1945:

(1) Consumers Price Index has doubled to 125.

(2) American Appraisal Construction Index has gone up almost four times to 147.4.

(3) Price Inflator Index has increased twice to 126.5.

(4) Dow-Jones Industrial stock market average has gone from 152 to over 800, or an increase of over 5 times.

The changes in price levels, coupled with deficiencies in accounting whereby costs are not properly capitalized, make the carrying amounts for many assets in financial statements misleading and void of usefulness. The carrying amounts are far removed from current realities and present-day values. We are not confronted in a dramatic way with the accumulation of these errors until a combination occurs. Then the inadequacies in our accounting become obvious.

Our objective should be to improve cost accounting principles, so that both parties to a business combination would have a proper cost evaluation of assets. We should not need to rely on the "new-start" principle for an acquired business to clean up past errors and thereby try to adopt proper cost principles on a retroactive basis. We must have principles for combinations that stockholders can understand as well as a procedure for stopping the constant accumulations of accounting errors in the carrying amounts of companies' assets. Then we can meet the combination problem directly and honestly without using the "new-start" theory as a camouflage to cover up our past errors.

If proper cost accounting principles were established to handle research and development costs, development of natural resources, carrying cost of plant during construction, carrying cost of long-term investments on an equity basis, proper tax allocation, carrying marketable securities at market value, etc., the problems we are facing today in the combination of corporations would be much less significant.

Price-level accounting could readily apply to both companies in a combination. If price-level statements had been properly used in the financial statements to stockholders up to this date, they would understand the meaning of the statements. In this manner, stockholders could instantly see how the accounts of a combined company would start. Now, however, we must work with deficient accounts for both the buyer and the seller. We should set up a procedure whereby as the cost accounting principles are improved, the proper accounting for combinations becomes effective. The Accounting Principles Board should commit itself to the rapid correction of our basic accounting principles, particularly as they relate to proper costs.

Solution to problem must take all relevant factors into account

The question before the accounting profession today is: What can reasonably be done within the framework of the basic accounting concepts and principles which presently exist, to make the necessary corrections in accounting for business combinations and to correct the most serious "abuses" which exist? Also, how can the solution be a forthright step forward toward eventual improvement of our concepts and principles and at the same time not appear to be simply a device to use the solution to the business combination problem as a "devious back door" to progress?

My associates and I have been studying this problem carefully and thoughtfully for several years. We are well aware of the practical and theoretical aspects of this complex problem. We are also cognizant of the difficulties in trying to make changes which have very far-reaching effects. Therefore, my recommendation to the Accounting Principles Board for action now would be as follows:

(1) Establish objectives for accounting and financial statement presentation that would lead to the establishment of accounting principles whereby the carrying amount of assets would include all of those costs incurred in establishing those assets and bring the carrying amount as close as feasible to value.

(2) Adopt the basic conclusions of AICPA Accounting Research Study No. 10 whereby—

(a) The concept of pooling of interests as we now know it, would be eliminated.

(b) Business combinations would be accounted for as acquisitions.

(c) Acquired goodwill would be shown as a reduction of stockholder equity at date of acquisition.

(3) In recognition of the fact that the accounting deficiencies I have referred to above lead to grossly understated amounts at which certain assets are carried, and in view of the necessity that these deficiencies be corrected in a forthright manner rather than having such significant adjustments result

only at the time of a business combination (and for only one member of that combination), temporary exceptions should be made to permit carrying through the recorded amounts for such assets pending the necessary corrections by the accounting profession to the original accounting for these types of assets. These exceptions would be:

(a) No recognition of increased value of LIFO inventories until such adjustment for accounting purposes is permitted by the Internal Revenue Code and required generally for corporate reporting.

(b) No recognition of price-level adjustment of plant and property until such adjustments are required generally for corporate accounting.

(c) No recognition of increased value over recorded cost for natural resources held and sold in the ordinary course of business until changes are made in generally accepted accounting principles to require proper accounting for costs incurred to enhance natural resource values.

To those who say these exceptions are fundamental to a "new start," let me emphasize that they have not been fundamental for the past twenty years of accounting. Further, the items exempted have not created any of the abuses of pooling. Assets other than those exempted have distorted mergers and have been responsible for abuses, and abuses arising in the past from such assets would be eliminated. The corrections relating to these exceptions are needed for the accounting of all corporations, regardless of whether such corporations are involved in mergers.

(4) Inventories should generally be carried forward on the same basis they will be accounted for by the acquiring company. Also, for acquired plant and equipment, it would not be necessary to make minor adjustments which would exist in many cases.

(5) Any profit from the sale of the acquired assets of the type referred to in (3) above, outside of the ordinary business operations, should be credited directly to retained earnings during the three years subsequent to date of acquisition. (This period is arbitrary, but it is intended to avoid what has sometimes been referred to as "instant earnings.")

(6) Financial reports of the acquiring or continuing corporation should include pro forma income accounts for the last year (or possibly two). Such pro forma report would give effect to a full year's operation of all acquisitions consummated prior to the date of the report issued. An additional pro forma income account should include acquisitions consummated after the annual report date. Income accounts of years prior to the last year or two should be provided in footnotes, or the net income should be added separately to reported net income of the acquirer. The SEC has recently required disclosures of this type for actual corporate earnings and retroactive pro forma accounts.

During the balance of this paper, I will discuss these recommendations further (particularly as related to goodwill) and explain my reasoning in support of them.

Goodwill not an acceptable asset for financial statements

Goodwill is, and always has been, at the heart of the business-combination problem. It has plagued the accounting profession for many years, and the problem cannot be solved under existing accounting concepts.

Goodwill is not an acceptable asset for inclusion in financial statements because it reflects a judgment derived in part from those financial statements. If goodwill were to be recognized in the financial statements, certainly the recognition must necessarily include all the corporate goodwill. To record as goodwill only the portion related to one specific unit of operation in a corporate combination is to make the financial statements untrue and lopsided on two counts:

(1) The goodwill value determined at any one particular date is not applicable to another date, as would be the case with the cost of a lathe, a computer, a house, etc. The latter are products of an engineering and manufacturing process that can be readily duplicated at approximately the same cost, if adjusted for price level. Goodwill cannot be duplicated from engineering drawings; rather, it is the judgment of investors of the stock in terms of market value. Consequently, goodwill is only as stable as the composite views of investors of the stock of the company involved.

(2) Goodwill of an acquired company, recognized by an acquiring corporation, cannot be placed on its balance sheet and be represented as being all of the acquirer's goodwill. Such a representation would be untrue. That amount is only part of the acquirer's goodwill, never all.

No corporate balance sheet that includes only a fractional part of the company's goodwill, without providing stockholders' information concerning the unrecorded goodwill, should be represented to stockholders as exhibiting the fair financial position. The total goodwill could be approximated for this purpose by adding to the amount recorded the unrecorded goodwill represented by the excess of market value over book value of equity. This, however, would be meaningless to a reader. The goodwill amount would have changed, possibly greatly, by the time the report reached the investor. Further, it is not a financial statement objective to present such information. Rather, financial statements should present financial information which the investor may use in his determinations of goodwill values. Thus, goodwill was not, and is not, an eligible asset for the balance sheet, even though it may be the most important asset to the investor or stockholder.

The importance of goodwill as an asset varies with every company. A company may have no goodwill value or an amount of goodwill many times greater than its producing assets. Chart B is a random sample of *Fortune's* 500 largest industrial companies showing the amount and importance of goodwill in 1950 and in 1969 as related to the net book value of all other assets.

CHART B

Company	Goodwill Value In Relation to Book Value of Net Assets	
	1950	1969
1.	2.00x	3.50x
2.	Neg.	Neg.
3.	1.00x	7.00x
4.	Neg.	.50x
5.	Neg.	Neg.
6.	Neg.	2.00x
7.	Neg.	2.00x
8.	Neg.	Neg.
9.	Neg.	Neg.
10.	.25x	.50x
11.	.50x	7.00x
12.	.25x	8.00x
13.	Neg.	2.00x
14.	.50x	2.00x
15.	.25x	Neg.
16.	3.50x	9.00x
17.	.50x	Neg.
18.	1.50x	5.25x
19.	Neg.	Neg.
20.	1.50x	1.00x
21.	3.00x	1.50x
22.	1.00x	5.50x
23.	.50x	3.00x
24.	Neg.	.50x
25.	1.00x	2.00x
26.	1.00x	1.75x
27.	3.25x	1.25x
28.	2.00x	5.75x
29.	Neg.	1.00x
30.	Neg.	.50x
31.	Neg.	1.25x
32.	.25x	Neg.

Company	Goodwill Value In Relation to Book Value of Net Assets	
	1950	1969
33.	2.75x	7.50x
34.	.75x	6.50x
35.	.75x	.50x
36.	Neg.	1.00x
37.	Neg.	.50x
38.	1.00x	3.25x
39.	Neg.	4.00x
40.	1.75x	8.00x
41.	2.00x	5.75x
42.	1.25x	1.75x
43.	Neg.	2.25x
44.	1.25x	1.00x
45.	1.50x	3.25x
46.	1.50x	2.50x
47.	.50x	1.75x
48.	Neg.	1.25x
49.	Neg.	.50x
50.	Neg.	2.25x
51.	Neg.	.50x
52.	1.75x	6.00x
53.	.75x	1.00x
54.	1.50x	.50x
55.	3.75x	1.50x
56.	Neg.	1.50x
57.	Neg.	.75x
58.	1.50x	1.00x
59.	1.50x	1.25x
60.	.25x	.25x

(neg. = negative goodwill)

Out of these 60 companies in 1969, 41 had goodwill value equal to, or greater than, net book value of assets. Several had goodwill as high as 7 to 9 times net book value of assets.

Any attempt by accountants or managements even to pretend to account for goodwill value, what gives rise to it, and what life it may have, would involve a miraculous achievement. Such effort should be their primary occupation—it is that important. In terms of value, goodwill is many times more important than all other net assets of many corporations. Yet, it is a product of the operating unit of all net assets represented by "net book value"—if no goodwill is recorded.

Pooling provided a way to circumvent the SEC's Accounting Release No. 50, eliminate goodwill from the balance sheet, and thus provide meaningful financial statements to the investor.

The wide application of pooling and the charge-off of goodwill to capital and earned surplus prior to 1945 have created the generally clean corporate balance sheets free of goodwill today. Can it be said that this absence of "goodwill" on corporate balance sheets has been wrong or misleading for the last twenty years? I know of no meaningful single criticism that the removal of this goodwill from balance sheets has been harmful rather than beneficial in communications with stockholders.

Goodwill, whether acquired or self-developed, should never be carried as an asset in the balance sheet. Such an asset is not only ephemeral and elusive, it is meaningless and misleading.

Amortization of goodwill against earnings destroys reliability and usefulness of reports to stockholders

If acquired goodwill is shown as a reduction of stockholders' equity at the date of acquisition, there is no question of amortization. However, since some accountants favor capitalization and amortization of goodwill, I will discuss briefly the question of amortization.

In my view, there should be no amortization of goodwill as a charge to income.

If the recognition of goodwill value as an asset and its subsequent amortization is proper accounting, it follows that in every mutual fund, in every insurance company, in every endowment fund, the excess market value of a security held over the book value of that security represents goodwill and should be arbitrarily amortized. Of course, such amortization is not required, and it should not be as long as the market value of that security supports the value of the goodwill included in it. The composite investors in a security are the only ones who value goodwill. Any valuation of goodwill must go to that authority.

Some people feel that goodwill should be amortized merely because no company can be assumed to exist in perpetuity. Some people arrive at a judgment that a 40-year maximum amortization period is appropriate. Such a decision disregards those who determine its life—the investors. They would promptly answer that if they thought the goodwill would expire, they would sell their stock.

Amortization of goodwill is, in effect, an amortization of the stock value that determines goodwill. After amortization (if accepted as a charge to earnings), goodwill must go down because the decrease in earnings in turn reduces the market value of stock until all the goodwill is written off. The bookkeeping mechanics create an impression that goodwill has lost its value. Upon completion of this cycle, the earnings are miraculously restored. The market value of stock increases which, in turn, restores the value of goodwill.

Let me illustrate with this assumed acquisition of IBM:

CHART C

ILLUSTRATION OF CONSEQUENCES AND CIRCULAR REASONING RESULTING FROM AMORTIZING GOODWILL

ASSUME STANDARD (N. J.)
OR
GM ACQUIRED IBM

(In a manner comparable to the way that all acquisitions are normally made.)

1.	IBM shares outstanding	113 million
2.	Market value @ $350 per share Premium in acquisition— 30%	$455 per share
3.	Total acquisition cost	$ 51.4 billion

4.	Book value of IBM producing assets..	4.6	billion
5.	Balance—goodwill acquired	$ 46.8	"
6.	Amortization over 40 years	$ 1.2	"
7.	IBM—1968 net income......	.9	"
8.	Net **loss** after goodwill amortization .... **(loss)** (for 40 years assuming same level of earnings)	.3	"
9.	Value of goodwill based on net income after amortization	0	
10.	Write-off of goodwill on principle of loss in value...	$ 46.8	billion
11.	IBM net income after write-off of loss in goodwill as recorded	.9	"
12.	Market value of stock after above circular reasoning.	$350 per share	

Someone is bound to say the above could not happen, and probably it could not with IBM. But the same circularity results with any acquisition—the effect is only a matter of degree. Below is the effect on two acquisitions on which I am working. The end result is the same:

ILLUSTRATION OF CONSEQUENCES AND CIRCULAR REASONING RESULTING FROM AMORTIZING GOODWILL OF TWO ACQUISITIONS NOW IN PROGRESS

(The names cannot be disclosed)

		Millions of Dollars Acquisition	
		A	B
1.	Total market value..	—	$ 75
2.	Premium	—	25
3.	Acquisition cost	$33	$100

CHART C (Continued)

	Millions of Dollars	
	Acquisition	
	A	B
4. Value of net producing assets	3	15
5. Balance—goodwill acquired	$30	$ 85
6. Annual income before goodwill amortization	1.5	2.5
7. P/E ratio using acquisition price ...	22x	40x
8. Annual amortization of goodwill—over 40 yrs.	.8	2.1
9. Annual income after goodwill amortization	.7	.4
10. Revised goodwill value (Based on market value of stock at same P/E ratio of company as before acquisition, less book value of producing assets)	12.4	1.0
11. Loss in goodwill value (Line 5 minus line 10)	17.6	84.0
12. Revised net income after write-off of goodwill	1.2	2.5
13. Market value after goodwill write-off at original P/E ratio	26.4	100.0
14. Revised goodwill value in market value after goodwill write-off	23.4	85.0

Actual goodwill lives based on last twenty years' experience

As I have previously noted, pooling accounting results in an elimination of goodwill values through a failure to have any accounting for them. Our experience with "pooling" since 1950 should provide some measure of goodwill values eliminated by the expiration of time. To show the results for that 20-year period, sixty companies picked at random from *Fortune's* 500 industrials were analyzed to determine whether goodwill value decreased or increased during that 20-year period. The results are shown in Chart D:

CHART D

	Goodwill In Millions		
Company	1950	1969	Relation 1969-1950
1.	$ 115	$ 800	7.5x
2.	Neg.	Neg.	No change
3.	60	2,500	41.5x
4.	Neg.	200	Infinite
5.	Neg.	Neg.	No change
6.	Neg.	2,900	Infinite
7.	Neg.	500	Infinite
8.	Neg.	Neg.	No change
9.	Neg.	Neg.	No change
10.	50	200	4.0x
11.	15	1,600	106.0x
12.	15	2,200	146.0x
13.	5	400	80.0x
14.	50	1,700	34.0x
15.	135	Neg.	Decrease
16.	425	4,000	9.0x
17.	135	50	Decrease
18.	60	1,600	26.5x
19.	Neg.	Neg.	No change
20.	240	1,000	4.0x
21.	2,700	3,000	1.0x
22.	300	10,000	33.0x
23.	5	250	50.0x
24.	Neg.	450	Infinite
25.	700	5,300	7.5x
26.	135	1,100	8.0x
27.	6,600	11,500	1.5x
28.	60	1,100	18.0x
29.	Neg.	800	Infinite
30.	Neg.	2,100	Infinite
31.	Neg.	145	Infinite
32.	50	Neg.	Decrease
33.	450	34,400	76.0x
34.	55	2,200	40.0x
35.	130	400	3.0x
36.	Neg.	100	Infinite
37.	Neg.	200	Infinite
38.	10	500	50.0x
39.	5	400	80.0x
40.	85	3,000	35.0x
41.	145	5,000	34.5x
42.	135	400	3.0x
43.	Neg.	80	Infinite

CHART D (Continued)

Goodwill In Millions

Company	1950	1969	Relation 1969-1950
44.	90	300	3.0x
45.	65	1,350	20.5x
46.	300	3,000	10.0x
47.	110	1,700	15.5x
48.	Neg.	700	Infinite
49.	Neg.	45	Infinite
50.	Neg.	400	Infinite
51.	Neg.	5,000	Infinite
52.	90	1,200	13.0x
53.	20	140	7.0x
54.	820	780	Decrease
55.	220	485	2.0x
56.	Neg.	440	Infinite
57.	Neg.	1,000	Infinite
58.	90	120	1.0x
59.	55	150	2.5x
60.	45	150	3.0x

(Neg. = Negative goodwill)

Of these 60 companies, only 4 had 1969 goodwill of a lesser amount than they had 20 years earlier in 1950. Of the remaining 56, 5 had no change and the rest had increased value of goodwill of up to more than 100 times the 1950 value.

If, in 1950, goodwill had been recorded for the above companies and had been amortized over a 40-year period, about one half would have been written off by now.

If goodwill had been amortized over twenty years, earnings reports to shareholders would have been understated by these companies. Earnings would have been charged with goodwill amortization even though no loss in value of goodwill occurred. Is that the kind of truth that the stockholders who own these enterprises deserve? I say, any amortization of goodwill against earnings is a gross miscarriage of truth to the stockholders. Amortization should be prohibited by our profession and the SEC if the objectives of the accounting profession and of the Securities Act mean anything in terms of preserving elementary truth for stockholder reporting.

Earnings per share

The proper reflection of business com-binations and of the securities issued in connection with such combinations requires the presentation of informative earnings per share data.

One cannot dispute the need to provide the per share data now required under APB Opinion No. 15, particularly under the varying circumstances of conversion or exercise of outstanding securities. To present only an amount for primary earnings per share on financial statements when there are so many ways this amount could be arrived at fails to provide proper communication to stockholders. In addition to the required disclosure of primary and fully diluted earnings per share, a footnote explanation should also be required to show the method by which these amounts were calculated. This explanation is extremely important in communicating the operating results of a business entity to investors in an understandable manner. An illustrative footnote is shown at the end of this paper as an appendix.

Conclusion

The problem of accounting for business combinations involves more basic concepts and principles than any other problem which has ever faced the business community and the accounting profession. It involves the effects of inflation and the vast differences between values on a current basis and original costs on a conservative basis. It reflects the effect of stock market prices and relatively high price-earnings ratios. It causes us to look at goodwill for what it is and not as a piece of a journal entry. It highlights in an embarrassing way the current deficiencies in accounting.

Therefore, it is recommended that the accounting profession take a practical step forward in the solution of a very complex and controversial problem in a way (a) that will represent true progress in the right direction toward more useful and meaningful financial statements, (b) that will not be too drastic a step to expect the business community to take at one time, and (c) that will represent a fair statement of the facts for the use of investors and others relying on financial statements.

Since accounting for goodwill is a basic element in any solution to the business combination problem, it is essential that this matter be dealt with in a sensible and reasonable manner. Capitalization of goodwill and its mandatory amortization will never stand up from either a theoretical or practical standpoint and neither the APB nor the SEC can sustain such a requirement, because it is contrary to the economic facts. Also, a great disservice will be done to the business and financial community and, particularly, stockholders if corporations are forced to record many billions of dollars of goodwill.

There is no easy solution to the problem before us. However, I am convinced that what has been proposed represents the best balancing of all of the factors involved.

FOOTNOTE RELATING TO EARNINGS PER SHARE

		1969			1968	
	Market at 12/31/69	Annual Current Income to Investor Per Common Share Equivalent	Effect on Earnings Per Common Share	Common Equity Portion of Total Capitalization	Effect on Earnings Per Common Share	Common Equity Portion of Total Capitalization
	(Col. 1)	(Col. 2)	(Col. 3)	(Col. 4)	(Col. 5)	(Col. 6)
(1) Outstanding common stock .	$ 60	$ .75	$2.00	36%	$1.50	48%
(2) Effect of conversion of securities that are common stock equivalents:						
(3) $5 preferred............	200	1.20	(.10)	5	(.04)	7
(4) $3.15 preferred..........	140	1.35	(.08)	7	(.02)	9
(5) 4½% debentures.......	180	1.35	(.20)	10	(.14)	13
(6) Primary earnings per share.			$1.62	58%	$1.30	77%
(7) Effect of conversion of other convertible securities:						
(8) 5% debentures.........	150	2.00	(.10)	10	(.06)	13
(9) 5% debentures.........	100	3.00	(.02)	8	Issued in 1969	
(10) 6% preferred..........	110	4.00	.34*	15	Issued in 1969	
(11) Earnings per share assuming full conversion............			$1.84	91%	$1.24	90%

*This item would not be included in a pro forma calculation under Opinion 15 since it does not result in dilution at this date.

In the above table these essential facts are shown:

(1) Dividends and earnings per share on actual outstanding common stock are shown as $0.75 and $2.00, respectively, on line 1, Cols. 2 and 3.

(2) The effect of the various convertible securities is segregated between those classified as common stock equivalents (lines 2 through 5) and those not so classified (lines 7 through 9).

(3) The market of the convertible equivalent to each share of common stock as of a specified date is shown in Col. 1 so that the reader who is

evaluating his position at another date can determine the factors on which the earnings per share were based and can determine whether he considers them to be currently appropriate.

(4) In Col. 2, the earnings actually received by investors in the form of dividends and interest is shown; these data are the major controlling factors in determining whether conversion will take place, absent a call. Unless the gap is closed between the dividend per common share on line 1 in this column and the senior dividend or interest per equivalent share on lines 3 to 10, conversion will not take place; therefore, any "common stock equivalent" security is, in fact, a prior lien or senior security as well as a common stock equivalent at any time until conversion.

(5) Col. 3 shows the dilution or addition to earnings per share on outstanding common stock, if the convertible securities were to be converted. The figures through line 6 relate to common stock and common stock

equivalents; the remaining lines reflect conversions of all other convertible securities.

(6) Col. 4 shows one of the most important facts—information that is overlooked in the preparation of all proxy and registration statements today. It shows the effect that conversion would have on the capital structure and the resulting increased safety to the common shareholder; this improved capitalization serves as an offset to any dilution that would result from conversion.

(7) Although the table does not show what investment value—that is, market value absent the conversion right—has been assumed for the various convertible securities, consideration should be given to including such information. In that way, the reader not only is supplied with all data necessary for understanding the earnings per share computation but also is in a position to substitute his judgment for that of the issuer.

Return on investment—a challenge to the growth of the paper industry

An address by Leonard Spacek and Robert I. Jones before the Fourth Annual Presidents' Forum of the American Paper Institute, New York, October 9, 1969

Accounting never makes the facts—accounting reports the facts.

COMMENTS BY ROBERT I. JONES

As WE LOOK into the future, both short term and long term, the capital requirements of the paper industry are immense. This requirement for capital exists at a point in time when the performance of the paper industry is looked upon by investment analysts as being below average. As each of you views the future, you must program your growth in terms of sources of funds. Significant amounts may be available from retained cash flow, but many companies will seek much larger amounts in the form of debt financing, possibly in entirely new forms, and equity capital as well. It is desirable therefore that your industry address itself now to the many factors which affect your ability to attract capital on sound terms. We will attempt to review some of these factors with you in our discussion today.

In following annual reports of your companies, we have been impressed with the emphasis on expansion plans and future growth prospects, particularly the:

Significance of industry capacity and demand conditions during recent years, and the effect thereof on pricing levels and profitability.

Emphasis on capital expenditure programs in process to provide new mill and other manufacturing facilities.

Planning for substantial future growth.

Diversification of product lines and emphasis on development of new products, many of them outside of the forest products packaging industries.

Integration of operations and programs to acquire woodlands.

Development of new concepts for reforestation, forest management and utilization of woodlands.

The reports provide a dynamic story of growth and future potential. Yet, as indicated by discussions at your 1968 Forum and as covered in various business publications, there has been general dissatisfaction with the industry's rate of return on shareholders' investment, particularly since the mid-1950's.

Since paper industry performance is important in relationship to the performance of other industries, it becomes imperative that the industry consider the overall fairness and quality of its accounting and financial reporting and how its standards in these areas compare to those of other industries. Let us ask ourselves these questions: Does the accounting, customarily followed by the industry, provide investment analysts and bankers, stockholders and others with the information which would be most useful for analysis purposes? Is traditional accounting reflective of the true economic financial position and operating results of the industry?

Reexamination of current financial reporting practices

Without suggesting that we are introducing any basically new observations to a group like this, let us nevertheless examine the facts related to these questions and see whether under current conditions they suggest some need for a new approach to communication with the investment community.

Integrated paper companies having extensive woodland holdings are vitally affected by the failure of present accounting conventions to give recognition to the substantial value of standing timber. It has been estimated by some companies that the stumpage value of woodlands which have been held for a long period of time may be 15, 20, or even 30 times the cost amount at which these assets are shown in the financial statements, and this is in addition to the land which may also be appreciating in value.

While this unrecorded value of the timber may reflect somewhat the absence of capitalization of costs and the depletion practices which are in effect (which we will discuss later), and also appreciation in terms of timber prices, a very important factor is generally considered to be the annual growth of timber holdings in excess of harvesting and other factors which decrease the stand. This same problem applies generally to other natural resource industries where the value of oil and gas reserves and mineral deposits do not find their way into the financial statements until the mining or extracting phase is completed, which may be many years after these assets were discovered.

In the case of other industries, however, the significance of these mineral deposits and reserves to the financial community and other users of the financial statements, comes at a much earlier date. It comes when the asset is first determined to exist, and the significance continues until the deposits are consumed. We recognize this need for accounting and reporting of values of natural resources as one of the important accounting and reporting problems of the accounting profession, and emphasize it here as an important distinction between the paper industry and other industry groups not having these same characteristics.

Paper industry companies have an important asset which, in almost all cases, is increasing in value each year, but neither the aggregate value nor the annual increment in value are available from the financial statements for purposes of determining return on investment (ROI) and earnings per share.

The problem of improving communication on timber values is common to all integrated paper companies and, consequently, you may find it advantageous to approach it on an industry basis through the Institute. Recognize that adequate disclosure is not accomplished within present accounting conventions because of the emphasis within the accounting profession and the SEC on original cost concepts. But that should not preclude you from an active program to stress the importance of timber values and to seek ways by which this information can become a part of financial reporting. Direct your efforts to the accounting profession, the SEC, investment analysts and bankers.

Possibly, some form of supplementary footnote presentation could be developed to serve as a first step in providing financial information on timber holdings. This form of disclosure has been adopted by the casualty insurance industry to cover a unique reporting problem of that industry. Of course, stumpage values and depletion policies would have to be reviewed carefully and procedures worked out so that the data would be reliable and useful, and the principles followed in developing such data would be universally adopted by the industry.

Timber represents an entirely unique asset, quite different from assets of most other industries. The extent to which costs borne by current operations are providing future values is not recognized by traditional industry accounting practices and is not considered in conventional calculations of ROI. Perhaps most important, timber holdings represent very substantial values which could become the basis for new concepts and techniques of long-term debt financing in the future. More effective financial reporting of these values may permit an expanded use of the aggregate credit pool available to a company.

In the meantime, under existing practices, increased significance should be attached to the cash flow of your industry, which in most cases is quite strong. A brief review, for example, indicated that for a number of large integrated companies the cash flow would support a much higher debt leverage than is now actually being utilized.

I made brief reference to the insurance industry as a precedent in summarizing supplementary data in a footnote, and I would like to explain this further. Because of the regulatory influence on the insurance industry, financial statements of insurance companies report substantially on a liquidating basis. It was well recognized, for instance, that an insurance company incurred "acquisition costs" in the year a policy was sold which amounted to far more than the first-year premium; these costs were expensed, but could properly have been deferred to future years. As a result, the concept of "adjusted earnings" developed. While the underlying reasoning for an adjustment was proper, the technique used for many years was not sound. Rule-of-thumb adjustments based upon increases in insurance in force were applied across the board for all companies to determine an amount which was added to statutory earnings. This became a company's adjusted earnings. The use of rule of thumb completely failed to recognize countless factors which were different as between companies and ultimately led to a good deal of confusion with respect to insurance company earnings. During the past few years, however, the casualty insurance companies, working with the accounting profession, have adopted a footnote reporting of these costs to arrive at an adjusted earnings based on the facts as developed for each company. Similar concepts are being explored for life insurance companies. This is a step in the right direction so long as it moves toward the day when such data is included in the financial statements.

This illustrates the reason for saying that information as to timber values must be based on reliable data, factual and carefully determined, and must be fully responsive to the need for the information. General rule-of-thumb estimates of growth factors per acre, for instance, would not answer the need and could result in confusion. Such estimates could hardly serve as security for long-term financing.

Now I would like to turn to other accounting areas, areas wherein you make decisions as to the accounting practices which you will follow. These practices are all sanctioned as generally accepted accounting principles. The decisions which you make have a direct influence on the timing and the amount of earnings which you report to shareholders, the income taxes which you pay and, highly important, your ability to attract investment capital.

I might also add that these are truly classical, in that the practices follow guidelines which have existed for many years, and the practices themselves have undoubtedly been discussed countless times. But perhaps it is timely to consider another dimension.

Accounting practices of the paper industry have been heavily oriented to their income tax consequences. Accounting followed on the books and for purposes of reporting to shareholders and others has paralleled the income tax handling of the costs. The primary emphasis has generally been to obtain the maximum tax deduction as quickly as possible, with the result that recognition of earnings to the stockholders may be deferred.

The LIFO inventory valuation method has been used extensively in the industry. As you well know, during periods of rising prices this method has the effect of charging recently purchased higher cost logs and pulp to operations and, thus, minimizes the valuation amount of inventory carried forward on the balance sheet.

Speaking in general terms with respect to woodland programs, the industry has followed the practice of absorbing as expense the costs incurred each year for forest management purposes. While some companies have capitalized or deferred certain costs for the development and planting of seedlings or for special seeding programs, it is reasonably accurate to say that, following the harvest of timber from a tract, only minor amounts are capitalized in connection with the development and management of those woodlands during the period until the next harvest, many years later. Similarly, depletion practices have the effect of substantially (if not entirely) writing off the original cost applicable to timber over the period during which the first harvest is completed. Recognition of annual growth factors has the effect of stretching out depletion charges over the harvest period; nevertheless, the investment as shown on financial statements of the company is ultimately reduced to a minimal or even a zero amount. This is the accounting treatment generally followed notwithstanding the fact that, through sustained yield management, the woodlands may have timber stands as great or greater than when the properties were first acquired.

The accounting followed by the industry over many years gave recognition to the fact that timber supplies were consumable, were subject to destruction by fire and disease, required very long periods for replacement through natural reforestation, and also that obsolescence factors might some day develop. Over a period of years, however, paper industry companies have adopted sustained yield concepts, introduced new plantation operations, emphasized continuing forest management, and developed new species of trees in some areas having faster growth and higher yield characteristics. Long-range forecasts indicate a very favorable future market for wood fibers.

Under these circumstances, depending upon their application to specific companies, present accounting may not result in the fairest reporting of operating and economic conditions with respect to forestry operations. For instance, costs associated with site preparation, nursery operations, including the upgrading of species, seeding and planting, disease control, and other management and carrying costs could properly be accumulated and allocated to woodland stands, to be depleted as woods are harvested. Care would have to be taken to assure that capitalized costs do not exceed the market prices for similar timbers of a marketable age. Such a practice is completely in accordance with generally accepted accounting principles. Similarly, under these operating conditions, present depletion practices may warrant close examination.

A related question can be raised with respect to the handling of costs on purchases of woodlands. Companies generally have tended to assign costs first to depreciable assets where the depreciation is deductible from ordinary income, secondly, to timber stands whereby the costs are deductible as depletion against capital gains, and the residual is then assigned to land. Final valuations may be made in connection with revenue agent examinations, with the result that the amount assigned per acre of land is increased to a negotiated amount. To the extent that judgments are involved in determining amounts to be capitalized as land vs. timber, any switch of amount to timber results in a tax deduction of 25% thereof but the remaining 75% is ultimately a reduction of earnings reported to shareholders.

What effect would changes in these accounting practices have and how would they apply to a particular company? Some of the costs can be determined quickly, while others, such as in the woodlands area, may be much more difficult to identify because phases of the forest management programs may be handled by harvest crews. While these costs are sometimes considered to be minor from an overall expenditure standpoint, they may be much more significant when related to corporate earnings, particularly for a company that is moving towards sustained yield programs and plantation concepts. It is not possible to generalize as to effect because of the many factors involved, some of which are counteracting, and it must be recognized that, while some changes could result in higher earnings, the interplay of amounts capitalized could result in a lower ROI.

What we are suggesting is that operating practices have changed over the years

and that accounting practices may not have kept pace with these changes. Accordingly, we suggest that they should be reviewed with the objective of determining that the accounting provides a fair basis under such changed conditions for internal management reporting as well as reporting to shareholders and others.

Recognition must be given to the income tax implications of any changes in accounting procedures. Present accounting practices have generally been considered necessary in order to assure continuation of the advantageous treatment of forest management costs as current deductions from ordinary income. Consequently, the tax benefits must be carefully measured.

These accounting questions may lend themselves to evaluation on an industry basis through the Institute and this approach may also be helpful in determining how to proceed on the income tax questions. How could the Institute or member companies proceed to consider the forest management costs? First of all, some of these costs clearly can be deferred on the books but expensed currently for tax purposes. Property taxes would fall in this category as would interest costs incurred to carry the investment. Secondly, each other classification of forest management cost should be examined to consider the tax impact of any change in accounting practices. Some of these could probably be capitalized on the books but treated as a period cost for tax purposes. Other costs, however, would clearly be of a nature whereby any change in the book-accounting treatment would logically cause the IRS to attempt to capitalize the item also, and probably consider the cost as a reduction of capital gains income (rather than ordinary income). Such an analysis could result in a partial solution to the question.

Possibly another approach can be developed to achieve the proper accounting for forest management costs. Earlier we talked about the failure of present accounting conventions concerning timber, in that neither the aggregate value nor the annual increment in value are available from the financial statements. At that point, it was suggested that perhaps the annual economic increment of timber should be recognized currently rather than defer such cumulative increment until the timber is harvested. Under this concept of accounting, it would be necessary that forest management costs be expensed as incurred, just as is done now. However, since these concepts are not permitted at present by generally accepted accounting principles, perhaps another approach could be followed. It may be appropriate to recognize in the accounting records and financial statements the annual growth up to but not exceeding the amount of maintenance costs incurred. With the proper supporting records and proper identification, it may be possible to develop a case whereby this practice would not disrupt the existing tax handling. You would have the immediate tax benefit and additionally have the benefit of proper matching of forest management costs with revenues. All of us must recognize that the IRS is developing an industry approach to technical examinations and can be expected to be increasingly critical of the present tax handling of these costs.

Another important omission in properly reporting the long-cycle economics of the paper industry is the financial carrying cost of timber. Where such timber investments have a reasonably assured future economic utilization, it would seem appropriate to consider a current capitalization of such costs to be matched against the returns to be received in the future as a result of incurring such costs. Such accounting practice would be justifiable under generally accepted accounting principles under the circumstances described, although it is admittedly an application with only limited precedent. The unique nature of this significant element of your capital utilization, however, demands that you apply accounting practices which are reflective of the actual economics of your own unique industry.

If an industry is conservative to the point of significantly understating its position in relation to true economic values and earnings, it places itself at a disadvantage in the securities markets with a direct impact on its ability to attract funds. Equally important, the industry becomes attractive prey to those who recognize the true values of hidden assets, at the expense of existing stockholders. This condition developed over a period of time in the example of the insurance industry previously discussed, and continues to exist today.

Managing assets for improved return on investment

With the emphasis on profitability and in view of the magnitude of capital expenditures, managements have increasingly sought new techniques by which it is possible to manage assets on a carefully programmed basis so as to maximize the ROI. I would like to discuss with you the type of systematic long-range planning that is required in this area and the important contribution that computer models can make to such a program.

While a great deal of attention may be given to ROI and profitability during conferences such as this and in top-level meetings within your companies, the success of a program to maximize ROI is dependent upon the degree to which it is expressed and related to the complete organization. If you are aiming at a 12% or 20% return on stockholders' investment, and your present rate is well below this, your new objectives can be met only through specific programs. Programs must be developed following organizational lines with profit objectives expressed by project and location and in terms of individuals in charge. This involves the basic concepts of budgeting and responsibility accounting and reporting.

Equally important, management must make available the necessary financial data and provide for the analysis techniques required to properly evaluate alternative projects. There may be cases where management will find it necessary to develop and use financial data in a fashion other than as it is developed by the accounting system.

Perhaps because of the very large unrecorded appreciation potential of woodlands, this area draws considerable attention in attempts to maximize ROI. How can this profit be realized and what can be done to assure that realization is at the highest level? I would like to discuss with you some of the key elements of a program in the woodlands area and, at the same time, emphasize the systematic planning and analysis which such a program involves. These points would apply equally to many other areas.

Recognizing the variation in appreciation and potential, evaluation of woodlands requires a systematic program of study on a tract-by-tract basis. This phase of the program must have as its objective:

Identification of those woodlands which are economically productive as a source of timber and meet overall company objectives including an adequate ROI and, thereafter, classification of these tracts as to ROI potential so as to shift production to the most efficient areas.

Identification of those properties which are not suitable for timber operations either because they are too valuable, having potential for industrial or residential development, recreational and certain conservation purposes or, on the other hand, are not of sufficient quality for utilization by the company as timber-producing acreage.

The degree of appreciation over book value varies substantially from tract to tract depending upon many factors. These would include the species and quality of timber, suitability of land for high production of timber, accessibility in general, location relative to mills and customers, and economic factors which suggest alternative uses yielding a higher return than can be achieved through normal timber operations. There is, of course, the overall consideration of company policy. Companies will continue to justify maintenance of large timberland reserves to assure a captive supply of basic raw material in the future despite, in some cases, relatively unattractive rates of return during long holding periods.

Having recognized objectives and the management approach to be followed, people should be appointed who have the capability of conducting the program. Specific organization stature should be given to the group so that management support is obvious. The department should consist of individuals having backgrounds in such diverse areas as forestry management, land development, operations research, computer programming and finance. The group should have authority to operate company-wide to completely analyze current woodland holdings, determine classifications of properties as to the contribution which can be expected, and make specific recommendations as to programs for concentrating timber development in the most productive tracts, disposing of uneconomical holdings, purchasing woodlands to complement mill-supply situations, and utilization of properties having high value for alternative purposes.

The group should proceed to develop a specific program which would clearly establish its objectives and timetable. At a very early stage in the project, the group must determine the analysis techniques and methods which will be employed in reaching conclusions.

Conventional methods of calculating return on investment generally do not apply because of the need to consider 25 to 50-year time spans corresponding to normal growing cycles. These fail to take into account the cost of money. For this reason, discounted cash-flow methods must be used for analysis purposes. Discounted cash-flow techniques introduce the time factor of the holding period and express the results in terms of present-day dollars. Most important, this permits the comparison of ROI from alternative project possibilities having varying time spans. The results of discounted cash-flow analysis may be quite different from the conventional accounting approach.

Budgets should be developed in terms of both program costs and benefits expected to be realized. A reporting package would also be required, entirely unique in nature, which would graphically, statistically, or in some other way, report on achievements compared with the objectives. Such a program must be viewed as being of a continuing nature, and tracts would be retested and evaluated from time to time.

A program to maximize ROI from woodlands may have other objectives, in addition to tract analysis and utilization. For instance, discounted cash-flow analysis techniques can be an integral part of programs to schedule cutting operations. Programs may be developed to evaluate tracts of timber which have reached a harvestable stage to measure the growth potential in terms of gross income to be received at various future dates as compared with the carrying costs and interest factors. Using discounted cash-flow analysis, it may be determined more advantageous from a net yield standpoint to cut at an early date, even though the tract continues to mature and will provide a higher gross income several years later.

The woodlands program may also have a direct responsibility or at least an interest in the establishment of the annual cutting program. These programs, as you well know, require innumerable calculations, assumptions as to costs, decisions as between alter-native sources, consideration of freight differentials, and many other factors. The final conclusions bear significantly on the ROI from woodland holdings. Yet many companies do not provide a reporting process to measure how well they did in the final analysis relative to their program and, thus, may repeat erroneous assumptions in future years.

Systematic analysis, budgeting and reporting along organizational lines are key concepts in successful programs to maximize ROI. We often refer to these as a form of responsibility reporting. The concept has been with us for a long time and remains one of the best.

The potential of corporate financial modeling

In the paper industry, it is commonplace for management to be faced with investment decisions measured in tens of millions of dollars and there never seems to be enough capital to take care of all the needs. It is not surprising, therefore, that many companies in the industry have adopted rather sophisticated techniques for evaluating investment alternatives and setting priorities. However, as the industry has grown and become more complex, it has become increasingly apparent that even these relatively modern and sophisticated techniques suffer from a major deficiency. That is because they are used to support a management evaluation process that tends to treat all investment opportunities as though they are independent of each other. Moreover, the analysis accompanying each investment proposal rarely gives an accurate description of the corporate-wide effects of a major capital investment.

In the paper industry today, such omissions can produce grossly inaccurate estimates of return on investment. Moreover, such omissions can and do result in the failure of management to see better alternatives for the deployment of capital. What is needed is a tool for measuring the entire corporate-wide effect of an investment upon revenues and costs. Such a tool is now available in the form of the corporate investment planning or financial projection model. This is a computer-based mathematical model. By taking advantage of linear programming and modern computer technology, the corporate investment planning model makes possible a valid projection of the economic effect of an investment upon all facets of corporate operations. And, equally important, it gives management the means to consider a vastly greater variety of investment alternatives than are possible without it.

Let me illustrate with a hypothetical example. The company in this example could be any one of many represented here today. It has been in business for several decades during which it has experienced about the same rate of growth as others in the industry. It produces about 30 different grades of paper, most of which are distributed nationally. Many of these grades of paper can be produced at more than one of the company's four mills. It is apparent that the company must obtain substantial new paper-producing capacity if it is to achieve its growth potential. Based upon a study of where the growth of demand is expected to take place, a tentative plan is developed to purchase timber and build a new paper mill in a central southern state. The total investment is established at about $60 million. Estimates of sales that will be served by this new mill and corresponding estimates of costs to produce and distribute the products to be sold indicate a very favorable return on the proposed investment.

As this plan is developed in more detail, however, it is seen that some products presently made at other mills could be produced and distributed much more economically at the new mill. This creates a new question. What products should be made in existing mills to fill the capacity made available by those products transferred to the new mill? This, in turn, raises a host of related ques-

tions, all of which make it apparent that there will be a great many company-wide effects of the proposed investment that have not yet been considered in the estimated rate of return. For example, if different products are to be produced at the existing mills, this will change the pulp requirements at those mills. Thus, it will be necessary to consider the cost differences between mills of producing each of ten different kinds of pulp as well as the possibility of transferring pulp between mills, or perhaps even purchasing it. It is also apparent that there will be an entirely new product distribution arrangement which will affect the freight costs of moving about thirty kinds of paper from five mill locations to nine marketing regions.

As the number of unanswered questions increases, the complexity of the problem becomes more apparent; any significant change of capacity in one part of the company will have a chain effect throughout all facets of operations, including both manufacturing and marketing. Until very recently, however, the difficulties of taking into account so many complex, interrelated variables were almost insurmountable.

Today, however, such difficulties are greatly minimized for companies that have developed corporate investment planning models. These models give management the opportunity to consider dozens of different capital investment strategies with assurance that the total economic effect upon all facets of the company has been considered. Thus, a more valid basis for measuring returns on proposed investments becomes available. And, of equal importance, it is now possible to search systematically for the best strategy in the deployment of available capital.

When reference is made to improved vision as to demand/capacity factors and relationships proceeding into the 1970's, the meaning is clear. Companies will develop and rely much more heavily on corporate models to assist in long-range planning of operations and particularly in evaluating the effect on operating results and financial position of alternative decisions in such areas as planning new mill facilities, determining various warehousing and other marketing strategies, evaluating the profit potential of new products, and many other areas. If you are not utilizing financial projection and other special purpose models, you should be actively considering them.

At this point, I would like to turn our discussion of this subject over to my partner and the chairman of our firm, Mr. Leonard Spacek, who will focus on some of the more important aspects of financial reporting for your industry.

COMMENTS BY LEONARD SPACEK

Mr. Jones has reviewed with you some of the traditional accounting practices of the paper industry and has discussed certain areas where present accounting conventions fail to recognize the fundamental economics of your business. He has introduced these thoughts from the standpoint of whether the accounting customarily followed by the industry provides investment analysts, bankers, stockholders, and others with the information needed for sound analysis purposes, and whether the traditional accounting fairly reflects the true economic financial position and operating results of the industry.

I have spoken out on many accounting issues where I have believed that the accounting profession has failed or has lagged in its responsibility to establish high standards for accounting principles and reporting concepts. In so doing, I have been accused by many of my contemporaries of advocating rigid rules of accounting. This is an interpretation of a contention which I strongly advocate—that accounting must be a reflection of the true economic facts as they exist. If the economics are absolute, so is the accounting. Accounting never makes the facts—accounting reports the facts. If

there is no way to stretch economics, there is no way to stretch accounting. Whatever is stretched will ultimately retract to the economic facts as they exist and in the interim will prove to be misleading.

The measure of progress from operations of any corporation in any given year is presumably shown in the income account. That statement provides a reporting of the net gain in a corporation's asset value for the year, if the price levels remain constant. The income account is a corporation's counterpart of the football scores you hear on the news reports every week. They are the net result of all the effort that was put into the game—errors, judgment, good work and bad. If these scores are not properly kept or are biased, then they are not reliable as a score of the game or a measure of the effort.

So it is with the income account. If the income account does not provide a full measure of the economic gain during the year by your company, then there is something wrong with the accounting and that accounting must be reexamined regardless of how extensively it is accepted by the industry and the accounting profession.

Operations in your industry involve very significant commitments of funds to programs having long-term cycles. This applies to your construction of converting facilities costing many millions of dollars and to your expanding programs in timber development. These long-term programs involve turnover cycles extending many years into the future and we sometimes forget the importance of properly allocating the total return from these investments and operations to the right year. This is highly important because the investor looks at results on a year-by-year basis. His appraisal is ultimately translated into the price the shares command in the market place and the capital costs that the company incurs for financing. Do investment people really know what your net gain is each year and do they understand and can they measure the effort that is going towards providing values which will be realized many years in the future?

One of the tests of good capital use is the return earned on capital invested. In the case of General Motors and other major industrial companies this is a good measurement because all of their plants are producing a current return. Their inventory is kept to a minimum necessary to achieve production on a relatively short lead time. In other words, their capital is working and the results flow currently into the income account. How does this compare with your operations?

You are carrying an inventory of standing timber adequate to cover your timber requirements for a period of many years. Some of this inventory is harvestable now but is carried into the future on a policy basis while other timber stands are in varying stages of growth. You charge to expense all of the cost incurred each year for carrying and developing timber, assuming that the excessive charges to expense in a year will be offset by the gain recorded that same year in harvesting timber that has only a nominal cost assigned to it. Little recognition is given to the growth of timber or to the carrying costs of maintaining that inventory. It is important for your shareholders to have reliable data on the value of the timber inventory just as shareholders of oil companies should have the most complete facts possible concerning oil and other deposits on leases in the Prudhoe Bay, Alaska area.

The cost of capital funds invested in timber for future use is a tremendous drain on the return to stockholders, and the investors have no way of knowing the complete facts so as to evaluate the return shown by the income statement. In the case of public utilities, because it takes four or five years to build a generating plant,

interest is capitalized at 6% or more on the entire investment during the construction period. This cost becomes a part of the cost of the plant and the credit is shown in the income account. Such a practice has become routine for utilities because of their major construction expenditures over long periods of time and the extensive use of borrowed funds. If these interest costs were permitted to be charged to operations during the period until the new facility was placed into service, neither the income for the period nor the cost of the plant would be properly shown. This is vitally important for a utility company since the amount of profit allowed under regulation is based on the cost of its plant in service as reflected in its financial statements, together with other factors. The interest during construction concept in the utility industry also includes a factor for the forbearance of return on equity funds used in the project in addition to the interest on borrowed funds. This is proper on the theory that it represents a part of the cost which must be recovered in the future from customers. The same principle applies with equal force to industrial companies, although the accounting profession does not yet recognize the accounting necessary to properly reflect the economics in the case of industrial companies.

It is entirely within the province of generally accepted accounting principles for industrial companies to capitalize interest on borrowed funds during the period that facilities are being constructed and until they are available for productive use. This has been done in a number of instances such as by financial institutions when embarking on a major project of constructing a new building to house operations and by an airline which borrowed funds which were advanced to a manufacturer on planes that were being constructed. The practice is often followed in the real estate industry where land is purchased and held for an extended period pending development of a project. There have also been cases of companies in your industry which have capitalized interest on major mill construction projects or where timber was purchased and held for a period until mill facilities were constructed and cutting could commence.

These are all situations where specific costs were incurred, and it is just as proper to capitalize the interest on funds borrowed to finance construction as it is to capitalize the labor and materials which are used. Certainly, if the facilities are purchased from an outside contractor, his interest costs would be a part of the purchase price.

In summary, we would urge you to re-examine your financial reporting practices with the objective of more effectively communicating the economics of your unique industry.

Gentlemen, we consider it a real privilege to have been invited to participate in this Fourth Annual Presidents' Forum, to exchange some thoughts and points of view as to approaches in meeting the financial growth requirements of the industry. While the business environment over the past decade has presented unique problems to be confronted and solved, we join you in looking forward with considerable optimism to the future of the paper industry.

Alleged improvements in accounting for mergers will result in deterioration in financial reports to the public

An article in *The New York Times*,
August 30, 1970

Proper standards can be established only when the true objectives of financial statements are determined and logical and persuasive reasons are given for the principles agreed upon.

AFTER TWO YEARS of debate and several years of research, the Accounting Principles Board of the American Institute of Certified Public Accountants is issuing two well-publicized Opinions. These pronouncements relate to the accounting for business combinations (mergers) and intangible assets (goodwill). Elaborate efforts have been made to justify these Opinions as representing a significant step forward in the improvement of financial reporting. However, quite the contrary will occur. These Opinions actually represent a complete failure by the accounting profession to face the real issues on these subjects and to deal with principles on a proper basis. The result is a horrendous group of arbitrary rules and regulations (17,000 words) which will further compound the difficulties in trying to present fairly the financial facts of corporations to the public.

Managements and public accountants will have extreme difficulty in attempting to follow these Opinions. But even more important, the resulting financial statements will be both incomprehensible and misleading to investors. The accounting profession should be establishing appropriate standards to give true purpose and meaning to the much used term, "generally accepted accounting principles." Instead, we continue to receive a flood of unrelated and unsupported directives from the APB which further pollute fair financial reporting to the public. The failures here go beyond their effect on the accounting profession and business; they are the best evidence to young people that the system is so involved in trivia that it can't identify simple, basic, and honest principles.

The accounting profession has not met its most important responsibility, that of establishing standards which will result in financial statements which represent a fair presentation of financial position and results of operations to the public. Such standards can be established only when the true objectives of financial reporting are determined and logical and persuasive reasons are given for the principles agreed upon. Otherwise, investors and other users of financial statements will be damaged by a vast array of arbitrary directives which are unsupported by any logical reasoning. The many uses to which financial statements are put, including the determination of investment values, are too important in our free enterprise system to have them based on such a questionable foundation of accounting. Real values can be destroyed and an illusion of nonexistent values can be created, without a legitimate basis for either one.

Why did the APB "fumble the ball" so badly in the case of merger accounting? The heart of the whole problem is the accounting for goodwill which arises in mergers. The difficulty can be traced directly to the refusal of the APB to face this issue squarely and to recognize that goodwill should never be shown as an asset in corporate balance sheets. This failure first led to an Opinion relating to goodwill which represents a farce insofar as fair financial reporting to the public is concerned. Then the Opinion relating to pooling-of-interests accounting and purchase accounting for mergers, with its lengthy and complicated rules, was primarily the result of trying to avoid the goodwill problem in part. The price which has been paid for this evasion of the real problem will be more and greater problems to deal with in the future.

The conclusions in the two Opinions are destructive rather than constructive for reasons such as the following:

1. The arbitrary criteria and conditions for determining how to account for the assets merged have no possible connection with accounting principles. These criteria and conditions which supposedly are aimed at undefined "abuses" are irrelevant to a proper accountability of the facts which occur.

2. A different accounting is prescribed for the same assets depending upon what kind of consideration, such as stock, cash, or debt, is used to pay for the acquired company. This contradicts a fundamental truth that asset values are neither changed nor determined by the type of consideration used to pay for them. Yet the Opinions erroneously direct that the assets acquired be reported to shareholders as though it was a fact that the vehicle for acquiring assets makes a difference in the assets acquired. Also, there is the ridiculous conclusion that the issuance of certain convertible preferred stock, which under another APB Opinion must be treated as equivalent to common stock for purposes of computing earnings per share, now is considered to produce a vastly different result than the issuance of common stock.

3. A different kind of accounting is required for merging a company, depending upon its origin and period of existence.

4. The books must be balanced by "plugging" them and recording an "unidentifiable" asset—goodwill—that, as time goes on, cannot be specifically found, cannot be measured, and cannot be priced. This will be the only asset in the balance sheet that will have no specific verification as to its existence or nature. Nevertheless, it must be presented to shareholders as a bona fide asset, but only for mergers that are made after October 31, 1970, and not even for all of them. There will be no opportunity for shareholders to learn what restrictive effects these double standards have on their investments—until is it too late.

5. Assets acquired after October 31, 1970, will be accounted for differently than assets acquired before

that date. This results in the same types of assets being accounted for several ways in the same balance sheet with shareholders not knowing why these double standards are adopted or what they are supposed to mean.

6. Earnings are to be artificially reduced by mergers after October 31, 1970, as a result of the mandatory amortization of goodwill, but not for earnings from mergers of an earlier date—with no way for shareholders to know what damage this double standard causes to their investment.

The accounting alternatives available before and after October 31, 1970, as well as alternatives resulting from choices whether or not to meet the various criteria, all of which will produce widely differing results, are most undesirable from the standpoint of investors.

The accounting profession, while trying to improve the basis for "generally accepted accounting principles," has only succeeded in establishing directives which place a serious burden on public accountants in giving opinions on financial statements. This burden is particularly significant when viewed against the background of recent comments of the legal counsel to our professional association relating to a recent legal proceeding involving public accountants found guilty of fraud:

"The trial court . . . gave instructions which said that the 'critical test' was whether the balance sheet fairly presented the financial position without reference to generally accepted accounting principles.

"The trial court also said in its instructions that evidence of compliance with generally accepted accounting principles would be very persuasive, but not conclusive. It also gave other instructions which the jury might have taken as an invitation to test the fairness of presentation, not against gen-

erally accepted accounting principles, but against their idea of what an investor or other layman might want to know."

These two Opinions of the APB will be under constant attack until they are replaced by other Opinions based on sound principles. Managements and public accountants will be forced to go through a trying period when enforcement of the Opinions will be subject to serious question. Appeals to the courts may be necessary to establish where legal responsibilities and rights exist, which could include a review of the rights of the Securities and Exchange Commission to enforce such arbitrary Opinions issued by a committee of a private association. The courts may well decide, in the end, what represents a fair presentation of the financial facts.

In this connection, Senator Scott Lucas from Illinois, who was a Democratic majority leader of the Senate, in a legal opinion written in 1947 stated with respect to the responsibilities of independent auditors under the Securities Act of 1933 as follows:

"In our opinion . . . although the form and content of the financial statements are subject to the rules and regulations of the Securities and Exchange Commission, the opinions expressed in the certificate are the accountant's and should reflect his knowledge of the actual facts in the case. Thus, in any case where the preparation of a statement in accordance with the Commission's rules and regulations results in a statement that is untrue or misleading, it is the accountant's duty to point out the fallacy in the statement and to show what, in his opinion, is the correct result."

Nothing is gained by sweeping an undesirable situation under the rug as some of my contemporaries seem to prefer to do. The desired goals can be attained only by a frank appraisal of what has occurred and then taking the necessary corrective steps.

What is profit?

Given in the summer course of The Institute of
Chartered Accountants in England and Wales
at Churchill College, Cambridge, England,
September 19, 1970

*The first order of business must
be the defining of objectives for the
financial statements in such
a way that the public can clearly
understand them.*

THE QUESTION POSED by this title
is a simple one, one which the public has
a right to ask. In turn, the public should be
entitled to receive a simple direct answer at
least in conceptual form. This question epit-
omizes the profession's greatest problem—
communication. It is these simple questions
that we, in our profession, apparently are
unprepared or unable to answer. This is
the kind of question that makes us face up
to the reason for our most serious inade-
quacy, failure to define the objectives of
financial reporting. It is the kind of question that remains unanswered, notwithstanding the requirement that financial statements
"fairly present" or give "a true and fair
view."

Certainly this question proved to have
many complexities for me as my thinking
evolved in preparation for this discussion.
There is no answer to this question in economic terms, either in theory, concept or
practice. Even so, the preparation for this
meeting proved to be most beneficial to
me, since a speaker generally does many
times the work and thinking that would seem
necessary to convey his ideas. Thus, I certainly have benefited greatly from undertaking this mission, and I hope that you will
find some things worthwhile in the observations to follow.

*Effective communication needs
anchor points*

When one has outlines of the presentations to be made by his colleagues speaking
on the program, outlines so excellently prepared, he is further motivated to find
"anchors," fundamental points of agreement
or disagreement, so that in the thinking
process we can turn square corners. Only
if such anchor points are found can one
expect to relate his observations to the thinking of his audience. I have always felt that

if I could attain a 25% success-level in the communication of my thinking, this would be a great achievement; therefore, I am particularly grateful for the discussion period that is to follow.

I feel at a great disadvantage, but highly complimented, to be here among practitioners whose abilities to express themselves are so much greater than my own. I am grateful for the opportunity to comment in a fundamental way on the forces that many of us in the United States feel are keeping American thought on accounting principles polarized according to group self-interests, and causing members of the profession to be petrified when we think of making an accounting of our responsibilities before our courts.

Financial reporting knows no national boundaries

When I examine the problems we face in the United States, and compare them with those in the United Kingdom and on the continent, I see that the obstacles to sound solutions are much the same. And this is as it should be. The economies of our nations are all highly developed. All have in common wide public corporate ownership and national interests. Furthermore, the economic interrelation among our countries is far greater than our predecessors ever could have visualized. Each one of us has a deep obligation to communicate to the public simply and directly on this common matter of sound accounting, since the reports issued by your firms and mine know no national boundaries.

Accountants in your country appear to be approaching the problems of defining accounting principles by addressing themselves to first problems first. In order for me to find some satisfaction in your more logical approach, upon which I will comment later, I have assumed that you have benefited somewhat from our unfortunate experience in the United States of failing to approach the overriding basic problem first.

Source of my views

My objectives and my views are based on twenty-five years of intensive occupation with the practical problems of reporting to public investors in the United States as a certified public accountant. These problems were encountered in actual practice in providing independent public accounting service to clients, and to public investors in those clients, in the one firm with which I have spent my entire business career of some forty-two years.

My views on accounting problems do not arise from a theoretical concern about the public need of the professional accountant's services. I take that need for granted, based on my practical experience, because that requirement is self-evident in any highly industrialized and developed society. My views stem from the problems of getting on with the job of meeting that need.

Need for independent financial reporting

The diversity of management multiplies as the economic entities in any society develop and grow in number, size and complexity. Reliable and sound financial reports to the public for each of these entities are an absolute necessity if the public is to have control of the nation's destiny and deal with the financial excesses that may be inflicted upon it.

The independent attestation as to the fairness of such a vast number of financial reports—reports on the accountability of these entities to the public—can be accomplished on a reasonably reliable basis only by nongovernmental practitioners, such as those comprising our profession, whose allegiance is to the public, not to the government, not to industry, not to labor, and not to management.

At the same time, such a nongovernmental body cannot allow itself to develop antagonistic attitudes toward any legally established governmental objectives that become law through the duly chosen political representatives of that society. By the very nature of organized society, we must have laws establishing property rights and the responsibilities of individuals and other entities. These legal rights and obligations differ among nations; therefore, the accounting for them differs among nations, but the principles and objectives of the accounting do not. We must, therefore, perform our work from a nonpolitical standpoint, subordinating all political activities to professional responsibilities nationally as well as internationally.

Our profession is an important part of the guidance systems of our respective economies. But if we fail as a profession to define our objectives clearly, and thus fail to achieve quality work that we ask the public to accept on faith, the overall guidance system of our national economies will fail the public. Our work can prevent financial failures in our countries, or at least keep them to a minimum, if our accounting clearly portrays the facts as to unfavorable and deteriorating conditions when they arise, so the public can take informed action on what it is told.

Accounting, however, cannot be expected to heal the economic ills of our nations; it will merely reflect the economic health, stability or instability of the economic system as experienced by the individual entities being reported upon. On the basis of these reports, presumably the public would act. Consequently, if government were allowed to control the accounting objectives it is reasonable to expect that overall national economic faults would be covered up just as corporate faults are apt to be covered up if corporations are allowed to control accounting objectives. Our reports must be based on objectives that will keep the public informed, if possible, before economic failures arise. It is easy to assess the results of disaster after the storm; but good and timely reports will advise shuttering the windows before the storm breaks.

There have been too many cases where our reports could have foretold trouble, but did not do so because the objectives of our principles of accounting were not clearly stated or were nonexistent. In those instances where our reports have failed the public, we have rightly been charged with some or all of the responsibility for the failures, particularly where we ignored obvious economic truths.

We cannot simply set up a body of practices and procedures that appeal to us, call them accounting principles, and assume that if we follow and observe them, this alone will constitute the discharge of our responsibility and therefore will be an adequate defense for us. Principles determined on this basis are self-serving to accountants; they are useless to the public, and they are held in contempt by business managers. Accounting principles will constitute an effective defense for us only if they are soundly conceived to attain the defined objectives of reliable and informative financial reporting to the public.

The legal counsel of the American Institute of Certified Public Accountants has told us unequivocally, as a result of the Continental Vending fraud case, what the distinction is between observing the application of an accounting principle and achieving the objectives of that accounting principle. He said:

> "The defendants had asked . . . for instructions that would have required the jury to acquit if it found that the balance sheet was in conformity with generally accepted accounting principles. The trial court instead gave instructions which said that the 'critical test' was whether the balance sheet fairly presented the financial position without reference to generally accepted accounting principles.

> "The trial court also said in its instructions that evidence of compliance with generally accepted accounting

principles would be very persuasive, but not conclusive. It also gave other instructions which the jury might have taken as an invitation to test the fairness of presentation, not against generally accepted accounting principles, but against their idea of what an investor or other layman might want to know." (*J. A.*, August 1970)

Profit as now reported is the result of a conglomeration of practices which defy definition

Our present dilemma in responding to the question, "What is profit?" arises from the fact that we have drifted into the practice of describing as being the fairly presented net profit an undefinable balance resulting from accounting practices that are not designed to achieve the objectives of financial reporting to public investors. The word "fairly" in this context is misused, and, in my opinion, results in a misrepresentation.

Thus, profit as now reported is the consequence of observing a great number of accounting practices which we and the business community have been in the habit of following. And this habit is the authority for their existence. These practices were not adopted because they were designed to arrive at some objective standard of measuring profit. They were adopted as patchwork compromises in bookkeeping to meet certain desired and often conflicting viewpoints at one time or another, and they have been continued regardless of changed conditions and the absence of basic objectivity. Their repetitive use is like copying last year's working papers in making this year's audit, a sure way to repeat all previous mistakes.

This is the history underlying the practices that we have inherited from the past and continue to pass on to the future. Obsolescence of such practices has accelerated over the years. During the continued use of those outmoded accounting practices,

investor ownership has greatly widened and has completely changed in character; and the needs of the investors have changed while our accounting to them has not.

The central purpose that used to underly the accounting, that of stewardship accounting to a private entrepreneur or a closely knit group, has been replaced by the need to respond to the self-interests of millions of public investors. Such self-interests are paramount because each investor is concerned only about his own shares, not those of any other individual or group. Overall large amounts merely make communication with the investor more difficult, hence the growing interest in one small amount—earnings per share.

Profit as we now determine and report it defies objective definition. We can say how it is arrived at only by listing bookkeeping entries that end up with a final balance we call profit. It has practically no common economic denominator to help the investor choose among investment alternatives, which is his paramount need. The term profit needs purging and expanding to meet an objective standard of measurement of financial progress or lack of progress by the entity to which it is attributed.

Steps to modernize accounting definitions and bring about improvement

The situation in which we find ourselves, as imperfect as it is, does not require that we throw out the whole financial reporting system and start anew. Such action would serve no useful purpose. An inadequate steering wheel is better than none when the car is in motion; and our economic car will always be in motion. The accounting that has evolved out of our past experience is the best we have, even though we are capable of devising far better practices. Our accounting system has a structure within itself which permits it to be changed without abandonment.

In order to move closer to objective standards, we must first put an end to the aimless improvisation we now follow in establishing accounting practices. This will require the injecting of defined objectives as the foundation on which all accounting principles are to be based. Then the application of such accounting principles in specific circumstances can be measured against the objectives to be achieved. Those objectives must be simply defined, even though the accounting principles necessary to achieve them may be complicated and often difficult to understand. It is the end result, the achieving of the defined objectives in presentation of financial statements, that is meaningful, and that should be understandable to the public and should control the practitioner's professional judgment. It is not necessary for the public to understand the practices followed in achieving the objectives; this would necessitate a reversal of the priorities for disclosure that we now emphasize. The first order of business must be the defining of objectives for the financial statements in such a way that the public can clearly understand them.

To make the public a party to the standards or objectives that we aspire to, we must involve that public beforehand in what it is that we strive to provide. This requires, first, the establishment of objectives and, second, the formulation of accounting principles to achieve them. This has not been done in the United States; that is, we have not determined the objectives before attempting to establish accounting principles. For that reason, we are constantly propelled toward the establishment of an "appeals court of accounting principles" to resolve our misunderstandings.

An appeals court of accounting principles

Such a court could be established either within the profession or outside of it. Today, appeals of accounting principles through our judicial court system are possible because the United States Supreme Court has recently established a basis of appeal from government edicts that unfairly damage the public. In this way, the quality of our accounting principles could now be monitored in behalf of the public through our judicial court system. But the decisions by our judicial courts, like the decisions in the BarChris and Continental Vending cases, would be made upon subjective standards unilaterally determined by the courts, not upon objective standards established by the profession. Such standards do not now exist; hence, the courts have had no other course but to set such standards for accounting performance as they saw to be required in the specific cases tried.

Creation of an accounting appeals court, either in or outside of the profession, would require the establishment of the end objectives of financial statements if both the public and the public accountants are to be treated fairly in the U. S. courts. Consequently, we shall not be ready for the creation of such an appeals court until these objective criteria have been established. The only criteria we have under our Federal Securities Acts are the ambiguous requirements that the reporting omit no material facts and that it be not misleading. Compliance with these criteria can only be accomplished subjectively and unilaterally by whoever happens to be the decision maker.

Management services a misleading term

A word should be added here about the participation of the public accountant (or the chartered accountant) in the field of what is commonly called management services. This term is likely to lead the public into thinking that we as professional accountants may be participating in the management of the business or that we may be monitoring managements' operating decisions on behalf of the public. We cannot do this. We do not have the competence; and even if we did have the competence, we could not do such work and at the same time pose as independent auditors.

While we may appropriately participate in designing and installing information systems and procedures, we must always remain verifiers and reporters of financial facts for those to whom management is accountable, not only the stockholders, but also labor, management, creditors and the public at large.

We cannot join in the responsibilities of management and at the same time measure the results of that management against accounting objectives without in the process measuring ourselves, and thus being guilty of duplicity. In my opinion, the use of the word "management" in describing any of the services rendered by the public or the chartered accountants either disqualifies them as auditors or makes them guilty of misrepresentation to the public.

How to change the present status of "profit" and "accounting principles" that determine it

The deficiencies that exist today in the determination of what is called "profit" do not arise from a professional failure that rests on some impersonal group of professional, governmental, academic, or industry people that we can point to as "they." You and I personally can and must step up to the bar and measure the deficiencies in the performance of our own individual work. When we identify our own deficiencies, we will also have determined those that apply to the whole profession. No excuse to the contrary is an acceptable personal defense for any one of us.

My thinking on the question of "What is Profit?" led me to focus on some existing realities.

First, we in our profession must come to a common understanding that the quality of present accounting practices followed in determining what we report as profit needs a major overhauling. To reach such a common understanding requires us to consider which of the accounting principles and prac-

tices we now observe are designed to achieve an acceptable objective, and thus can serve to guide us in judging the end result flowing from application of those principles.

We know that we now follow many practices only because they are widely used. We can explain how those practices came about. But if we try to identify the objectives they are intended to achieve, we often find them to be in contradiction to the objectives of other principles followed. And this goes on ad infinitum. Thus, the present accounting practices in determining what we call profit reveal contradictory objectives.

We must first isolate all present practices that do not meet the specific common end-objective, i.e., the accepted measure of profit. In doing this, we must create a measure that defines what profit is. We need to get a horse for the cart that we are using, because we do not now have one.

Next, we need to acknowledge the fact that imperfections and limitations in accounting practices do exist, and to recognize what they are, what they mean, and that they will be with us for some time even if we succeed in identifying clearly what the objectives of accounting reports should be. We do not possess the power of instant solutions that can be made effective at once. Nor can we guarantee that future experience will not produce the need for further change or improvement in any practice we may now adopt to meet an objective.

Thus, our need is not only to determine accounting objectives, but to couple them with an accounting communication system that can accommodate practice changes as they are found desirable and, in the meantime, reflect separately the effect of present accounting practices which do measure up to the present objectives. The recognition that instant change cannot be accomplished is no excuse for sitting back with hands folded waiting for evolutionary changes to force themselves on us. Nor is it an excuse to bury, unidentified, the consequences of those accounting practices that do not meet objective standards and to rely on the disclosures the professional accountant makes in his audit reports. The public has a right to demand from professionals proof that they are aggressively pursuing the steps that are within their capabilities to meet the public needs. Thus, we need to establish a program that will provide for a transition from where we now are to where we must go.

Out of my experience, I have concluded that our difficulty in defining accounting principles that will produce realistic profit reporting lies in different points of view or in the lack of understanding among us that follow from the differences in our individual experiences. This is the same problem that the proverbial three blind men had in agreeing on the appearance of the elephant. Perhaps of even greater significance is the fact that many of us view proposed accounting principles as unacceptable if they cannot immediately be applied to the letter with bookkeeping perfection. We call such proposals impractical and lose sight of the fact that every balance sheet and every profit statement is, at best, an approximation reflecting many estimates. Such statements are somewhat blurred instant pictures of history in motion. A reliable approximation of usable facts is far better for the information of the public than accurate bookkeeping results that are useless to individual investors in deciding whether to act or not to act in their own behalf.

We are so devoted to the philosophy of accuracy in bookkeeping that we lose sight of, or forget entirely, the objectives of sound reporting of the end result. But the observance of such objectives does not require abandonment of accurate bookkeeping practices; we must have both, because they are as interrelated as Siamese twins. The trouble stems from our devotion to the practice part and the ignoring of the objectives, although the objectives should be the guiding stars for our public reporting.

The means (accounting practices) to an end have tended to become more controlling than the objective of the end result. For instance, the recognition of fair value in reporting is often rejected because of the difficulty of determining it. We then devise an accounting principle as a substitute for fair value, such as cost. Cost is, of course, ordinarily the best evidence of value as of date of prudent acquisition, and it has continuing usefulness if coupled with depreciation, provided that price levels remain stable.

But we proceed to lose sight of the real objective, the reflection of fair value, and to become content with the poor substitute, which is cost. The consequence of this practice is the crediting of capital to profit since, over the life of the property, operations are charged only with cost depreciation rather than fair-value depreciation. He who accepts cost-depreciation practice as an end in his work does not even see the occurrence of this transfer from capital to profit; but he would be aghast at a direct bookkeeping entry that did the same thing. The practitioner who properly identifies the objective for depreciation practices is (or should be) conscience-stricken by the transfer from capital to profit, which he sees being reported to the public under the guise of cost depreciation principles.

How much happier is life for the accountant who is oblivious to the contradiction between practice and the objective of practice as illustrated in only this one instance. The cumulative effect of this specific erroneous practice is far greater in the United States where it is fostered by government to conceal the effects of inflation, than it is in the United Kingdom where you recognize fair values from time to time when cost has lost its usefulness as a measure of asset value.

Another reason for resisting changes that eliminate obsolete accounting practices is that we are loath to change methods to which we have become accustomed. Like the child who takes his blanket to bed regardless of how beaten up and ragged it becomes, we

like to hold on to familiar accounting practices and principles. Historical accounting
data lose their usefulness in up-to-date economics, where shareholders, in fact, live and
die today. They ask for meaningful financial
communication that connects them with the
reality of their daily-life problems as they
now experience them. They care not for
theories of accounting related to the past.
They are living for today. We fail to meet
the test of relevance for them because we
do not remeasure our so-called accounting
principles and practices against our goals
(if we have any), and then adjust our practices to meet those goals as conditions
change. Our present attitude applies yesterday's obsolete practices as today's required
principles. They would be rejected out-of-
hand if we would first identify the objectives
which should control them.

Continue to use old practices until officially replaced

If we were able to define the real objectives of our financial reporting and thus
establish accounting principles to achieve
them; if we then acknowledged that it would
take time to revise and apply practices to
achieve those objectives; and if we were to
formulate profit and loss statements that
disclosed the effect of the application of
those principles that conformed to our objective standards and those that did not so
conform, we could at least be honest with
ourselves and to the public investors we are
serving.

We could then sort out our principles
between those that meet the objectives and
those that need revision. The public could
then be told the amounts involved in those
practices that properly met the objectives
and the amounts involved in those that did
not meet such objectives. As revised accounting principles that met the desired
objectives were authoritatively established
and applied, the amounts affected in the
reported accounts would be moved into the
category that met the reporting objectives.

Let me illustrate this suggested approach
by referring to a compass. A compass shows
the direction to a given point; this point may
be compared to our ideal accounting objective. But in following the direction shown
by that compass, one does not necessarily
travel in a direct line. To get to the desired
point, it is sometimes necessary to digress
temporarily by turning off from a straight-
line course to avoid mountains, storms, or
other impediments.

We have a similar problem in achieving
the desired accounting objectives. Professional judgment and practicalities may lead
to the approval of accounting practices and
principles that temporarily call for turning
off from the direct course while working
toward our objective; but in so doing, we
reach an acceptable or practical approximation of the objective, and we say so.
However, if the objective of every principle
is not clearly stated and does not become
the guide for our actions, there is no way
of measuring how far off course we may
be in the application of any given principle
or practice.

Our judgment as professional practitioners
can be used to appraise the gap between the
result achieved with a given principle or
practice. In this process we would close the
retrogressive loopholes caused by the use
of less desirable alternative accounting practices. Since permissible alternative practices
or principles would be only those which
more closely achieved the objective to be
attained, choice of alternative practices that
failed to achieve the closest approximation
to the objective could be identified by the
reporting accountant and his disapproval
expressed.

This would permit users of financial statements to understand that as practitioners
we take the responsibility that the practice
or principle used is not only an approximation of the guiding objective, but is also
believed to be the closest practical approximation. Then, as conditions permitted, we
could improve the practices and principles

to reach a position closer to our objective.

As we move the practices and principles toward our guiding objective (our compass point), we could identify the conditions that justify stopping short of the preferable solution. Then, no matter who used results based on the alternatives applied, he would know in what regard the results approximated the desired-end objective. If further improvement can be made, the user will know the direction of the change that will result from such improvement. Thus, as a minimum standard, each accounting practice or principle would relate to a specific objective and, if changed, could only go further in the direction of the objective. Personal preferences would be confined to those practices that best achieved the objective sought, rather than being the personal choice of the management or the accountant without regard to the controlling objective.

Such a restructuring of our accounting thought would get us off dead center and away from blindly accepting accounting practices and principles as an end result in themselves. Such a restructuring would place emphasis on what is to be achieved and would avoid emphasis on bookkeeping practices without measuring the results against the objectives. In fact, changes in practices and principles as among companies should be encouraged if such changes result in better achieving the objective standard for financial statements.

Accounting Principles Board (APB)
procedures and those of the Institute of
Chartered Accountants (ICA)

In inaugurating a program of professional determination of accounting principles in the United States, we established the Accounting Principles Board some twelve years ago. The Special Committee of the American Institute of Certified Public Accountants which formulated the plan to establish the APB avoided spelling out the criteria, the objectives and the process to be followed in establishing the principles, and the nature of the opinions thereon that would be issued. This deficiency in the plan left the APB without sail or anchor, and it has continued to drift on a conglomeration of ideas having no common objective.

The idea that objectives be stated in the masthead of each opinion was rejected in favor of the limited goal of narrowing the range of alternative practices and principles by the use of persuasion. This effectively struck down all semblance of quality control based on objectives. Time and experience have resulted in opinions of low quality, based to a considerable extent on the personal preferences of, and pressures on, the APB members.

The program of your Institute of Chartered Accountants is similarly based on broad objectives, with one basic but great difference that makes your ICA program and our APB as different as day and night. It is a difference that makes it possible for you to achieve progress with quality such as was never possible for us, given our APB charter.

I must commend your Institute for undertaking as the first step in your program a study to describe the basic purpose and meaning of the accounts and then to follow this with a recommendation of specific problems to be considered, such consideration to require reexamination of accounting principles in the light of the purpose of the accounts. If the APB in the United States had followed this order (incidentally, such a plan was recommended to our Special Committee) its accomplishments to date would have been legion.

I note, too, that pending completion of the first part of your program, you have begun recommendations as to accounting practices on specific problems; this is necessary to keep your guidance system functioning. I commended the ICA on its first exposure draft on one of these specific problems, "Accounting for the Results of Associated Companies." It is superior to those that we have been receiving from our APB, superior because it conveys the reasoning for its issuance and the consequence of its findings in terms of usefulness to the investors, in short, it states the objective to be achieved. It does have a masthead explanation, and in paragraphs 3 and 4 states what will be accomplished by the accounting proposed. It should be controlling on the practitioner in exercising his professional judgment.

I venture to say that this excellent start by ICA will be improved by experience. I hope it will be a guide to us in the United States in improving our approach, and that it will prevent such destructive pronouncements as the recent APB Opinions Nos. 16 and 17 on business combinations and goodwill.

These two APB Opinions, in 17,000 words, contain directive after directive with no showing of relevance and with no statement of the objectives of financial reporting or profit determination to be achieved by those Opinions. With no statement of the objectives in these Opinions, there is no target for the reader; and we have found that because of this omission, these Opinions fail to communicate their purpose, either within the profession or to the public. The result is two Opinions representing an assortment of ideas held by the various Board members which, in total, will produce reporting that will be meaningless and misleading to the whole profession and to the public.

Responsibility for progress

One cannot expect an individual firm to accept responsibility for observing proper principles of accounting when the profession has no cohesive opinion on the purpose or objective to be achieved by financial statements. A unilateral determination of objectives by one firm would serve no useful purpose to it, to its clients, or to the profession. Yet our courts have stated clearly that the individual accountant has no defense against failure to fulfill his responsibility for fair presentations that show what

the investors or other laymen might want to know, irrespective of what so-called generally accepted accounting principles may call for. At present in the United States the public accountants are between the devil and the deep blue sea. Which term refers to our courts and which to our accounting principles, I will leave to your speculation.

Once the profession establishes objectives for financial reporting to the public, we can, as individuals and as firms, establish for use in our professional practice suitable principles of accounting to meet those objectives. We then can also establish individual identity of performance to the public. In the meantime, one cannot expect an individual firm to assume responsibility for accepting and applying APB accounting principles that serve no useful purpose or objective for the investor or layman.

This is the condition that we have in the United States today, and it is acceptable to the public accountant only if the courts in some way give authority for the observance of practices that are not documented as to what the investor or other layman might "want to know." The one condition precedent in serving the public with which our courts have charged us is that we must establish the fact that each principle of accounting applied, reasonably achieves the objective which underlies it. Since the objectives have not been established, achieving the impossible is what we are now charged to do.

Basic objectives of financial statements presented to the public

I have always advised my associates that the diagnosis of an accounting illness is of no use if, as practitioners, we do not know how to treat that illness. I now find myself required to perform under the standard that I have urged. My diagnosis is finished. The two remaining tasks are:

   1. To state the basic objectives of financial statements, and

2. To illustrate a system of communication to investors, consisting of financial statements based on accounting principles which in part conform to the objectives and in part do not.

We can describe in rather short, simple language the objectives of our three basic financial statements, if we release our ties to all existing accounting principles and practices that we use. These objectives should be defined as though everything as to facts needed were available at the financial statement date. The definition of objectives for the balance sheet, income account and cash-flow statements should not be complicated or burdened with extensive rhetoric. They should be like the Ten Commandments, simple and to the point—the point toward which all accounting principles must focus.

The objectives of the three statements setting forth the financial position, results of operations and cash flow of any entity, could be stated as simply as this:

A. The objective of a balance sheet is to present to its readers:

(a) an inventory of all assets and deferred charges, reasonably but briefly described, at their fair value, i.e., at amounts estimated to be recoverable under the economic and political conditions of ownership and use at the date of issuance of the balance sheet;

(b) a summary of all liabilities and reserves at present estimated amounts payable at date of maturity; and

(c) the net balance, that is, the assets and deferred charges less the liabilities and reserves, representing the equity, showing the accumulated amounts of the entity and by the various classes of owners or stockholders.

B. The objective of the income account for any period is to analyze for readers the nature of the net change in the owners' equity, exclusive of dividends paid and new capital received, including changes in old capital for price-level variations. The net change in equity thus defined would be described as the "net profit" of the entity for the period.

C. The objective of the cash-flow statement for any period is to show (a) the balance of cash funds at the beginning of the period, (b) the additions to such funds, with the amount from net profit separated from other sources, (c) the uses made of funds, and (d) the balance of funds at the end of the period. This statement should be divided between those funds applicable to parent and all subsidiaries having no significant minority interests or debts outstanding that have priority over the parent ownership, and those subsidiaries that do have significant prior lien minority interests and debt outstanding.

When agreement about the objectives is reached, their authorship should be by or in behalf of the whole profession. No individual claim to authorship is desirable.

These objectives would represent the ideal as to what investors and other laymen could reasonably be expected to want in a fair presentation of financial position, results of operation, and cash flow. But, we cannot expect to achieve perfection in accounting any more than we can expect perfection in any other line of human endeavor. The actual conditions, facts, and costs of accomplishing accounting tasks make attainment of total perfection in preparation of financial statements beyond the possibility of our achievement. However, this realistic condition in no way detracts from the ideal goal of reaching for specific objectives against which to measure our performance.

It follows from the foregoing objectives of financial reporting that:

1. "Net profits" for a period are the net gain in fair value of net assets during the period (or conversely that "net loss" is the net decrease in net

assets), exclusive of changes in value of old capital attributable to price-level variations, new capital received, and dividends paid.

2. Any error in establishing net assets at fair value, or from omitting recognition of liabilities has an equal effect, which may be in part on net profits and in part on owners' equity.

3. Only when all assets, net of liabilities, are recognized at fair value will we have a fair measure of profit for the period and a fair presentation of financial position.

The purpose of accounting principles is to establish practices that will produce results which most nearly approximate those called for by the objectives of the financial statements

As previously noted, a compass always points the exact direction, even though to follow that direction it may be necessary or advisable to digress from a straight-line movement because of overriding practical obstacles. Practical obstacles always will be present in seeking to achieve reporting objectives, but the digressions caused by such obstacles should be clearly identified so we can recognize and measure them.

While disagreements would arise in identifying the digressing practices, the reporting objectives would provide a philosophical base or compass point to which they could be reconciled.

The profession should develop an inventory of all the principles necessary to reach the desired financial-reporting objectives. This may involve polishing and perfecting some principles now followed, but in the process their description should be tightly related to the controlling objectives of the financial statement. Opinions relating to accounting principles should state the practicalities or other necessities that may cause the end result of their use to produce less than a bull's-eye hit on the objective. An

alternative practice that meets the same degree or a greater degree of perfection in reaching the objective can be readily approved and accepted by the practitioner. In fact, in specific instances, some of the anticipated obstacles in establishing an accepted principle of accounting might be found not to exist, and, therefore, the digression that was allowed for would not be necessary.

Each present practice found in such an inventory of accounting principles that falls short of the objective would require revision or substantiation. Deficiencies in principles would be classified by degree of failure to achieve the objective, with priority of revision and substantiation being given to the more significant deficiencies. For those deficiencies in principles for which correction is to be delayed, the practical reasons that underlie continued acceptance of the deficiency would need to be clearly established.

Forthrightness should govern our judgments so that we do not submit to continuation of hidebound practices that seriously impair the attainment of our objectives. On the other hand, life is not so perfect that we can afford to look at a molehill as we would a mountain. Being forthright as to the basis for temporarily continuing deficient practices should enhance the public confidence in our profession.

To classify deficiencies in order of priority for correction or justification, we must also define "fair value" of assets on a basis that is free of exorbitant expense and minute technical aspects of determination. Fair value,* as applied to cash, securities with quoted market values and receivables, is already a widely accepted basis of reporting. Explanation of the basis used in determining fair value is desirable, such as indicating that the fair value reported for marketable

---

*For a discussion of means of obtaining current-cost (fair value) data, see "A Statement of Basic Accounting Theory," Appendix A, American Accounting Association, 1966.

securities is derived from published quoted values. The related accounting principles should clearly state that the quoted market value does not necessarily represent fair value at the statement date, but is only an indication of approximate fair value for the securities involved. Furthermore, the quoted market value at the later date when the financial statements are released may not be equally required in order to meet the objectives of what the investor wants to know but, if there has been a significant subsequent change, disclosure should be considered.

Fair value for inventories would ordinarily represent estimated realizable value, less cost of completing and selling and a fair profit margin. Average cost commonly approximates this result, and this is why use of average cost would usually qualify as a generally accepted standard to meet the objective, provided it is determined that no significant lack of recoverability exists.

The fair-value principle for deferred charges (including prepaid expenses) would permit deferral only on the basis of reasonably expected recoverability from future revenues. Fixed assets (plant and equipment), other than land and natural resources, would need to be adjusted for the change in general price level as a step toward approximation of fair value. In some countries periodic appraised value of plant and equipment is recognized (rather than price-level adjustment of cost) in determining fair value. This may be acceptable under some conditions where it does not produce amounts that exceed economic value. However, for the present, at least, I would prefer to start with price-level adjustment of cost. The question of economic value—of reasonable expectation of realization through future operations—should also be considered in applying price-level adjustments. Natural resources, including land, would need to be valued periodically, probably on a regular basis with dating stated.

Liabilities and reserves are generally recognized in accordance with proper standards today, except for those leases for which neither the liability nor the asset is presently recorded. But such leases should be recorded because the liability thereunder remains constant while the asset value fluctuates. The present deficiencies in lease accounting are based on the theory that the value of the leased property is an offset against the liability. The offset assumption clearly violates valuation measurement principles.

What are some of the major present deficiencies in attaining sound balance sheets, which therefore result in unsatisfactory profit determinations for investor use? I would suggest the following:

High Priority

1. The nonrecognition of current fair value of the equipment, at least to the extent of price-level changes.

2. The nonrecognition of current fair values of land and natural resources.

3. The noncapitalization of development costs of new products and the resulting failure to include such costs as assets to be evaluated by investors.

4. The nonrecognition of increases in quoted value of marketable securities (except in some situations such as investment companies and insurance companies); and in underlying value of long-term minority investments in other companies.

5. The erroneous capitalization as "goodwill," of unidentifiable amounts often representing nothing but speculative future earning power of the entity.

Low Priority

1. The nonrecognition of the price-level (inflationary) shrinkage in purchasing power of working capital of companies situated in developed nations. This shrinkage is frequently

recognized in developing countries where inflation is rampant.

In the United States, the accounting profession is currently giving attention to all of the above high-priority problems, except the recording of current fair values of land and natural resources. But if past practice continues to prevail, none of these problems will be resolved in relation to the objectives of sound financial reporting. This deficiency is already evident in the recent APB Opinions Nos. 16 and 17 on business combinations and goodwill.

The nonrecognition of the price-level changes on working capital in developed nations is of lower priority because the effect is not relatively severe as yet in the developed countries. It is, however, a part of the broader problem of recognizing price-level changes generally.

Improvement should be provided by the passage of time

Use of the valuation bases suggested above will not always lead to precise current valuations. Normally, however, reasonably satisfactory measures of current fair value can be made on a periodic basis. Their use will improve the financial reporting and permit the best balance sheet that can be prepared and, hence, will provide the best measure of net profit. Hindsight, however, will afford the basis for improving the fair-value determinations made at earlier dates, just as hindsight is enlightening in practically every other fact-finding endeavor.

Financial statements previously prepared for past dates or periods should reflect the most accurate reporting of net assets and net profits currently possible. Consequently, the profession should adopt a principle calling for subsequent revision of prior-year statements to reflect significant improvements in practices or the effect of further information that becomes available with the passage of time.

Unfortunately, recent court cases in the United States have caused both legal counsel and public accountants to become very reluctant to revise prior-year statements to reflect possible improvements in presentation when again included in current reports. This reluctance is due in part to a misguided strategy for court defense of public accountants, and tends to injure rather than serve the public investor. It is blindness of a high order to refuse to improve prior-year reporting just to maintain a defense against possible allegation of error or negligence in reporting in the first instance.

To provide the best defense strategy for the accountants and to best serve the investors, the accounting profession should establish a principle requiring subsequent retroactive recognition of significant facts which meet high standards of accountability any time prior-period statements are issued, irrespective of the reporting contained in the prior reports. Without such discipline, how can the practitioner claim to be an independent professional? A standard of this nature would be understandable to the courts when lawsuits require specific accountability for service given.

If all financial statements of an entity could be issued, say, three years after the entity's demise, it is probable that such statements would be as close to perfection as it is humanly possible to achieve. However, all entities must live and operate in the current environment. We as accountants must prepare periodic financial reports under those current conditions as events take place. Even though we utilize all the knowledge and known facts available at a given moment, we must also recognize that this knowledge will be augmented by the passage of time.

The tests of fair financial statements at any given date must be both the exercise of proper diligence and prudence in obtaining all facts at that date, and the fair reporting of the facts available at that date. Therefore, facts affecting a prior period must be presented as a part of the accounting for that period if present readers of prior-year statements are not to be misinformed about the results of prior as well as current periods. How can we permit a reader to make a comparison with prior-period results where, on the basis of subsequent knowledge, we now know the reporting for the prior period to have been significantly deficient?

A principle calling for appropriate revision of prior-year statements would be consistent with our present practice of reviewing transactions subsequent to the date of financial statements, but prior to issuance of our reports so as to take into consideration as much additional hindsight information as we can. It would not be possible in a calendar-year enterprise of any size (except perhaps banks) to issue year-end statements on the morning of January 1; the more the elapsed time, the better the statements can be.

Why financial statements are given "baths"

In determining what is profit, we cannot overlook that phenomenon commonly called a "bath" which some companies give to their reporting of profits from time to time. These baths often result from the failure to recognize changing conditions and the accumulation of inferior accounting practices which practices are nevertheless considered permissible within the wide spectrum of generally accepted accounting principles. Under these circumstances, I would generally recommend that such a bath be taken, in order to clear the accounting tubes and to persuade the management (often a new management) to lead a better life accountingwise from then on.

In the United States we have a second-rate practice that results in carrying as an asset an item called goodwill. This arises where a company acquires another business for consideration having a fair value in ex-

cess of the fair value of the net assets acquired. Although this so-called goodwill is an intangible item that is not separable—it cannot be sold or realized—it appears in the balance sheet as an asset of value. I have strongly urged that such so-called goodwill be promptly written off against, or at least deducted from, the owners' equity. But the APB has been unwilling to adopt this practice. Consequently, this goodwill often is one of the items that awaits the bath for final disposition.

The majority of such bath items that eventually have to be charged off to profit can be attributed to the lack of sound objectives in financial reporting. If sound objectives were established for such reporting, they would promote greater reliability in profit determinations for companies that are now inclined to take the primrose path of second-rate accounting practices that usually leads to a day of reckoning. The practicing accountant is now unable to demand that better standards be observed because there are no objectives for financial reports to back him up.

Retribution accounting

In the United States, we also have a somewhat dubious principle which might be called "retribution accounting." It is a first cousin to the philosophy of absorbing prior-year adjustments, usually charges, in the current-year profit and loss account. Its basic "justification" is to punish management for adopting second-rate accounting practices in the first place, and also to protect the public accountants from having to admit they were in error in allowing such accounting in the first place.

The idea is that if any imprudence occurred in prior-year accounts that resulted in erroneous reporting for that prior year, the correction when discovered must be absorbed in the accounts of the later year, thus going against the sound old adage that two wrongs do not make a right. The injured party in such cases, if the effect is significant, is the public investor who by reason of this strange reporting practice is given at least two annual statements in which the profits reported were wrong. We should be petrified at the thought of what our courts would say if we tried to defend such accounting treatment as presenting what the investors want to know. Objective standards would give the practicing accountant the tools to prevent such practices from taking root; and if they did, both the issuer and the accountant would have to face the facts objectively.

*Illustration of a communication
system in which the statements
are based on principles that in part
do not conform to reporting objectives*

There is no such thing as instant construction or building. Every step of progress is preceded by a well-defined plan for progress, and we in the accounting profession have no special competence to break out of this pattern. We need a program to guide us in approaching the compass point of ideal financial statements, even though it is probable that, in human existence, we shall never reach that point. Confidence of the success of any plan is always so much greater among the young; but it tends to fade as experience brings us face-to-face with the obstacles involved. Despair or frustration often comes with age, and it is this that has thwarted much of the progress that otherwise would be obtainable in our profession.

Assume for the moment that we have arrived at a fair definition of the objectives of financial reporting by which profit is determined. Assume further that our present accounting principles do not produce results which square with those objectives, but that these principles must be used until revisions can be made. What then about the quality of the profit figures communicated to investors in the resulting financial statements in the interim?

The response must be that the profit determinations during this interim period necessarily will be second-rate. However, if the objectives of the financial statements are established, the principles of accounting used by the individual companies can be improved by the companies themselves and by the practicing public accountants, by adopting more appropriate practices geared to the reporting objectives.

Even at present, the observance of an accounting principle by an individual enterprise might closely approximate the objectives, while in another instance application of that same principle will not do so. For example, the price-level effect caused by inflation is far greater for companies with older plants than with companies having mainly newly purchased or constructed property.

These being the conditions we have to work with, the suggested approach to the problem of reporting to investors lies in the design of the form of financial reports issued. With financial reporting objectives defined, the statements can be custom-designed to make the most informative presentation practicable in the circumstances instead of simply following the customary form.

The communication value of a profit and loss statement, or a balance sheet, is not solely in the accounting-principle ingredients applied, even if such principles meet the ideal objectives in all major respects. These statements are not just pills to be swallowed whole, or even to be swallowed at all, particularly the one popular figure of earnings per share. The nature of the items shown therein is equally as important as the accounting standards underlying their presentation.

Therefore, I would like to propose a change in the form of profit and loss (income) statement that would reconcile the accounting results based on objectively determined amounts for assets and liabilities and revenues and costs with the net income or profit as now reported with its imperfections.

Such a presentation would set out separately those items which have major imperfections in their determination. These items will vary among companies, as will the degree of their impact; therefore, their importance will also vary from company to company. But investors would thus be told what they want to know about the profit figures given them, even though objectively determined profit amounts, which they would also want to know, are not available or determinable.

As improvements are made in accounting principles to achieve the reporting objectives, either by the issuers or by the profession, the items having imperfections that appear in the profit and loss statement and the impact of these items on profit reports will diminish and eventually disappear. We will then have profit statements that are as near the ideal sought as it is possible to achieve. What is also important is that the defined objectives for those statements will serve as a magnet on issuer and practitioner alike to constantly improve the reporting.

Illustration of profit and loss statement embracing such imperfect accounting principles

Communication between us can be facilitated by an illustration of the type of profit and loss presentation I have in mind. It is a combination of the usual U. S. form and a form designed to set forth the effect of the deficiencies resulting from application of some of our present accounting principles. The design is secondary to the usefulness to the investor, and is intended to communicate as much substantive data as the issuer and the practicing accountant can pack into a brief presentation.

Attempts to reconcile a balance sheet prepared according to presently accepted accounting principles, with a preferable one based on fair value of net assets, will be thwarted as long as the ingredient of fair value is not available. Corporations do not presently determine fair values for assets and are not likely to devise ways to do so overnight, even though they do approximate such values for insurance purposes. The establishment of sound accounting principles, in this regard, should provide the basis for use of acceptable substitutes, such as I have previously discussed, that are generally available.

We will, however, move closer to our objectives, step by step, as we adopt new principles, such as the recognition of earnings on long-term investments (as called for by the proposed pronouncement of your Institute, which I hope we in the United States will also adopt), the recognition of fair value based on present price-level adjustment of cost of plant and equipment, proper accounting for development of products and natural resources, etc.

In this way, profit or income reports would localize and identify those elements of income and costs which are in a transitional state, elements which accountants feel need greater refinement in order to achieve better reporting of profits and values. Such reporting would clearly isolate the entire area in which accountants need to make rapid progress, progress that will bring about a better matching of revenues with the real cost expirations of producing them. Such separations can be readily made by the practicing accountant when objectives of financial statements are clearly defined.

We have but one avenue for partial correction without forcing immediate change in accepted accounting principles and practices, and that is to put all the black sheep (mismatched income and expense) in one pen until we have the time and the tools to do the shearing.

I would not mislead you by predicting that all of the items in the second category can ever be fully eliminated. As a matter of fact, it may be impossible to square some

Line No.		1970	Per Common Share Equivalent	1969	Per Common Share Equivalent
1	SALES AND REVENUES EARNED DURING THE YEAR:				
2	Sales..$	$	$	$	
3	Dividends.................................				
4	Interest.................................				
5	Total sales and revenues...............$	$	$	$	
6	COSTS, EXPENSES AND TAXES THAT MATCH THE PRODUCTION OF THE ABOVE REVENUES:				
7	Cost of products sold (excluding depreciation) .$	$	$	$	
8	Selling expenses...........................				
9	Administrative expenses....................				
10	Taxes on current income....................				
11	Interest expense on operating property........				
12	Total production costs that match above sales and revenues..................$	$	$	$	
13	Net earnings from sales and revenues less matched expenses...................$	$	$	$	
14	REVENUES (COSTS) RECORDED DURING YEAR WHICH ARE NOT DIRECTLY MATCHED AGAINST ABOVE NET SALES AND REVENUES:				
15	Depreciation provision based on price level values, or costs, of prior years............				
16	Interest expense on construction work in progress not capitalized..................				
17	Sales and revenues earned in prior years but recorded this year......................				
18	Cost of development or search for products to be produced in the future....................				
19	Provision for loss on contracted production of future periods...........................				
20	Recoveries on production losses of prior years .				
21	Profit on sale of plant for which carrying costs were absorbed in prior years..............				
22	Profit on sale of investments for which earnings in prior years were not reported and carrying cost was absorbed as expense in prior years.				
23	Tax credit (cost) applicable to above..........				
24	Reported net profit for the period........$	$	$	$	

( ) Deduction.

of them with the revenue-matching concept, even though they may meet the precise definition of asset value for the balance sheet. One such item is the provision for loss on contracted production of future years. Since a known future-year loss should be provided for currently even if the amount can only be estimated, it becomes a charge against current profit rather than against profit when production occurs. At that latter date the reserve provided in the prior year becomes a credit to profit to offset the loss that occurs when revenues and production costs are matched.

Nevertheless, this proposed form of income account would disclose those items which cause by far the largest part of the trouble investors are now having in understanding the makeup of reported profit as against the real profit.

Such a statement as I am proposing would not at this point achieve the ideal determination of profit for the period, since we do not yet have the objective standards or the facts to make such a determination. However, such a statement would permit one with reasonable understanding to grasp the makeup of what is reported as profit, which is the next best thing to an objective determination of what the profit is. That is the best we can do today.

The understanding of such a statement may appear to place a formidable task on the reader, if he cannot cope with it, but he still is no worse off, since today most users have no idea of what judgment should be applied before the reported net profit is accepted as being objectively determined. At least he would then have the information which he could take to his advisor for enlightenment.

Design of profit and loss statement is also a subject for treatment by accounting principles

As stated earlier, accounting principles that merely regulate bookkeeping practice do not finish the job expected of them. The form and content of both the balance sheet and the profit and loss statement should be covered by prescribed accounting principles if the objectives of financial reporting are to be achieved. This is a large area that warrants a full seminar discussion itself.

Here, I shall refer briefly to only one phase of profit and loss reporting that in many instances destroys its effectiveness, irrespective of the quality of the accounting followed. I refer to the practice of using the customary form of statement that combines both profitable and unprofitable divisions or subsidiaries in one total and gives net figures, as though the results on a combined net basis communicate to the investor what he wants and should know. A reasonable consideration of investors' requirements would call for a principle of presentation that requires separate or supplemental profit and loss statements, or segregation within the statement, showing the combined profitable operations and the combined unprofitable operations.

Such a reporting requirement, however, would be a complete failure if its pronouncement consisted of many pages of declaratory directives, such as APB Opinions have in the past. An opinion to accomplish this reporting should be limited to the principles involved; and if it were simply and clearly drawn to implement the objectives of such financial reporting, it would require only a few pages. Such an opinion would be exceedingly beneficial to the public investor, to the issuer and to the independent auditor.

Misuse of the word "fairly" in auditors' opinion

I cannot leave a discussion of "what is profit" without reference to the use of the word "fairly" in the opinion of the independent accountants on our side of the Atlantic. This word, "fairly", refers to and qualifies the opinion on every presentation of financial position and results of operation in the United States.

There is no objective standard of use for the word "fairly" as it appears in the auditors' opinions. Until the objectives of financial reporting are defined, our opinions mislead the public investor into believing that some such objective standard does exist, and that it has been used to measure the whole presentation made by the financial statements. This is not so. Still, we use the word by rote.

Since the principles of accounting adopted by our profession are in no way documented or supported by reasoning which leads to a "fair" presentation in the financial statements, the only use we should make of the word "fairly" in our opinion is in regard to the application of the principles. Our opinion paragraph would then read:

> "In our opinion, the accompanying balance sheet and statement of income presents the financial position of the company and the results of its operation, in conformity with a fair application of generally accepted accounting principles."

Incidentally, the inclusion of the word "fairly" in the U. S. form of auditors' opinion is not required by the Federal Securities Acts, or by the Securities and Exchange Commission.

Concern about the interim reporting of profits

There is a growing concern and criticism among investors, at least on our side and I believe on your side, about some of the seemingly unexplainable differences that show up between the interim unaudited reports of profits and the annual audited reports of profits. Where these differences arise, they generally are traceable to inadequate accounting and bookkeeping practices on which the interim reports are based.

Such criticism of interim reports is the exception rather than the rule. But here again we, as professionals, have a responsibility to assist as much as practicable in eliminating the causes of errors in interim reports before the exceptions compel continuous audits during the entire year.

Decision-making by investors is a continuous process. It does not occur only after the audited annual reports are issued. Many investors closely watch the interim, usually quarterly, unaudited earnings reported, and rely on them. In addition, corporate directors of many companies are demanding greater protection against possible errors in the interim reports, for which their responsibility is considered equally as great as for the annual reports.

The reader's reliance on the annual audited report is impaired unless interim reports of profits are also acceptable and conform to reporting standards that are reasonably similar in quality to those required for year-end statements. Such conformance is in a large part dependent upon the objectivity and continuity of the housekeeping standards of a company's accounting system between annual audit dates.

Reporting responsibilities of independent auditors do not require a statement of opinion as to whether, so far as he can determine from his audit, the accounting practices and record-keeping followed by the company are up to recognized standards and are being maintained in such a manner as to produce reliable interim reports. At present, when accounting records of a client are not up to acceptable standards for the preparation of proper financial statements, or when they are not well maintained, the independent auditors must supplement their normal audit work to satisfy themselves that the financial statements are properly presented, even though internal controls over assets and liabilities leave something to be desired. However, the auditor now reports on these conditions only to directors or stockholders, and then in confidence. The risk of such inadequacies to the reporting of financial position and results of operation at interim reporting dates may be greater than that of many of the conditions reported to the investors in the financial statements.

This suggests that the independent auditor should be required to express his opinion on this condition in his annual report, and thereby contribute materially to the quality of interim reporting of profits by all corporations. If there were such a requirement, corporations would be under greater pressure to maintain proper records, and the independent auditor would provide an improved service in reporting on profit data; and he could include in his annual opinion a statement to the effect that the records were poorly, fairly, or well maintained.

The requirement that the auditor make such an observation and evaluation would create an incentive for every company to justify the highest marks for its accounting system in its auditor's opinion. This evaluation would contemplate a much more extensive review than that presently made by independent auditors in their check of internal controls for the purpose of establishing the scope of the audit as a basis for expressing their normal opinion on the financial statements.

This annual comment by the auditors on the company's accounting practices and the condition of its records would not eliminate the growing insistence by Board members that something more reliable be provided on interim profit reports in place of the so-called comfort letters now often given by the independent auditors. Such letters are practically useless in increasing the confidence of the directors in the interim profit reports, and probably will be required to be replaced with more positive comments by the auditors, based on the interim performance of portions of the annual audit work. This may result in some duplication during the year of the verification process followed in the annual audit.

The auditor as arbiter of disagreements on cost determinations

The multiplicity of individual entities in our societies is constantly increasing, and these entities, for the most part, perform different services or supply different products. Consequently, they frequently serve each other as suppliers and users under contracts. These contracts, no matter how well written, often result in disagreements as to cost determinations.

Independent auditors are, more and more, being named in these contracts as cost-determination arbiters, frequently without the auditor's knowledge until he is called upon to act. I have personally recommended the use of other auditors' names in certain cases, and lawyers do this constantly. The public requires that such arbitration services be available from someone. The auditor is a logical person to perform this service because he should have the maximum independent capability to appraise the cost determinations. The decisions are not the King Solomon type—they are the accounting facts type.

To arbitrate such cost-accounting facts requires the auditors involved to be completely disassociated from management judgment and from the regular auditing of the financial statements; but even more important, this service needs the authoritative establishment of objective cost standards. We are in dire need of such standards having a high quality and clarity of definition.

For government defense contract work in the United States, the determination of such standards has been put in the hands of a government agency, primarily because we as a profession clung to the position that the task could not be done. When the handwriting of government determination was seen on the wall, our profession flip-flopped and admitted it could be done.

Regardless of history, the effectiveness of cost determinations will rest on the definitions of cost standards, and the profession is the place where this defining should be done. The ability of the public to understand cost-standard objectives and financial-statement objectives will depend on the description of the differences in their purposes and of how these differences are reconciled by the profession. These are the prerequisites for writing understandable contracts in the first place, and also for determining whether the auditor's performance as the arbiter of cost determinations under those contracts can be well done. If such objectives are simply but well defined, the independent auditor is in a position to provide one of the most valuable services needed by the public.

Conclusion

It is difficult to contain one's excitement in contemplation of the progress that would be made in the United States in the determination of what profit is if the profession would but define the purpose of financial statements in a sufficiently simple manner to be understood by the public.

I believe this will be done as the deficiencies, and the disenchantment resulting from these deficiencies, continue to mount. It will not be done through government action, because it is not authority or coercive power that is needed; this is all that government can furnish. What we need is accounting competence and ability and a way to organize such talent to assure its effective use. This is the key to breaking the log jam that has stratified and frustrated the thinking of the profession in the United States.

Defining these objectives of financial statements will give to the accounting profession the overall controlling target that the Hippocratic oath gave the medical profession in 400 B.C., which has lasted for centuries among all nations, all continents, all tongues and all races.

Discrimination against stockholders of small businesses through accounting legislation

Before a Business Forum of the
Regional Industrial Development
Corporation of St. Louis,
October 13, 1970

*Accounting Principles Board
Opinions Number 16 and 17 amount
to discriminatory legislation against
stockholders of small companies.*

THE PREVIOUS SPEAKER'S comments are exceedingly revealing in showing how the protection of a person's property rights necessitates political participation.

Until now one never has had to think that political participation was necessary in preparing accounting reports. That condition has changed. We in the accounting profession are now legislating for and against stockholders by adopting rules of reporting that are as conclusively discriminating as would result from placing a discriminatory law on the books. This has happened in two instances; in the first case few of you were even aware that it happened. It is history now and would be unimportant except that we have a repetition of it today in the accounting for mergers under Accounting Principles Board Opinions Number 16 and 17.

Because of a Congressional outcry against mergers, per se, (particularly against take-overs) and because all of our accounting was bad in some areas, regardless of mergers, the Securities and Exchange Commission came under increasing pressure to enact new rules. Like a wife who has been scolded by a husband and in turn scolds her children, the SEC took its scolding from Congress to the accounting profession. Even though neither the profession nor the Securities and Exchange Commission knew what the objectives of financial reporting were (and we still don't), the profession proceeded to legislate, through the imposition of artificial financial requirements, against the stockholders in smaller companies seeking to merge. These requirements are known as APB Opinions Number 16 and 17.

Let me state here that legislation against mergers is a prerogative of Congress. If

57

anti-merger action was the sense of Congress, it should act accordingly. But legislation against mergers through rules of the accounting profession makes accounting and accountants lackeys for the individual demagogue, and that was the situation behind APB Opinions 16 and 17, in my opinion. The Securities and Exchange Commission behind the scenes supplied the blueprint for the legislation against the stockholders of the smaller companies in a merger.

Now what were those actions? I can't cover them in detail in ten minutes. While APB Opinions 16 and 17 were being debated, the profession, with SEC backing, attempted to prescribe different accounting depending on the size of the company involved, the so-called "size test." Under this test penalties would, in effect, be assessed against any merged company that was one third, later reduced to one tenth, the size of the other company in a merger. This discrimination against the smaller company was so blatant and so obvious that it was finally eliminated by both the SEC and the accounting profession.

However, other discriminations equally as great, but much more subtle, remain in APB Opinions 16 and 17, discriminations which have nothing to do with accounting but are imposed through accounting processes. Whether by design or otherwise, larger companies got a windfall, without their asking for it, in the form of price reductions under the merger accounting made possible by APB Opinions 16 and 17. What is more, these price reductions are noncompetitive; all smaller companies' stockholders must pay the penalty in price to any merger partner they seek. Therefore, APB accounting in Opinions 16 and 17, in my opinion, is price-fixing made easy.

I set out the specific causes of these price penalties against the smaller company and discounts to the larger company in a merger in an article in the *New York Times*.

The newly appointed Chairman of the Accounting Principles Board replied through the same paper. He did not deny a single charge, but asked time to see what happens. That is like saying to smaller companies' stockholders, "Let APB Opinions 16 and 17 cut off your right arm and see if it is true that you could lose a lot of your blood."

In a nutshell, the one blood-letting requirement is in APB Opinion 17; it is the amortization of so-called goodwill by the acquiring company. This requires the acquiring company to artificially reduce the earnings of the acquired company by not less than 2½% per year of the difference between the market price of his stock and the book value of its stock as it appears on the company's books. Since this 2½% is not deductible for income tax purposes, the effect is to reduce net earnings by twice that amount, thereby greatly reducing the price at which the smaller company's stockholders can sell their stock.

However, provision is made so that if, instead, the smaller company's stockholders will agree to take the acquiring company's less attractive common stock, usually with a lower dividend, and if they will give up any right to an additional purchase price for superior future performance of their own company and also push the merger through in one year, they are not required to suffer the penalty of reduced earnings for merger purposes by recognizing this goodwill. Under those circumstances, the so-called "goodwill" asset vanishes. An illustration of how this works follows my comments.

Remember, the acquiring company in the merger is not imposing these penalties on the smaller company's stockholders; we in the accounting profession are doing it. Insofar as I know, we are doing so contrary to the wishes of the managements of the possible acquiring companies. The Securities and Exchange Commission enforces all accountants' opinions so that they have the force of legislation.

ILLUSTRATION OF COMPUTATION OF MERGER PRICE PAID TO SMALLER COMPANY STOCKHOLDERS IN A MERGER

	CPA Certified Earnings Without Merger	Merger Price	
		Without Goodwill Amortization— Prior to Oct. 31, 1970	With Goodwill Amortization Required by APB Opinion #17— After Oct. 31, 1970
1 AGREED METHOD OF DETERMINING MERGER PRICE...	15 x earnings	15 x earnings	15 x earnings
2 NET INCOME OF SMALLER OF MERGED COMPANIES..	$ 1,000,000	$ 1,000,000	$ 1,000,000
3 MERGER OR MARKET PRICE—BASED ON AGREEMENT OF 15 X EARNINGS................	$15,000,000	$15,000,000	$15,000,000 Less 15x Amortization of Goodwill
4 GOODWILL COMPUTATION PER APB #16			
5 (a) Book value after all assets at fair value...........	$ 3,000,000	$ 3,000,000	$ 3,000,000
6 (b) Earnings for purpose of computation of market or merger value................	$ 1,000,000	1,000,000	1,000,000 Less Goodwill Amortization
7 (c) Goodwill amortization—per APB #17.............	None	None	$ 225,000*
8 (d) Earnings after goodwill amortization.............	$ 1,000,000	$ 1,000,000	$ 775,000*
(e) Market or merger price at 15 x earnings...........	$15,000,000	$15,000,000	$11,625,000*
9 Artificial loss imposed by accounting merger legislation of APB #17............................	—	—	3,375,000*
10 Percent loss to stockholders of smaller of merged companies.................................			22½%*

*Subject to algebraic refinement.

The significance of recent and pending opinions of the Accounting Principles Board

Before the Conference on Public Disclosure and the Corporation, the Conference Institute, New York, November 19, 1970

In the Continental Vending case the Court said the critical test of accounting was whether the balance sheet fairly presented the financial position, without reference to generally accepted accounting principles.

"Entropy"

I AM INDEBTED TO Professor Shenkir of the University of Virginia in diagnosing the ills of the Accounting Principles Board as "entropy." He states:

"The concept of entropy, which is a fundamental law of nature, may be stated as: 'In a closed system, there is a tendency for organization to change into disorganization, or for the amount of information available about the system to become smaller as time goes on.' Stated another way entropy denotes the general tendency of closed or isolated systems in the universe to 'run down,' to move from a state of organization to chaos. Entropy, therefore, is a measure of disorder and confusion, and the tendency is for entropy to increase.

"Increasing entropy in a profession reduces the public's confidence in the profession's service and is a potential contributor to the growth of a credibility gap between the public and the profession."

This is a good description of the disease that has overtaken the accounting profession and its consequences. Professor Shenkir also states the treatment that should be applied by saying, "The accounting profession needs to recognize the operation of the second law of thermodynamics in its activities . . . by creating feedback processes to control entropy."

I submit that to many of us in the profession who are outside of the Accounting Principles Board, the Board not only is disorganized but also is completely oblivious to the consequences of its acts as they affect the public investors through financial statements prepared in accordance with APB edicts. The Board has refused to take note of the responsibility placed on the profession by the courts in the Continental Vending case. In that case, the Court said, the "critical test" of accounting was whether the balance sheet fairly presented the financial position, without reference to generally accepted accounting principles.

Why then is the Board grinding out directives which it calls generally accepted accounting principles when these principles standing alone are not addressed to the critical test of fair financial presentation, the critical test being what is fair to the investor?

APB Opinions Nos. 1-15

Let me review the Board's productivity since it was organized in 1959 and give a fair scoring of its achievements as I would appraise them.

Opinion No. 1, issued in November 1962, provided that deferred tax provisions were required where guideline depreciation was used for tax purposes but not for financial reporting purposes. It stated an objective, but immediately proceeded to nullify that objective for public utilities whose rates are set without recognizing the objective set forth in the Opinion. In other words, as soon as some backbone was required in carrying out the objective, the APB collapsed. Since then, this objective relating to utilities has been repaired to the extent possible through Congressional legislation. Rating this Opinion on the basis of a score of 100 for complete success, I would give the APB about 5 points for this Opinion.

Opinion No. 2 on accounting for the investment credit was issued in December 1962. I will comment on this a little later in connection with Opinion No. 4.

Another Opinion was issued in October 1963, on the subject of including a statement of source and application of funds along with the other financial statements. The objective was rather completely stated and the Board carried the ball right down to

the one-yard line—and then fumbled. This fumble occurred when, after setting up an important objective, the Opinion merely recommended that funds statements be included but did not require them. My viewpoint, which is attached to that Opinion, read in part as follows: "Since the Board believes that a funds statement should be presented in financial reports and yet does not require such presentation, it fails in its primary responsibility of determining standards that meet the needs of investors and others who use financial statements." The SEC gave no encouragement to the profession to recover the fumble in that Opinion. Yet, seven years later in 1970, after liquidity problems took their toll, the SEC has now made funds statements mandatory in annual reports filed with the Commission. We shall see whether the Board will now tag along behind when it could, and should, have been the leader. The score for this Opinion must be about a minus 10.

Next we come to the infamous APB Opinion No. 4, amending the accounting for the investment tax credit by giving authoritative support to accounting completely contrary to the "objectives" of Opinion No. 2. Of course, it did so after the SEC had pulled the rug out from under the Board by accepting an alternative accounting treatment, even though such accounting alternatives could not serve the "objectives" of usefulness for public investors. Opinion No. 4 set the Board in a decline from which it has never recovered. The score for Opinions No. 2 and No. 4 is a minus 50.

Next is APB Opinion No. 5, which covers the reporting of leases in financial statements of lessees. Here again the Board had the ball, and then proceeded to head for the wrong goal by omitting any significant requirement that would result in leases being recorded as liabilities. These liabilities today are some of the greatest corporate headaches as well as some of the greatest corporate assets. But the use of this information is denied to the public investor, because the leases are not recorded in the financial statements. The Board proceeded to do what appears to be impossible. Authoritative support was given to the proposition that a particular lease was not a liability to the lessee; whereas a year later in Opinion No. 7, the Board gave equal authoritative support that the same lease was an asset in the accounts of the lessor. To the investor it was "heads you lose, tails I win." Without a guiding objective, the Board went in opposite directions on the same set of facts, and we ended up with ridiculous consequences. The net score for accomplishment in benefiting the investor for these two Opinions would be generously appraised as zero.

Opinion No. 6 declared that the bulletins of the predecessor committee would be continued in effect by the Board. In this process, an important disclosure to the investor of the effect of an accounting practice (flow-through of deferred taxes for certain regulated companies) was dropped for no good reason, merely because of the objections of some companies. Therefore, the net gain was negative. Score—minus 5 points.

Opinion No. 8, covering accounting for the cost of pension plans, was the first good Opinion. We could give it a score of 25 points.

Opinion No. 9, on reporting the results of operation, was a much needed Opinion. The Board, however, could not in this Opinion bring itself to face up to a meaningful distinction between adjustments affecting the earnings reported in prior years and extraordinary income charges or credits arising from current operations. If, in retrospect, certain errors which occurred in one year are corrected in another, they are, under this Opinion, to remain as errors in both years. Thus, two years are to include erroneous information for investors only because the results of the year in which the error in reporting initially occurred, often with justification, was deemed to be inviolate once financial statements have been issued

for that year. A score of 10 points could be assigned to this Opinion.

The Omnibus Opinion No. 10, in 1966, was not intended to be a momentous document, but it did include a major mistake in the accounting for convertible debt. The Board's view was not originally thought out because there was no objective standard by which to measure its fair reporting to investors. This mistake was corrected in Opinion No. 14. Net accomplishment, perhaps 5 points.

Opinion No. 11, on the accounting for income taxes, was a big step forward, but the Board found it necessary to grant special exemptions to certain industries in order to get the necessary votes for issuance, which is a bad practice. But again, this was pragmatic action by the Board that was necessary in the absence of an "objective" which would require relating the results of the Opinion to its impact on investors. Score for this Opinion—25 points.

Opinion No. 12 was an Omnibus Opinion for 1967 which was primarily interpretive in nature and did not include the promulgation of any principle. Score—5 points.

Opinion No. 13 amended Opinion No. 9 so that the prescribed form of income statement was applicable to banks. Here again, the new Opinion was not appropriately considered from the point of view of what best presents the facts for investors. The importance of defining and presenting bank operating income to the investor was missed completely. Opinions No. 9 and No. 13 did not properly distinguish between operating earnings and net income with respect to banks, and it prescribed accounting for portfolio securities that destroyed the comparability of income among banks. Score—5 points.

Opinion No. 15 on earnings per share was good in concept, but again failed to consider the proper objectives for presenting data to investors. Common stock equivalents for purposes of earnings per share were not related to what changes would occur for purposes of stockholders' equity in the balance sheet under the same assumptions. This relationship is important in appraising the quality of reported earnings. Consequently, the interrelation between reported earnings per share and the debt-leverage position pertaining to those same earnings cannot be obtained by the investor from the financial statements.

In addition, the investor cannot relate earnings per share figures to the conditions existing after the balance sheet date when, for example, the market prices of common stock equivalents may have changed significantly from those used in the earnings per share computations. Thus earnings per share reported in the financial statements may be obsolete and misleading by the time the annual reports reach the shareholder, particularly if wide swings in market prices occur during the interim as has been the case in 1970. While a security under the Opinion remains a common stock equivalent, it might in fact have no effect on earnings per share. There is no requirement in the Opinion to let the investors know how changes in market security prices can seriously change the character and effect on the balance sheet and earnings of securities which are common stock equivalents. Opinion No. 15 does not require setting forth how the earnings per share were computed or that last year's common stock equivalent is now strictly a debt that is driving the company to the wall.

What score can be given to an accounting procedure that possesses 90% of the requirements and then fails to properly inform the investor? A score of 10 points is more than adequate for Opinion No. 15.

APB Opinions Nos. 16 and 17

Now we come to APB Opinions 16 and 17, which became effective on Halloween night—the night of tricks or treats. This truly was an auspicious date to introduce these Opinions involving the accounting for mergers and acquisitions. Never in the history of the accounting profession were there two accounting bulletins that were more destructive to a fair presentation to stockholders of the assets and income underlying their investments. These Opinions were conceived with an attitude of regulatory and legislative action and driven to completion under a cloud of fear and incompetence. The accounting principles involved, if there were any at all, were not related to the specific objectives required to tell the truth to investors. The score for these Opinions would be at least a minus 100 points.

We in the accounting profession were trounced by a Federal court in the Continental Vending case and three of our colleagues were found guilty of criminal conspiracy because they were judged to have failed to use the test of "fairness" of presentation of financial information, without reference to generally accepted accounting principles. The question at issue was whether the "objectives" of generally accepted accounting principles had been presented. The jury found they were not. Thus, we have a judicial finding that generally accepted accounting principles, no matter how determined, are just a means by which to reach investors' objectives. For any accountant to know that investors' objectives are achieved in any given case, he must know what the objectives are.

In Opinions 16 and 17, there is not one word as to the merits of the conclusions in relation to the interests of investors and not one word as to why the consequence of applying those Opinions would result in "fair presentation of financial position or results of operations," insofar as investors are concerned. Those Opinions require assets to be recorded and shown in financial statements even though the Opinions themselves state that these so-called assets are unidentifiable. Opinion No. 17 states:

"The cost of unidentifiable intangible assets is measured by the difference between the cost of the group of assets or enterprise acquired and the sum of the assigned costs of individual tangible and identifiable intangible assets acquired, less liabilities assumed."

If we can measure "unidentified intangibles" as assets this way—why not unidentifiable cash, inventories, plant, deferred assets, investments, etc.? Where or what is the "objective" of fair presentation that distinguishes one "unidentifiable" asset as being good and another not good?

Why do we have to identify and verify every other asset on a balance sheet other than "unidentified intangibles" to qualify that asset as a fair financial presentation to investors? Can the existence of "unidentifiable intangibles" be measured and priced? The answer is—obviously not. What do they represent? They are the presently computed monetary values placed upon the future expectation of profits from the net working assets. They are based on investors' stock market trading opinions of value of this future production, and, consequently, are not corporate resources or assets used up in or contributing to future production. Naturally, the more optimistic an investing public, which determines stock market prices, the greater the "unidentified intangible values." Do such "unidentifiable intangible values" change? They change with every trade in the stock market. In times like these, such values are considerably below what they were a year or so ago. Of what use or value are such obsoleted "unidentifiable intangibles" to the investor, to whom they could now be reported as an asset and as a part of his "capital stock equity value?" The answer is none.

A fair presentation of current net working assets of a corporation and of the current net results of operation to a present investor is for his determination (together with other data) of what valuation he wants to make of the present net working assets and "unidentifiable intangibles" of the company.

If "unidentifiable intangibles" have been recorded in the presentation of assets in financial statements, the first thing the investor must do is remove such a recording in making his own valuation of that company. Consequently, we should ask, if knowledgeable investors in evaluating a company remove "unidentified intangibles" from a presentation of assets in financial statements, why would the accounting profession put such "unidentifiable intangibles" on the balance sheet and thus impair its usefulness?

The "unidentified intangible asset" valuation can be made only by the investor and only at the moment of such determination. It is only the owners who determine the selling price of a company. Management, which is responsible for valuing all other assets, can only recommend terms to the owners.

The procedures of the Board are devoid of objectives that would require this kind of analysis and, therefore, there are no sound answers to the "whys" on any of the directives in Opinions 16 and 17. The procedures have been legislated into required practice by these Opinions.

The apparent basis for the directives of the Opinions is some sort of "stewardship" concept. Under this concept, cost in terms of current market value of stock is deemed to be the same as cash, even though the only resources received for that stock are the net working assets acquired, plus the future opportunity value inherent in owning those assets. Since a substantial portion of current market value of stock was for this "future opportunity value," the stewardship concept would require an accounting by management for this unidentified intangible asset. The directives of the Opinions accomplish this by requiring amortization of this intangible against income. Thus, they imply that until the "future opportunity value" has been received in earnings out of future operations, the total resources received are short of the market value of the consideration issued. Of course, the unidentified intangible of "future opportunity value" could continue forever, could increase or could decrease, but stewardship accountability supporters believe the books are not balanced until resources equivalent to cash are received—even though "future opportunity value" is still intact.

The error is in adopting a procedure which tells the investor that earnings of the future have decreased until this opportunity value has been replaced with cash equivalent resources irrespective of the continuing value of the unidentified intangibles. In so doing, the information necessary for the investor to make his own evaluation of "unidentifiable intangibles" is destroyed. Thus, the accounting required by the Opinions results in destroying the very information the investor needs to know—that is, what performance is behind his stockholding. He thus has been severely damaged without cause or reason by these Opinions. If accounting to stockholders and future investors is designed by individuals who destroy rather than serve the investors, relief in some fashion must come.

Correction of Opinion No. 17

I have contended that stewardship accountability should be made on a supplementary basis, just like the accounting required for any special project. If in the case of mergers and acquisitions an accountability of all resources received—both real and potential—should be made on the face of the balance sheet, a method can be devised for doing so without destroying a proper presentation of net working assets on the balance sheet or by destroying the basis of measuring investment values by distorting the income of the corporation in reporting it to stockholders. This could be done by:

a. Following the Opinion No. 17 concept of computing unidentified in-

tangibles in all cases, regardless of whether the consideration is cash, notes, stock, or earn-out provisions.

b. Appropriating all income attributable to each acquisition from retained earnings as a reduction of such unidentified intangibles until the corporation has received resources through earnings equivalent to the value of consideration given up at date of merger or acquisition.

c. Deduct the net unrecovered unidentified intangibles from stockholders' equity on the face of the balance sheet until eliminated by the appropriation of net income earned by the business acquired.

This change in procedure would result in:

a. Properly recording all mergers and acquisitions, regardless of the type of consideration given.

b. Presenting to shareholder investors a balance sheet that includes all net working assets—but only net working assets—at their values or cost as associated with their physical and verifiable existence.

c. Presenting for use of shareholder investors all net income from all acquisitions and mergers without distortion.

d. Requiring management to make a stewardship accounting for each acquisition until total resources received from each one were equal to the total consideration given, independent of the continuing value of unidentified intangibles.

This would certainly be the best of all worlds and I would welcome a criticism of this presentation by my fellow speakers.

An illustration of the balance sheet and retained earnings statement presentation of this viewpoint is as follows:

BALANCE SHEET PRESENTATION

STOCKHOLDERS' EQUITY:

Preference stock—no par value, stated value $50 per share, callable at $80, $3.00 annual dividend cumulative—authorized 1,000,000 shares, issued 500,000 shares . . . . $ 25,000,000

Preferred stock—par value $100 per share, $6.00 cumulative dividend—authorized 1,000,000 shares, issued 500,000 shares 50,000,000

Common stock—no par—stated value $1.00 per share—authorized 1,000,000 shares, issued 500,000 shares 500,000

Capital surplus 194,500,000

Earnings retained for use in business (see attached statement) 75,000,000

Total gross stockholders' equity $345,000,000

Less—

Unidentified intangibles remaining at beginning of year from mergers and acquisitions since November 1, 1970 . . . . $100,000,000

Reduction—equal to net income earned during the year on these properties 13,750,000

Unidentified intangibles yet to be recovered in income from properties merged or acquired since November 1, 1970 86,250,000

Equity in net working assets applicable to capital stock issued $258,750,000

EARNINGS RETAINED FOR USE IN BUSINESS

	19———	19———
Balance January 1	$ 70,000,000	$ 58,000,000
Add—Net income for year	35,000,000	37,500,000
Total	$105,000,000	$ 95,500,000
Deduct—		
Cash dividends—preferred and common	16,250,000	14,250,000
Appropriation of income earned on acquisitions and mergers since November 1, 1970—applied as a reduction of unidentified intangibles recorded at date of acquisition or merger (see balance sheet)	13,750,000	11,250,000
Balance December 31	$ 75,000,000	$ 70,000,000

If the foregoing procedure were adopted, it could be applied to unidentified intangibles arising prior to November 1, 1970, as well, and thus eliminate the double standard of accounting inherent in Opinions Nos. 16 and 17. Imagine the confusion and the obvious meaninglessness of accounting standards that will result in a different treatment of mergers, acquisitions and "unidentified intangibles" only because of the date of October 31, 1970, which has no significance at all.

Great damage to investors

The potential damages to stockholders and investors and the liability arising from such damages, because of Opinions Nos. 16 and 17, are overwhelming. These damages occur because the penalty to an acquiring company in reporting its earnings net of amortization of "unidentifiable assets" must be covered by the acquired company stockholders taking a reduced value for their company to compensate the acquirer for the fictitious loss of earnings.

We in the accounting profession have subjected the shareholders of the acquired company to this loss in their stock values, and even have prevented the acquired company shareholders from avoiding the loss by going to another acquirer. The profession's action has legislated out of existence an acquired company's value in an amount equal to the annual amortization times the price/earnings ratio of the consideration given. I have already observed actual negotiations where this reduction in terms has been put in ultimatum form as the penalty for not reaching agreement prior to November 1, 1970. This is not speculation, it is a fact of life. If price fixing was the profession's motive, which I know it was not, in issuing Opinions 16 and 17, we could not have accomplished that end more effectively than by the accounting prescribed.

The acquired company's earnings must be discounted for the arbitrary reduction of income caused by amortization of unidentified intangibles. Thus, the damaged stockholders are those of the future acquired companies, and there is nothing in the Opinions which is even addressed to their now existing dilemma. You might ask, which company in a merger is the acquired company, and, therefore, which stockholders are subject to this damage? Opinion No. 16 answers this by stating, "The acquiring corporation normally issues the stock and commonly is the larger company." This makes the acquired company the smaller of the two. In the minds of the stockholders of the smaller company, they could conclude, with some logic, that the profession was in collusion with the larger acquiring companies, if it was not for the fact that prospective acquiring companies were the major critics of the penalty imposed on the owners of the smaller company by Opinion No. 17. My colleague on this panel is in a better position to state whether the SEC will enforce, through the Federal Securities Acts, these discriminatory provisions on the shareholders of the smaller company that are imposed by Opinions 16 and 17.

However, even if the SEC does enforce the requirements of Opinions Nos. 16 and 17, which we understand it will, who would be liable for the damage caused in case of a lawsuit? It cannot be the acquiring corporation since it only states the terms of merger or acquisition. It does not compel any company to accept those terms. The company seeking a merger partner finds the accounting penalty assessed against his fair price is the same, regardless of who is the acquirer. He is, in fact, locked in. He finds this loss placed on him by the accounting profession even though many in the profession disagree with the results, but to no avail. The disagreement within the profession means little, however, because the acquiring company must conform to the profession's pronouncements of "generally accepted accounting principles"—as represented by Opinions 16 and 17—or the acquiring companies' financial statements will not be accepted by the SEC. If the Board members are liable for damages, we all are. The public investors of the merged company are the ones damaged, not the SEC and not the accountants, except to the extent they are compelled to observe the Opinions.

The last case of prescribed accounting which went to the courts on the basis of its impact was in 1959 when several power companies complained of an interpretive letter requiring the exclusion from surplus of the reserve for deferred taxes. That letter, in effect, also had the backing of SEC after a long and tedious hearing. However, the merits of that accounting principle were soundly grounded on facts and the conveyance of a true state of conditions to the investor. The District Court's decision, sustained by the U. S. Court of Appeals, 2nd Circuit, and the U. S. Supreme Court, stated:

> "There is no allegation that the method of accounting proposed by

defendants is inherently false or fraudulent. On the contrary, it is supported by respectable authority. Neither is there any allegation of special damages except in the most general and speculative terms.

"The plaintiffs may have grievances, but they relate to the distribution of honest opinions, not facts. No threat of intentional, unjustifiable harm to plaintiffs' business rights or property exists."

There is no question in my mind that Opinions 16 and 17 create unjustifiable harm and damage and that they do not properly state the facts. Evidence of this damage is yet to be gathered, but it will be as acquisitions and mergers occur after November 1, 1970.

In my opinion, therefore, Opinions 16 and 17 must go. The only questions are what is to replace them and how are they to be eliminated. I know of no opposition (except as to inconsistency among other accounting principles) to the recording of all acquired net working assets at their fair value—without exception in any acquisition. The recording of unidentified intangibles as a reduction of stockholders' equity and the future appropriation of all earnings from the merged properties against such unidentified intangibles, as I have already described, would meet most objections as to what should replace Opinions 16 and 17.

As to how Opinions 16 and 17 are to be eliminated, or modified, it could be done in several ways. First, by SEC action not to enforce them where the certifying accountant and the company take responsibility for a proper alternative presentation that includes a proper accounting for all items, and there is precedent for such an approach in the SEC's previous action with respect to the investment credit. Another way would be for the Board to put its house in order and correct the Opinions, including a clear state-

ment of the objectives of the Opinions and the way in which they result in proper information being given to the public investors. Also, as evidence of damage becomes available in future merger negotiations, the Opinions could be eliminated by successful suits against the Board and the public accounting profession. And, last, the Opinions could be corrected through legitimate legislative action as legislators learn about the discrimination imposed against stockholders of the smaller acquired companies, just as flow-through accounting abuses by utilities were corrected by legislation.

Any one of these avenues may be used to correct erroneously issued Opinions. I have no doubt that the profession can do the job if it properly organizes itself and addresses its accounting principle decisions to reach objectives that clearly state (1) why the accounting adopted provides the investor with a reliable fact, (2) what that fact means to the investor, and (3) why the investor is required to have the factual result attained in making his investment evaluation.

When that is done we, on the practicing side, can make those objectives our absolute target in applying the correct accounting principles, and put our reputation and fortune on the line in getting that job done. Then we will have "authoritative objectives" for what we are trying to accomplish in the application of "authoritative accounting principles." One without the other leaves us crippled in trying to discharge our responsibilities in assuring the SEC that financial statements "do not fail to state a material fact" or that so far as we know the financial statements are "not misleading."

One of the pending opinions in process is to record earnings on an accrual basis for investments owned that represent ownership of less than 50% but more than 20% control. The objectives, so far as the shareholders of the owning companies are concerned, are good but are not well described in the present drafts of the opinions. The opinion when issued will serve a good purpose to shareholders.

APB Statements Nos. 1-4

The Accounting Principles Board has also issued three Statements. They consist of innocuous observations on Research Studies No. 1 and No. 3, disclosures of supplemental financial information by diversified companies, and a Statement on price-level accounting. That accounting should be required, but the effect of inflation on financial position or results of operations is still only a matter of optional disclosure, even though its effect in real life results in unreported losses and possibly eventual bankruptcy.

We are about to receive Statement No. 4 entitled "Basic Concepts and Accounting Principles Underlying Financial Statements of Business Enterprises." This is a masterpiece in double talk on accounting. No document could be issued that would more aptly qualify for the recent title of a magazine article relating to the effort to improve accounting, "Words, Words, Words." This Statement is a 30,000 word document that can be read only with difficulty and determination. It is full of meaningless statements, obvious elementary observations, and plain misleading statements. To describe some of its contents to you is possible, but nothing can take the place of attempting to read it for yourself. Under no circumstances could we expect investors to read the statement or for them to understand its contents. Therefore, we cannot expect investors, the APB, or anyone else to receive any informative benefit from it.

Those of us who seek understandable and reasonable objectives find no meaningful response in this document. It states that the qualitative objectives are relevance, understandability, verifiability, neutrality, timeliness, comparability, and completeness. Every one of these terms is violated by Opinions 16 and 17. It also states that

constraints on full achievement of the objectives arise from (1) conflict of objectives, (2) environmental influences, and (3) lack of complete understanding of objectives. If this means that the profession itself is throwing in the towel and does not know how to do its own work, I am wrong in saying it can do the job.

Objectives and responsibilities

Objectives of accounting can be stated in terms like the Ten Commandments, but they must be related specifically to assets, liabilities and income because these are what we must work with. The accounting principles that implement those objectives may be complex and technical, but that is the job that should be assigned to the practicing accountant; it is his responsibility.

The job of establishing objectives is the responsibility of the Board and the accounting profession. The objectives should be expressed in words that an investor can reasonably understand so that he can hold the practicing accountant responsible. That is not asking for an oversimplified accomplishment. The alternative is to put the whole matter in the hands of the government where the only communication of reliability for the investor is—since the government did it, it must be right. Nothing could ever be further from the truth.

What the practicing accountants and corporate mangements need is not to be relieved of their liability to investors for the results of accounting (which is what would be accomplished if the SEC adopts the rules), but some reasonably explicit "objectives" that serve investors, and under which corporate managements and practicing accountants can function and perform under penalty of liability for nonperformance. On such a basis the investor would be served.

As things now stand, management and the practicing accountant are operating under accounting rules that have no objectives, but are enforced by the SEC without the SEC issuing a rule. If the SEC issued the same rules that the Board has, say Opinions 16 and 17, such a rule would then hold the practicing accountant and management free of liability for following it. However, bad accounting principles presently have all the force of SEC rules with no elimination of liability for those who perform under them. This is completely untenable for both corporate management and the practicing accountant.

The issuance of Statement No. 4 on concepts confirms the fact that the profession has not only failed in defining usable "objectives" for investors, but it indicates either a lack of understanding of what its responsibility is in setting "objectives" or a refusal to accept that responsibility. This does not seem possible after a jury in a Federal court case has pointedly stated that "generally accepted accounting principles" have only a subordinated role to the "objectives" of investors.

Who will initiate the action required to set the profession on a corrective course? This authority could be one that represents the public investor and that authority is the SEC. The SEC knows that if the profession does not do the job, the final responsibility is theirs. A former Chairman of the SEC acknowledged this responsibility before a Congressional Committee on February 19, 1964,—six years ago.

Another authority that could put the accounting profession into action is Congress. The Senate did initiate an action to create a Board of Uniform Cost Standards, which is now law. Several Senators have indicated that legislation is probably the way to remove the log jam to the establishment of "objective standards" for financial statements so that the accounting principles established by the profession have some meaning to public investors.

The unanswered question is who will act in behalf of the public—the accounting profession, the SEC, or the Congress? We in the accounting profession have had all the chances to do the job that we can ask, but I know from experience that avoidance of real responsibility has pervaded every effort. If the profession is given one more chance, can it do the job? It can, if it will, but the public will not condone another experience such as has resulted from Opinions 16 and 17.

Utility accounting must reawaken to the true economics of operations

Before the AGA-EEI Accounting
Conference, Cincinnati,
April 20, 1971

Failure to maintain equity capital to correspond to inflation dilution is the greatest risk that overhangs utility equities in today's seemingly endless inflationary economy.

I HAVE BEEN IN public accounting for forty-two years, and have spent a good share of that time with utility leaders from the time of Samuel Insull and Howard Hopson to the managements of the present date.

Prior to 1928 when I entered public accounting, I was employed by utilities for four years, specializing in utility accounting and economics. I come before you today with forty-six years of association with utility operations and their relationship to accounting and economics. During this time I have carried on debates and have testified before commissions and courts, which placed me alongside, as well as on the opposite side, of utility managements, utility commissioners and utility-baiting demagogues. They have come and gone during these forty-six years; many of them used every argument and every scheme possible to achieve the particular end result which they sought. Their motives were numerous, ranging from hate of utilities or socialistic public ownership of utilities, on the one hand, to the other end of the spectrum where some utility managements and experts viewed utility service as personal and private business, based on the most open application of "laissez-faire" philosophy.

I, too, was not without a motive; my motive was to build a professional competence in the utility field which would be based on a philosophy of advocating an accounting for utility economics which in retrospect, say, twenty-five years later, would prove to be the only fair accounting for consumer, investor, management and the general public. Such a philosophy could be the only enduring one for a professional firm, whose responsibilities had to continue from one generation to another over a period hopefully extending into perpetuity.

With this explanation of my life and my connection with your industries, I accepted Ralph Heumann's invitation to speak before you; first, because I would be with old allies and antagonists and their successors, both close friends over the years; second, because I regard this as my last appearance before you; and third, because I wanted to survey this last forty-six years of my life in your industry to determine if an overriding long-term deteriorating condition exists that, in my opinion, faces you and your industries from an accounting and economic point of view. If a problem which could cause your financial collapse, say, in the next twenty-five years is in the cards, what is it and how can it be removed? In other words, how does one avoid problems as serious as those now encountered by the railroad industry and stop them from creeping up on you to strike you down?

I could speak at length about (a) the economic justification of interest during construction concept and the need for changes in the present accounting and rate-making practices, (b) the cost consequences to you, your investors and your customers of pollution and environmental pressures, (c) the lack of fairness in the rate making for wholesale rates to municipal or cooperatively owned distribution systems and the risks assumed by the investor-owned utilities whose production facilities are used to serve these consumers, (d) the necessity of including and reserving deferred income tax or tax credits for rate-making and accounting purposes in a manner that results in equitable treatment to both consumer and utility without windfall to either, and (e) the lack of intellectual honesty of those who sponsor and support government-owned utility enterprises but who, at the same time, decry the lack of capital for schools, nursing centers, hospitals and other public services, which are the first responsibility of government, when public capital invested in utilities would go far to eliminate these public service deficiencies, ad infinitum.

I visualize all of these matters and others as grave problems for you and me, but I also visualize them as current problems that will be solved under current procedures. Even if not solved immediately on a proper basis, it will take only a short time to show that the solution was in error, thus pointing the way toward correction. Proper accounting for deferred taxes has taken thirty years to achieve; after less than ten years we see the error in the investment credit accounting.

The problem that I want to talk to you about lies in our accounting area, and it will relentlessly destroy or, at best, weaken the foundation for effective utility service in this nation, and thereby permanently cripple one of our indispensable services which the public has come to take for granted. This problem is combating the effects of inflation as it affects utilities. I say "combating the effects of inflation" because it is not within our ability to prevent inflation. This should be the first objective of the national policies.

Inflation as it affects equity capital provided in prior years is the most important long-term problem facing utilities

Inflation is your single, overwhelmingly important long-term antagonist. While a common enemy of everyone, it has a special importance to you. While practically every other industry, except railroads, are combating its effect on all fronts, utilities are at best combating successfully only about one-half of its damaging effect. The half that you are meeting or combating is belated coverage of the cost of inflation as it hits your employees' salaries, expenses and the cost of new capital. The relief sought for these people is absolutely necessary if they are to keep on eating and living, and thus be able to work. When they were and are hired to provide their services, paying them enough to combat the consequences of inflation on their wages is an inherent part of the contract of their employment. They are entitled to what you do for them, but that is only half the job facing the company. The other half is the equity investors who have furnished you capital over the past years, and are responsible for the plant development to this date. Are they being compensated for their services to counteract the effects of inflation on them? Politicians and utility critics like to make us believe these equity capital providers are financial moguls sitting at their Wall Street desks counting their money.

There is little public relation effort to show who these people are. Utilities' equity, in general, is the most widely owned capital of any industry in the nation. When utility stocks are referred to as the widows' and orphans' stock, they are correctly named. There are probably several times as many individual stockholders of utilities as there are of any other industry, regardless of size. Pension funds, profit sharing funds, insurance companies, trust funds—in short, all of the places the little investor puts his savings—invest heavily in utilities. Should these people draw their belts tighter, eat less or pay less rent than the employees of the utilities, or the providers of new equity capital? If there is to be a double standard for equity providers, one for the past and one for new equity providers, why not apply the same double standard to wage increases? Old employees would not get increased wages while new employees are hired at higher wages. That would be logical if the present principle of paying equity providers were also applied to employees.

What are the consequences of the utility double-standard treatment of equity providers?

If the equity providers do not kick, why stir up a hornet's nest by telling them how inequitably they are being treated? There are two answers to this question. For each year that this inequitable treatment is allowed to stand, a greater and greater number of equity providers realize that when they bought utility equity securities they bought them under assumptions that are intolerable in the face of substantial, persistent inflation. As equity providers, they knew that they could suffer losses caused by unexpected economic conditions, failures of plant, product failures, strikes, etc. With this expectation, investors nevertheless bought these equity securities because they assumed that the other side of equity security compensation also applied, i.e., if properties for which they provided capital proved productive, valuable and serviceable, they would receive returns comparable to current standards of compensation. Many investors who ran up market prices of utilities in the early 1960's, assumed that commissions would allow for inflation in the fair rates of return. To some extent this was done by not limiting the return to actual cost of capital. However, this practice was soon replaced with totally inadequate returns and stock market values slumped as the realization of regulatory practices, based on cost only, became evident.

Instead of fair compensation on current standards as inflation occurs, are equity providers to be treated as though they bought bonds with fixed income? At the same time, are they to assume that, as equity owners, when conditions grow worse and wages decline their compensation will decline? Must they now take as fact that, as owners of utility equities, they have the worst of both worlds? As the reality of this condition becomes apparent, equity providers will leave the utility business for good. Like pollution and environment problems, we can't avoid seeing inequitable treatment forever. There will come a time, and it may now be here, when this condition is revealed and the piper will have to be paid. It is not the truth that hurts but the sudden realization of what it is. Can this consequence be avoided by not telling the equity holder the facts? Honesty requires that equity holders be informed of the facts by us, the fact finders, and be treated fairly by utilities, rate commissioners and the courts for the capital they commit to consumer use. Let me illustrate the case more aptly and free of all "financially originated jargon."

If two widows had $10,000 each 15 years ago and one widow invested her $10,000 in rental housing to provide her with eating money while the other widow invested her $10,000 in utility common stock, which widow comes out ahead? The second widow provided the capital to make the first widow's home livable and usable, and this first widow has seen the value of her house and her rental income increase as inflation dilution occurred, while the second widow has seen the market value of her utility investment unprotected against inflationary dilution and has gone without the increase in income attributable to inflation dilution. Which widow has learned a lesson to pass on to other equity capital providers?

Why tell all this to you as financial officers of utilities rather than chief executive officers?

At this point, you might very well ask "Why belabor us; we are only the financial officers of utilities. Product pricing and compensation policies are the responsibilities of the chief executive officers who run the business?" That is true, but if the chief executive officer is to have the facts from which he can make his decision, he must rely on fact finders, not only for the pitfalls and consequences, but also for the options available for corrections. He must rely on financial officers for the proof and testimony to demonstrate those facts to commissions and courts. There is no one in the utility business who is more qualified to be the general economist for the utility management than its financial officer. It is he who must lead the legal minds on economic facts, not the other way around. Once the facts have been marshalled, it is the lawyer who can best establish procedure and strategy with the executive officer, controlling its reasonableness, timing effect on

the public's ability to pay, public reaction, etc.

Inflation is striking the utilities just as it has the railroads and certain manufacturing companies who failed to price their product as inflation dilution occurred

Because the equipment of most manufacturing companies has a relatively shorter life than utilities, the more rapid turnover of their plant forces manufacturers to reflect inflation more promptly in product pricing. Companies such as Rolls Royce and Lockheed, which did not or could not adjust prices to reflect inflation, suffered serious consequences.

The most vivid example to project the future path of the utilities, unless there is a correction of the manner in which equity securities are compensated, is the railroad industry. If railroads had properly amortized and depreciated their property, even at original cost, and paid their income and property taxes on that basis, they would still be in difficulty today but with less severity. This failure to record current costs put a double load on railroads. Railroads had assumed that they would be able to compensate their equity stockholders permanently for their investment in right-of-way, tunnels and track, etc. without amortization against the users. As the capital committed to these services was not decreased by appropriate depreciation, the costs became in excess of competitive services, leaving a huge capital loss in the accounts of railroads for their investors to absorb. Railroad roadway, for all practical purposes, is just like our streets, but the equity providers were never paid for it and cannot get paid for it under today's economics. It is a loss for which there is now no full recovery yet, in part, it is represented by bonds that must be paid off ahead of equity capital. For equipment that demanded periodic replacement, such as bridges and rolling stock, railroads were forced to adopt depreciation accounting for capital recovery and adjusted their product pricing accordingly. But that was only half the change that needed to be made. Financing railroad-capital needs with equity money today is unheard of and their bonds and trust certificates are being avoided. Providing equity capital for railroads is pretty much a governmental affair. When the practices of railroads are followed, they compel this confrontation with disaster, because inflation dilution accumulations eventually wipe out equity values. Thus, neither was adequate annual current return compensation secured nor was the recovery of the capital itself at original cost secured. Apparently the railroads expected that their position and status in the economy would remain static regardless of how the economics for the rest of the nation changed. The simple truth is that all invested capital and compensation for it must be equated to the changing economics of every other business, or its demise is only a matter of time. That is the underlying support for the United States Supreme Court's standard of compensation to the equity owner "commensurate with the returns on investments in other enterprises having corresponding risks."

The inflationary consequences to railroads are the same for utilities; therefore, the existence of inflation without recognizing it in equity compensation is like a wet rawhide strap around your neck. It is only a matter of time before it strangles you by cutting off equity capital. Unlike the railroads, utilities do amortize long-term capital investment in structures, dams, tunnels, conduits and cast-iron pipes. It took thirty years to get Internal Revenue Service to recognize the depletable characteristics of right-of-way costs for utilities. Utilities, unlike railroads, probably have as adequate original dollar capital recovery and amortization procedures for tax purposes as can be devised under present income tax laws and regulations.

But utilities, commissioners and IRS have neglected the consequence of inflation on the maintenance of the original equity investment. Some commissions allow an undetermined and usually an inadequate amount of compensation for inflation as part of the return on original cost. Failure to maintain equity capital to correspond to inflation dilution is, in my opinion, the greatest risk that overhangs utility equities in today's seemingly endless inflationary economy.

Does the same problem apply to fixed income securities?

Many theorists often listen to this argument on inflation dilution of equities and relate this to the consequence of inflation on the bondholder and then reach the conclusion that if the equity provider is entitled to an adjustment for inflation, the bondholder is entitled to compensation for the effect of inflation dilution also. This ignores the difference between the contract the bondholder has made and the rights and risks of the equity provider. When the bondholder furnishes capital funds, he places on the equity owner, as owner of the business, all the risks of successfully investing such capital funds and all the risks of plant failures, strikes, economic obsolescence, deflation, etc. If the bondholder wanted the right of ownership and, therefore, the right to compensation for inflation, he would have to be an equity provider. He contracted away his protection against inflation in return for protection of his principal and interest and protection against other risks which by his contract were 100% assessed against the equity provider. Further, inflation is causing the bondholder to seek protection through higher interest rates on all new capital. Therefore, the bondholder is in a completely different category than the equity provider in seeking compensation on his capital at today's equivalent dollar of capital invested successfully in producing utility plants.

*How much would utility equity capital
be after reflecting inflation dilution?*

The amount of a utility's equity capital at
original cost, less inflationary dilution, can
rather easily be determined. It would be
the original contributions of capital, plus
reasonable fair return, less dividends, less
hazard losses assignable to equity capital.
This sum is then price-indexed up or down
from date originated to the present time to
reflect changes in the purchasing value of
the dollar. In short, each year's increment
to the equity accounts of the company is
converted to the current year's level of
purchasing power. If this calculation produces an amount substantially greater than
the aggregate present market value of the
utility's equity capital, the equity capital has
been inadequately compensated if the utility
has otherwise been a successful operation.
But for this formula to apply, stock market
values must be based solidly on a full disclosure of the rate-making treatment of
inflation. Stock market prices, which are
based on pure speculation of what utility
rate-making practices are, are bound to be
misleading and will result in loss in utility
values, as the market reflected from 1965
to 1970.

*If the computation shows equity capital
has been compensated sufficiently to offset
inflation dilution—what then?*

In making the computation referred to
above, it may be that a utility's dollar contribution of equity capital has been kept
whole after inflationary dilution. If this be
the case, every utility should so state in its
annual reports, so that investors are ap-
prised of this fact and the manner in which
it is done. This consequence cannot be
generalized, it can only be specifically computed, because the rate-making practices
may allow for some compensation for inflation without specifically stating so.

*Is the equity owner entitled to inflationary
dilution of bond money invested?*

Some argue that since bond money is
guaranteed by the equity owner both as to
interest and principal, the equity owner
should also have added to his capital the
inflationary dilution applicable to bondholder capital. The fairness of this position
from a purely proprietary position of the
equity owner cannot be totally denied. This
does occur in manufacturing and other
enterprises where total proprietary ownership principles operate. However, the
utility business is not a purely proprietary
business of the equity owner. He receives
many concessions from the public as compared to a proprietary owner, some of which
are the right of eminent domain, protection
against dual utility systems (some say protection from competition), but this is only a
half-truth at best. It is sufficient for me to
say that if the utility equity provider's
original capital is placed in the rate-making
procedures at his original contribution of
capital, after pragmatic adjustment for inflation dilution, the equity provider, in my
opinion, would regard that maintenance of
capital as competitive to his other options
to invest. If concurrence in this view were
shown by the investor in the marketplace,
it would establish proof of adequacy of
equity capital maintenance compensation,
without including also the inflationary dilution applicable to bondholders. Only time
and experience will prove the point, but it
will be entirely academic if regulatory procedures do not even recognize the minimum
fair compensation to equity capital providers based on maintaining the purchasing
power of their own equity capital.

*Maintenance of equity capital purchasing
power versus original cost rate making*

Any examination of the original cost procedure of rate making will disclose that it
originated and was conceived during a
period of relatively stable prices. Furthermore, compensation in terms of annual fair

return to equity providers of capital on the original cost rate-base method is equitable whenever there is a parity of purchasing power between the date capital was provided and the date of rate determination. Under such circumstances, the purchasing power of the equity capital to build a successful and efficient utility plant would be maintained, and if compensation comparable to equity risks involved were allowed, the equity provider should not have cause to complain. However, when inflation sets in on a continuing basis, all the support of the original cost base for equity capital collapses; and the very reasons advanced in support of original cost rate base now call for a recognition of inflationary price dilution adjustment, as do these same reasons support labor's demands for fair wage adjustments based on inflationary dilution of the dollar.

The Hope Case decision stated when original cost rate base did not apply

The Hope Case has been generally accepted as establishing original cost as the base for rate making under the Federal Power and Natural Gas Acts. It was decided on January 3, 1944, based on the supporting test year and rate-base data of the year 1940. However, that case did not state that original cost was the proper method of rate making. State commissions which are not required by their statute or state constitutions to do otherwise, rely on this case in adopting the original cost rate base. The original cost method was determined by the Federal Power Commission at that time under the unique conditions existing at that time. However, the U. S. Supreme Court's opinion in that case stated that it was a pragmatic determination at that time when analyzed in the light of the historical financial treatment given to the equity capital providers. The FPC brief in that case relied on these facts in arguing its position. The case was not based on theoretical arguments unrelated to the his-

torical treatment that had been accorded the providers of equity capital in that particular case. The Supreme Court's decision, in my opinion, established the authority of pragmatic adjustment consistent with the economics at that particular time as they related to the equity stockholders' position demonstrated to be true in that case. In so doing, in my opinion, it also established the theory of pragmatic adjustments for times and conditions such as we now have. The words of the court on these points were as follows:

"We held in Federal Power Commission vs. Natural Gas Pipeline Co., supra, that *the Commission was not bound to the use of any single formula or combination of formulae in determining rates. Its rate-making function, moreover, involves the making of 'pragmatic adjustments.'* Id., p. 586. And when the Commission's order is challenged in the courts, the question is whether that order 'viewed in its entirety' meets the requirements of the Act. Id., p. 586. *Under the statutory standard of 'just and reasonable' it is the result reached, not the method employed, which is controlling.* Cf. Los Angeles Gas & Electric Corp. v. Railroad Commission, 289 U. S. 287, 304-305, 314; West Ohio Gas Co. v. Commission (No. 1), 294 U. S. 63, 70; West v. Chesapeake & Potomac Tel. Co., 295 U. S. 662, 692-693 (dissenting opinion). *It is not theory but the impact of the rate order which counts. If the total effect of the rate order cannot be said to be unjust and unreasonable, judicial inquiry under the Act is at an end. The fact that the method employed to reach that result may contain infirmities is not then important.* Moreover, the Commission's order does not become suspect by reason of the fact that it is challenged. It is the product of expert judgment which carries a presumption of validity. *And he who would upset the rate* order under the Act carries the heavy burden of making a convincing showing that it is invalid because it is unjust and unreasonable in its consequences. Cf. Railroad Commission v. Cumberland Tel. & T. Co., 212 U. S. 414; Lindheimer v. Illinois Tel. Co., supra, pp. 164, 169; Railroad Commission v. Pacific Gas & E. Co., 302 U. S. 388, 401.

"The rate-making process under the Act, i. e., the fixing of 'just and reasonable' rates, involves a balancing of the investor and the consumer interests. Thus we stated in the Natural Gas Pipeline Co. case that 'regulation does not insure that the business shall produce net revenues.' 315 U. S. p. 590. *But such considerations aside, the investor interest has a legitimate concern with the financial integrity of the company whose rates are being regulated. From the investor or company point of view it is important that there be enough revenue not only for operating expenses but also for the capital costs of the business.* These include service on the debt and dividends on the stock. Cf. Chicago & Grand Trunk Ry. Co. v. Wellman, 143 U. S. 339, 345-346. By that standard the return to the equity owner should be commensurate with returns on investments in other enterprises having corresponding risks. *That return, moreover, should be sufficient to assure confidence in the financial integrity of the enterprise, so as to maintain its credit and to attract capital.* See Missouri ex rel. Southwestern Bell Tel. Co. v. Public Service Commission, 262 U. S. 276, 291 (Mr. Justice Brandeis concurring). *The conditions under which more or less might be allowed are not important here. Nor is it important to this case to determine the various permissible ways in which any rate base on which the return is computed might be arrived at. For we are of the view*

that the end result in this case cannot be condemned under the Act as unjust and unreasonable from the investor or company viewpoint." (Italics supplied.)

From that decision one can find only one standard of rate making, and that is one of "justice" and/or "just and reasonable."

We are in a period today when justice and just and reasonable are not found to be observed by fiat or by observing rules laid down generations ago under conditions different from those existing today. The question of justice to equity providers of capital is just as pertinent as the application of justice in the Calley Case or in racial discrimination toward minorities in housing, jobs, and opportunities. It is just as relevant as reviewing the pros and cons of environment and pollution practices of the past, all in light of the conditions of reality as they exist today. The economic conditions affecting the compensation of utility providers of capital have grossly changed in 1971 as compared to 1940 and prior. Like most of these injustices, they have been accepted blindly as a practice, because everyone else did so and no one challenged their obvious inequities. There is no way to make restitution for past deficiencies. All that can be done now is to immediately eliminate the practices for the future, consistent with the changed conditions of today. For utility rate making, the practice of accepting original equity capital dollars for measuring compensation for that capital requires, as the Supreme Court stated in the Hope Case, "pragmatic adjustments."

It is one thing for me to declare this injustice and quite another for you or me to prove it. The court said he who challenges a rate determination by a commission "carries the heavy burden of making a convincing showing that it is unjust and unreasonable in its consequences." This burden requires us to furnish this proof if we are to do an honest job for consumer and investor alike. In my opinion, such evidence would prove beyond a shadow of a doubt that original cost rate making in utility regulation is inequitable to the providers of equity capital and is taking the utilities down the same path to incapacity to serve the public that regulation that took the railroads. Thus the conditions that are now unjust and unreasonable to equity capital providers will also result in equal or greater unjust and unreasonable consequences to utility consumers. This proof of the obsolescence of "original dollar cost" as a basis of regulation for the providers of equity capital is on your shoulders and mine as "honest determiners of fact." Our responsibilities as independent auditors is not to be biased toward you or your management, your investors or your customers. Facts can know no bias. I am not so sure that a fair presentation of financial position of utilities to the stockholders on this point shouldn't include an explanation and demonstration of the results of rate making on the maintenance of equity capital values, and that such explanation should be confirmed by the regulatory body involved and required to be disclosed on each financial statement by the Securities and Exchange Commission, so that investors can properly evaluate their investment. If all of us were forthright in presenting the most important facts to the public investor, this information would be among the first.

The Supreme Court in the Hope Case, in addition to not endorsing any particular rate base, stressed that "If the total effect of the rate order cannot be said to be unjust and unreasonable, judicial inquiry under the Act is at an end. The fact that the method employed to reach that result may contain infirmities is not then important."

What does this mean? It means orthodoxy of rate making in itself is meaningless; consequently, original cost ritual is meaningless in the face of unjust and unreasonable consequences. It means imperfections of rate making, regardless of how wrong in principle, are not wrong if the end result is "just and reasonable."

"Unjust and unreasonable consequences" that "invalidate" original dollar cost for measuring equity capital providers' compensation

In the Hope Case, the Federal Power Commission argued that "a sound test to measure a complaint that rates are confiscatory is actual financial experience of the public utility thereunder" (FPC brief p. 13). The FPC contended that "reproduction cost new" and "trended original cost" of plant were illusory. It stressed the experience of financial consequences to the providers of capital. In that case the consequences were shown to be favorable over a rather long period of time.

An overall feel of the changes that have taken place in the financial experience of the providers of equity capital to utilities can be demonstrated by the following charts. They show that the changes in the purchasing power of the dollar for the twenty-five years preceding the Hope Case required no pragmatic adjustment of original cost as concluded by the court, while comparable changes during the thirty years since do require pragmatic adjustments in the rate-making processes.

No wonder the court could not find unreasonableness in accepting original cost based on the most part on twenty-five years of stable prices at a time when dollar purchasing power was deflated. The variations in the constant purchasing power of the dollar prior to 1940 were relatively microscopic, and to the extent existing were favorable to the provider of equity capital. The trending of property by the use of construction indices did not necessarily measure the change in the purchasing value of the dollar because labor cost increases were presumably offset in whole or in part by greater productivity. Since the Hope Case, the charts show that the value of the dollar has

CHART "A"
Based on Cost of Living

DECLINE IN THE PURCHASING VALUE OF THE EQUITY CAPITAL DOLLAR SINCE THE HOPE CASE COMPARED TO THE PURCHASING VALUE OF THE DOLLAR PRECEDING THE HOPE CASE

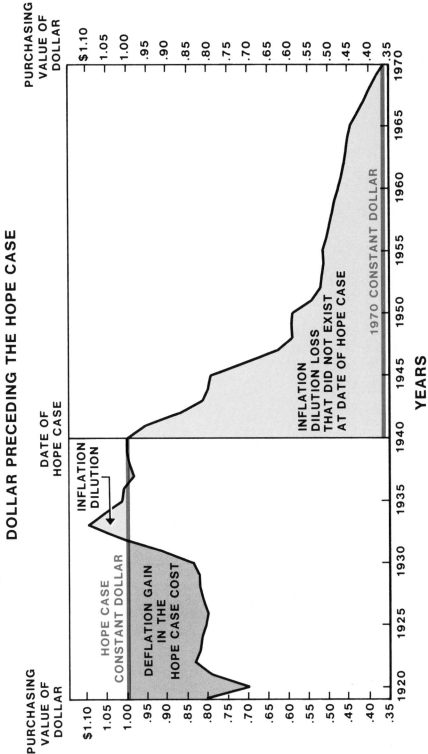

**DECLINE IN THE PURCHASING VALUE OF THE
EQUITY CAPITAL DOLLAR SINCE THE HOPE CASE
COMPARED TO THE PURCHASING VALUE OF THE
DOLLAR PRECEDING THE HOPE CASE**

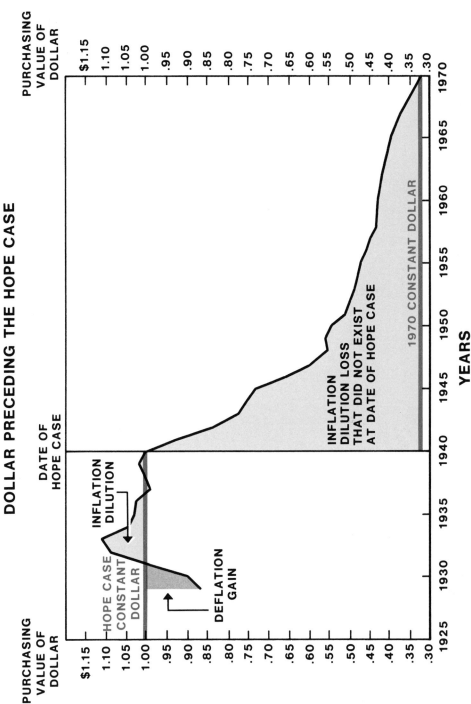

PURCHASING VALUE OF DOLLAR

DATE OF HOPE CASE

INFLATION DILUTION

HOPE CASE CONSTANT DOLLAR

DEFLATION GAIN

INFLATION DILUTION LOSS THAT DID NOT EXIST AT DATE OF HOPE CASE

1970 CONSTANT DOLLAR

PURCHASING VALUE OF DOLLAR

$1.15
1.10
1.05
1.00
.95
.90
.85
.80
.75
.70
.65
.60
.55
.50
.45
.40
.35
.30

YEARS

1925   1930   1935   1940   1945   1950   1955   1960   1965   1970

83

been decreased by inflation dilution in almost every year measured by the cost of living index or the GNP price inflater index. It shows that conditions have changed tremendously since 1940 on these points of evaluation upon which the U. S. Supreme Court relied in finding a just and reasonable result.

Generalizations do not prove "unjust and unreasonable consequences" for a particular utility

We cannot assume that the inflation shown by the preceding charts of dollar purchasing power has an automatic unjust and unreasonable effect on providers of equity capital for each company. These charts merely demonstrate that the conditions to produce an unjust and unreasonable result are present. They must be demonstrated for the particular company under consideration, and it is hardly conceivable that the result is exactly similar from one company to another in a manner that would justify establishing a general rule applicable to all rate cases. It must be proved that the damage to your providers of equity capital is significant, that its consequences are unjust for your particular company, and that relief is required under the very pragmatic principles of fairness laid down by the court. The Federal Power Commission won the Hope Case on specific financial conditions that demonstrated justice and reasonableness. Those same specifics, in my opinion, are already in the record but, contrary to the results in the Hope Case, they show that today the "original dollar cost" is used blindly, resulting in an unjust and unreasonable consequence on the equity provider of capital.

Procedure to be followed to get new direction

One last word on procedure and proof of injustice and unreasonableness is in order. As fact finders, you and I have been mesmerized by obsolete procedures and legal jargon that property "values" were in fact the only proper base for equity capital compensation in utility regulation. To prove the unjust and unreasonable consequences to the provider of equity capital, we need to deal, in addition, with three other facts which may be the most important of all, assuming a successful and efficient utility operation. They are the capital contributed by annual increments, the computation of inflation-dilution loss on that capital suffered continuously over the years, and comparison of the sum of those two amounts with the present market value of that equity. We should demonstrate year by year what the inflation loss is on equity capital contributed to a specific utility company, and thus demonstrate the damage that has been and is being suffered, if any, and that this damage is an unjust and unreasonable consequence of the present rate-making process.

Considering the long period of ritualistic use of original cost as a basis of setting equity providers' compensation without pragmatic adjustments, we cannot expect utility commissioners to abruptly make or initiate a pragmatic adjustment in rate procedure for changed conditions unless the utility advances and proves that one is required, and that the change conforms to the U. S. Supreme Court's decision in the Hope Case and/or state constitutional requirements. The reasons for now changing, both pro and con, must be forcefully argued in getting a new, more responsive direction. This is the mutual responsibility of commissioners and managements alike to the equity providers of capital. The change should not be requested in a manner that suggests an anti-regulatory commission attitude, and we must remember the responsibility for change is not theirs alone. Finally, the issue can probably best be decided by a case appealed from one of the Federal commission orders, so that it is not confused with different statutory language and precedent under state law.

ONE UTILITY'S EQUITY PROVIDERS' ORIGINAL CAPITAL CONTRIBUTIONS
COMPARED WITH THAT CAPITAL ADJUSTED FOR PURCHASING POWER
DILUTION AND WITH QUOTED MARKET VALUE

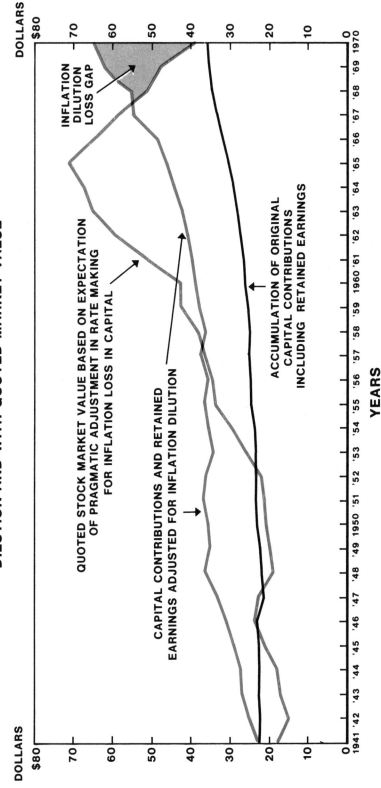

85

*Damage cannot be assumed, but if no
damage exists, equity security
owners must be informed to prove
the merits of their securities*

We should not be unmindful of the fact that the rate-of-return allowances in the past could result in the maintenance of the purchasing power of equity capital, even though the rate orders when issued did not specifically state that this was an objective.

Where such a result has been achieved and shown by an analysis of past financial history, current financial statements should explain this consequence. It is important to inform investors that the use of original cost rate base, which does not provide for the loss in purchasing power, cannot be assumed to have that undesirable end result if the consequence of actual earnings on the equity security values in fact did result in maintaining the purchasing power of such capital. Such a disclosure and explanation of the historical consequence on the equity owner (which was how the FPC won its position in the Hope Case) will go far to enhance the attraction of utility equity securities to investors. If this result can be achieved by the present rate practices or by changes in practice, it would prevent utilities suffering a fate comparable to that of the regulated railroads.

*One illustration of the growing gap
of inadequate compensation to equity
providers of capital*

In my opinion, you as financial officers should prepare for your management a computation which compares the effect of inflation on the suppliers of your equity capital with what the current purchasing power of that capital should be and its market value. I have made one such chart (pg. 85) and would like to present it.

While the chart presents an interesting history, its greatest impact is in the consequences to the equity suppliers' dollar purchasing power during the last three years. Unless this result is abruptly reversed, utilities' equity securities are destined for trouble.

Utilizing what is new in accounting

50th Anniversary Lecture Series, General
Accounting Office Auditorium,
Washington, D. C., July 15, 1971

*The benefits of using what is new in
accounting can be nullified by not
pruning out what is old, obsolete,
and decadent.*

Introduction

To YOUNG PEOPLE a fifty-year anniversary celebration probably sounds like
commemorating a great historical event. To
a person like me, it is a 50-year young anniversary. My business career covers forty-six
of those years, and I am frankly surprised
that G.A.O. is only fifty years old. I guess
even I took its existence and its services for
granted. The citizens of the United States
have been extremely fortunate to have enjoyed the excellent management that G.A.O.
has had. The theme of this meeting is, therefore, most appropriate in the light of past
good management foresight. I feel fortunate
to be among those asked to appear before
you because "Accounting Procedures and
Reporting" is literally the gut prerequisite to
"Improving Management for More Effective
Government." Furthermore, improved management is the connecting link between a
"System" or "Establishment" anchored to
the experience of past growth on the one
hand and the freedom to experience new and
more dynamic growth in the future on the
other hand.

Furthermore, it should be stated at the
outset that at no time in the past fifty years
have we been faced with the great accounting
problems we face now—caused by inflation.
This is brand new in the life of G.A.O. and
its fifty years of existence. But I must hold
my comments on this subject until later in
this presentation.

Quality accounting serves an ignoble
as well as a noble purpose

While I know that most all of you are
particularly interested in "Government," the
theme of this meeting, "Effective Management," is applicable to every phase of life
that exists in the United States. Furthermore, "Effective Government Management"
must be accepted, supported and demanded

by the productive forces of this nation as a prerequisite to their efforts to produce the wealth and the requirements to sustain life. Otherwise, the nation itself will not long exist as we know it.

Therefore, the breadth and application of good accounting is infinite in a country like ours. I say a "country like ours" because we have a democracy dedicated to balancing freedom and the fruits of that freedom to all of its people. Notwithstanding all of the complaints which this freedom permits and encourages, this nation stands alone in opposing oppression of all descriptions. Our risk, as a nation, lies in our taking freedom so much for granted that we think it will always be there even if we leave it for a moment to indulge in some suppressive digressions.

I have been exposed to accounting in at least one country which is not dedicated to the freedom of its people. I was impressed by the high quality of accounting in that country, and it, too, is used to establish "Effective Government Management." However, the accounting and management which rests upon it is used to deny freedom to its people. As a consequence, since freedom does not exist, the fruits of freedom are not available for distribution to that nation's citizens. The citizens of that nation suffer the absence of freedom and, therefore, absence of the plant that bears the fruit that will sustain wholesome life.

Thus, let us not forget that "Quality Accounting" is like an explosive. It can be used inwardly to destroy and outwardly to preserve freedom for the public. In our nation, the same dual use of accounting can injure one segment of our citizens at the expense of another segment. It can be used by government to oppress one or more segments of our people as well as to provide justice to all. Good accounting, like good government, knows no bias. If this premise for accounting were not preserved, the citizens injured would suffer the loss of some of their free-

dom from mismanagement by government institutions and corporations just as surely as if guns or bombs were used by one group against another. Since we are fortunate enough to have had forefathers that preserved freedom for us, we as individual accountants are, through the quality of our work, an important link in the preservation of the rights to assets and their use and the assessment of liabilities among our citizens.

The citizens of this country are entitled to receive the honest facts on costs and revenues, irrespective of whether they are labor or management, irrespective of whether they are consumers or investors, irrespective of whether they are employed, unemployed, or retired, irrespective of whether they are government or public contractors, irrespective of whether they represent government or are plain citizens, ad infinitum. Proper accounting knows no classification of its facts according to who receives them. If it were otherwise, accounting would be completely destructive of its purposes and would produce a fundamental violation of basic relationships among United States citizens.

Mechanics of accounting need major restructuring

We sometimes get mesmerized with the procedures by which accounting is performed and thus lose sight of its substance or bury its communicative value. Mechanical processes of accounting are fun to the nonaccountant, and often we confuse up-to-date mechanics with the quality of the product. The computer has made this diversionary tract even more attractive than when handwork was necessary. With computer speed we can build more useless accounting castles than we could ever imagine with handwork or mechanical machines.

As a consequence the computer has at times created a wall between the needs of management to use it effectively and the facts needed to improve management decision-making. We must keep in mind that decision-making by readers is the end use of all accounting products.

One solution is for management to dictate and approve the facts it needs for effective operational decision-making, and for technicians to determine the mechanics of programming and building of computer systems to supply those facts. Too often we let the computer mechanics dictate which facts are provided to management, without requiring management to state its needs and assume the responsibility of the architectural design of the information needed in order to make the most effective decisions. If the architectural design and the responsibility therefore is supplied by management, it becomes the accountant's and auditor's responsibility to fill in the specifications.

The communication of a quality accounting product from the computer to management has not improved in the same degree as have the mechanics of codifying, sorting, and tabulating. New accounting procedures require that this be reversed. In the area of procedures we certainly are not utilizing effectively what is new in accounting and, therefore, the opportunities for increasing the utilization of the computer in accounting at a lesser cost are legion. However, the need for improvement of form and greater simplification of computer communication for effective management is not the subject of my discussion with you today. I would rather emphasize the improvement of raw data upon which the computers feed. Until that is done, the computers cannot produce and management cannot have reliable data that is the prerequisite of effective management.

Internal and external reporting must be coordinated in a single accounting system

The difference between internal and external accounting and reporting is like the difference between underclothing and top clothing. They supplement and support each other and one cannot be eliminated without destroying the effectiveness of both. In articles, speeches, and textbooks we often confuse readers by placing undue emphasis on one or another of these levels of reporting as being more important. Neither is more important than the other. If the internal reporting among a train crew were not reliable and accurate, the engineer could not use the train externally. Both are needed for effective management of the train. Our accounting systems function the same way.

Over the past forty of the fifty years about which we are speaking, we have advanced a new concept for internal reporting, that is completely disengaged from external reporting but constitutes the only reliable basis by which external reporting can exist. This concept is (1) to formulate internal reporting around the concepts of management dictated by the personal habits and talents of the particular manager in charge, and (2) to base internal accounting on concepts of cost accounting which represent as accurately as possible true economic costs at each level of management supervision.

I want to spend a little time on these two steps of internal reporting before moving on to external reporting.

Use of modern personalized management internal reporting systems

Success in the use of modern personalized internal reporting systems under Step 1 has been achieved in some instances through the use of "Responsibility Accounting" and "Functional Accounting." The use of the adjective, personalized, is to emphasize the communication root of a proper system. The system must answer questions for the manager which he personally believes must be answered in order to maximize the utilization of his talent as a manager. The label on the system is of no consequence, responsibility accounting, functional accounting, or any other name. Internal accounting systems are too often designed to solidify procedures around some precedent or stereotyped form of communication of costs that does not give the particular manager what he needs in order to be effective. Such a system acts as a Berlin wall to the manager because he can't get through it or can't change it.

The system is often a bookkeeper's concept of what management should have, and he assumes the internal reporting system should be the same for all managers, regardless of their individual abilities and methods of thinking.

Breaking down this wall is one of the most important steps in utilizing what is new in internal reporting. Therefore, modern personalized management internal reporting must be audited periodically to evaluate its communication value to management. Adjustments should be made where needed, just as we would adjust cost figures to proper amounts as a result of an audit. A periodic audit of the efficiency of management information reported is equally as important as auditing the cost figures themselves. Very seldom, however, does the auditor-accountant go to management and audit the sufficiency and timing of the receipt of the right information. Thus, deficiencies in the information may be crippling or preventing the manager, without his knowledge, from making the best management decisions of which he is capable.

Modern personalized management reporting systems have probably been most widespread among electric and gas utilities. In this industry external reporting was required by law to be uniform for intercompany comparison purposes. That straitjacket activated the design of a system which enabled management to get what it needed from its internal system without impairing uniform external reports in the process. Thus, both internal and external levels of effective management were preserved, insofar as reporting was concerned.

The staffs of the Federal and State commissions readily saw the advantages and approved the use of personalized management reporting systems to enable these regulated utilities to reduce costs of operation and thereby benefit the public. At the same time, the internal systems developed provided analytical detail which facilitated the preparation of external reports in accordance with Uniform Systems of Accounts applying to all such utility companies. Consequently, electric and gas regulated companies had the traditional straitjacket of external reporting removed internally, and were able to design effective internal management accounting systems. Yet most commercial and industrial company personnel still believe that their companies must live with external reporting restrictions when they are developing internal systems. It is not so.

Commercial and industrial companies, except for service companies and similar organizations, have not utilized personalized management internal reporting systems as they should have to achieve effective management. Neither have governmental agencies. An extension of internal reporting systems in these areas should greatly improve management and result in reduced operating costs that will benefit the public and our economy.

Room must continue to exist for personalized internal reporting systems in defense and other industries that will be subject to the Uniform Cost Accounting Standards (UCAS). The real bite of UCAS applies to the definition of "cost" as used for internal reporting, on which I will comment later.

Thus, in the matter of getting greater management effectiveness from personalized internal reporting systems, much is yet to be done in all walks of life—corporations, all levels of government, hospitals, and welfare activities. We in the accounting field often confine too much of our attention to verifying recorded costs, without first placing on management the crucial decisions of what information is needed for its effective management. We, as auditors or examiners, cannot assume that we are qualified managers and thereby take responsibility that the information provided is adequate to manage effectively. At best, such systems are poor substitutes for those which management itself would design.

If management admits it doesn't know what information it needs for decision-making, that fact is probably more conclusive than any other fact that management is not capable of managing effectively. Disclosure of this admission is one of the most important points that can be made in any accountant's report. However, once responsibility for data identification is placed on management, effective management usually eliminates a bulk of trivia and trash in internal reports. This in turn eliminates substantial costs incurred all the way from the field to the top office in gathering raw data that is to a great extent useless.

As auditors and examiners we give far too little attention to the job of requiring management to assume the responsibility for determining the information it needs. As management changes, the new management should be required to restate the communication reporting system it needs to meet its particular way of management. This does not mean that the auditor, examiner, or accountant should abdicate his responsibility to assist management in developing an internal reporting system and evaluating the cost of producing it. He must continue to build the specifications for the procedures to meet the architectural design of management decision-making information as dictated by management. He must continue to be accountable for evaluating the internal control of the system.

The cost of producing an internal reporting system must always be measured against its worth for decision-making and internal control. The system should make clear where the costs of accounting outweigh the benefits to be achieved, and where sampling

will serve the same purpose of complete tabulation, etc. This procedure, in styling a personalized reporting system, is so new that it is seldom used—and yet so old that few people recognize that it was the system that existed when one-man managements were common. Management often does not know that personalized decision-making data can and should be available; therefore, the accountant must take the responsibility for pressing management to appraise this approach, and should not wait for management to demand it or criticize accounting for its failure to communicate the proper data to management.

Personalized management internal reporting systems are like being fitted with a new suit that must be tailored to fit; that fitting may be perfect now, but it may not last forever. Conditions of all descriptions change. Like the need for a new suit to fit the changed conditions, so we need new and revised internal reporting systems to repersonalize the system for a continuing management that operates under changing conditions and different requirements for effective decision-making. How often this review is needed varies from company to company, but a review every three to five years is generally advisable to prune useless data and gather new data.

How do these responsibilities tie into government staff and my work as a member of the external accounting profession? I would say our responsibilities are just about the same. It is true that the government staff, as it works with other agencies and other institutional or corporate problems, is more guided by a "questioning" posture on behalf of the public than is the outside public accountant. However, the intensity of questioning should be much the same. Too often the outside public accountant seems to have a blind spot with respect to his own management abilities. As a result, he confuses a substitution of his own ideas on management information for the necessity of placing on management the responsibility for factual data needed for effective decision-making. As government staff, you are often placed in the position of writing laws or regulations about management responsibilities and reporting requirements prior to management's participation in a project. Thus, you must exercise a greater degree of care in placing revision responsibilities on management.

One of the best illustrations of this double responsibility is the assignment to G.A.O. through the UCAS Board of the major responsibility for Uniform Cost Accounting Standards. The standards must be set up so that they can be fitted with the personalized management internal reporting desired by and necessary to each individual contractor. The standards must also be designed to delineate clearly and uniformly the true economic cost of production and cost divisionalization so that third-party review of management's prudence and effectiveness is possible. At the same time this cost divisionalization must provide for the application of pricing policies established by third parties—in this case, the government.

If UCAS is successful in meeting all four objectives, they will place on management of both contractor and government the clear opportunity to discharge their responsibility for effectiveness; if not, we can expect more Lockheeds and Penn Centrals in the future. UCAS will not eliminate management problems or ineffectiveness. They will only enable such problems to "surface" early enough so that effective management of both government and contractor can take action on them.

Use of economic costs in internal reporting system

Concern at all levels of proprietary ownership for the quality of management, whether in government, corporations, institutions, etc., has led to questioning the internal reporting of practically every entity. This interest in "knowing" is consistent with a proprietary right to know. The day of owner-management in corporate affairs in the United States is about over, except in the very small entities, and secrecy from public proprietary interest in government is warranted only at the most sensitive level. Management in all other walks of life in this country is hired help.

Each segment of the public is very "nosy" as to the results of operations for every entity in our economic system. This is only possible in a free country, in which we have a basic consistency between these two conditions, i.e., the demand to know and the right to know. Thus, internal accounting reports of all entities are now constantly perused by, and on behalf of, the proprietary public.

When most internal reports were conceived and designed, management did not expect them to be used by proprietary interests not versed in the loose vernacular used in such reporting systems. As a consequence, when used in internal reporting, such terms as "cost of so and so" or "profit of division X" or similar ostensibly conclusive or unmodified nomenclatures, are completely untrue. Such terms would more properly be "certain incurred costs" or "revenues or sales net of certain costs" but certainly not "cost" or "profit" in any total or defined way. Such loose reports and loose terms are about as communicative of reliable data as that fill-in figure of speech phrase, you know, that punctuates all oral communication today. Both are meaningless and carry no values of communication. In internal reports, however, we have great responsibility for making the terms we use meaningful, so that they mean what they say to our boss, the "nosy" public. A refinement of terms so that our reports are more communicative will greatly improve our accounting systems and will increase their usefulness to all of us. I am positive that such a disciplining will double the thinking power put into such reports by accountants. More important, the usefulness of reports thus prepared, either through elimination of unnecessary data or through increased accuracy, will be doubled.

Internal reports cannot include all costs in an economic sense, as I will later discuss in relation to external reports; therefore, accurate descriptions are important for not only what they state positively but also for what they do not say. A fundamental standard in the design of internal reports is to limit revenues, income, expenses and other costs of a division to those supervised by the manager of that particular division. Other economic costs of that activity may be supervised by and be the responsibility of other higher echelon managers. These costs should be included in the latter's reports. In this way each tier of internal reporting includes only revenues and costs for which the particular managers of that tier are responsible. The final report of the chief executive to the public would include an accounting for his tier costs and all prior supervised tiers. The sum should be total "economic cost." Therefore, the new exposure of internal accounting reports requires new accounting systems that are more accurate in defining the particular revenues and particular costs being reported upon.

It has been an old habit to use hackneyed words and phrases in internal reporting, almost slang. Only by long association with such reports does one develop the ability to interpret them. When used by strangers, such as the public and government staff who are not constantly living with them, they are obsolete and can be dangerously misleading. For instance, the use of the term "profit" when one is referring to pretax profit is a complete misnomer, yet it is commonly used under the "you know" concept of communication.

These reports are particularly wasteful in leading public readers down a wrong path and to a wrong conclusion. For instance, I recently had reason to hear a report that the Defense Department had a very large supply of ice chains on hand in Vietnam.

Since it is natural to question how much ice one might reasonably expect to find in Vietnam, the existence of these chains in inventory seemed a self-evident indication that ineffective management existed. However, the report was incomplete, misleading, and wasteful, since the chains were used to provide traction on mud roads. If the report had called these items "mud chains" instead of ice chains, the conclusion as to the effectiveness of communication to management for action decisions would have been quite different.

Likewise, in practically all instances, internal reports should refer to "supervised cost" subdivisions of the particular department or division and not lead a reader to conclude such cost is total cost of that activity. I believe this point is particularly applicable to all levels of government, and I know it applies to all levels of corporate activity. We provide reports on "cost" as though such costs were total "economic costs," when they are not.

I recall reporting on the accounts of Bonneville Power Authority many years ago and qualifying the final results applicable to that division of government, since no taxes had been charged. The final results should have been properly labeled as being before allocation of government services and carrying costs of government investment. A similar condition applies to practically every department of government when "costs" reported to the public are not complete economic costs. Reports on Vietnam costs should say "incremental costs" so as to distinguish clearly between total economic costs and those which are on-going irrespective of Vietnam, if the reports are to show these facts for effective government management.

Similar deficiencies in internal reports of corporations lead to misinterpretations, and may be misleading when such reports are given public distribution. All misleading reports to the public undermine the public trust and are therefore damaging to all of us, regardless of the phase of the profession in which we practice. This result is probably not intentional but certainly arises from lack of attention.

Some in our profession do not agree that reports should reflect costs that economically tell the "whole truth" to the proprietary owners of all government and all business representing the public. Their counter argument is often that the public would loudly protest many of the things a minority of us think are desirable. However, to provide the public with incomplete reports in order to secure their approval is lying, and reports constructed for such purposes fail to maximize the ways in which accounting can be used for more effective government. The public must assume the burden of understanding proper and accurate explanations of true costs and accept the consequences of such factual reports in the action it takes. We, as accountants, and you, as the government staff, are guilty of bias when our reports do not clearly state carefully worded descriptions of what costs are or are not.

I hope that progressive accountants will eliminate incomplete phrases and titles that convey half-truths. The use of a few more words often enables one to tell the whole truth. All of us in accounting are guilty of intentionally misleading the public on this score. I will cover this point in more detail later, but we must emphasize the use of terms and explanations that at least have an opportunity to convey the truth to the public, the collective and ultimate owner of all resources on which we report.

Misleading reports too often provide those who wish to criticize reported results with half-truths or untruths that can be damaging. We must eliminate such reports. An attorney in his role of an advocate will use various approaches to try to get the witness to weaken or damage his case if he can, regardless of the facts. We in accounting cannot indulge in the same sport.

We must make a sincere response to the public, so that the public can impose more effective management on governments, corporations and legislators.

No purpose is served in not making a full accounting of the facts to the public, even though at the moment knowledge of all the facts may be distasteful to that public. This is the newer look of accounting reports. Neither the government and its representatives, corporations, or other institutions should be permitted to slant internal accounting reports on the effectiveness of management. To do so is to ignite a time bomb that will explode at a later date. Experience has shown this to be more damaging than if the actual facts were made known on a timely basis when corrective action could have been taken. This principle is true even if timely internal reports prevent election of presidents, senators, congressmen or awards to corporations, cities or states. I well know how naive this viewpoint is in terms of total accomplishment, but without the accounting profession striving to reach it, no forward progress will be made.

This concludes my comments on personalizing and designing internal reports and on the use of economic costs in internal reports. Both of these aspects should encourage new uses of internal accounting reports for more effective management.

Cost accounting principles vs. generally accepted accounting principles

Generally accepted accounting principles have a new look today that needs to be understood before it can be appraised. The economics under which the United States produces its wealth has completely changed in the last twenty years. At the beginning we were an independent unit in world production. Today we have lost a great share of that independence and we are almost a dependent unit. We have been so accustomed to thinking we have "made it" that we won't even tell each other that we have practically "lost it" in international competition.

Some fifteen years ago the accounting profession began a serious discussion of these so-called "generally accepted accounting principles." The very existence of a standard of "general acceptance" for accounting principles was and always has been confusing, so that the application of such principles has been nebulous and difficult to explain to each segment of the public. With the economic status of our country in a tailspin we cannot afford not to have the real facts. The greatest gap in understanding in the United States today is not among the races, among the youth, or in environment. It is in our loss of economic muscle. To tell that story requires accounting based on true economics. The absence of jobs for youth today is not attributable to the downturn of business but to the export of jobs that economically could not survive here. Who is telling the young people these economic truths so that they can put their minds to pressuring the right to survival. The politician is a novice in this field and runs helter-skelter, destroying the country he has pledged to protect and help.

Since the dictionary states that a principle is a "fundamental truth," it is natural that interested public segments would expect a principle of accounting to have a crisp and apparent certainty in its meaning. Reconciling that definition with the double talk and double interpretation by professional accountants when applied to reports to the public was bound to bring a reaction of criticism of the profession from that public, as well as from those within the profession, who can't reconcile truth as shown by our reports with truth as it exists.

Most of the criticisms and comments are leveled at accounting principles as affecting corporations, but they apply to mutual institutions and to government accounting as well. Since public capital invested in corpo-rations generates most of the wealth needed by the public, the defects of corporation accounting automatically call for improved management, and management demands more effective accounting. The criticisms of accounting principles and the defective principles that exist color the effectiveness of management of every company.

These defects must all be faced by the Cost Accounting Standards Board when it determines the Uniform Cost Accounting Standards that are now in process of determination. If the precedence of "generally accepted accounting principles" is to be blindly followed by the Board, the standards which emerge will cause grave injustices to various segments of the public. It will result in freezing into regulation the obsolescence of past practices that have denied the public the economic truth that it must have to adjust itself, so that it can survive in our international economy that is so new to the world we now live in. The benefits of utilizing what is new in accounting can be completely nullified by not pruning out what is old, obsolete, and decadent.

The Cost Accounting Standards Board must justify the reasoning behind every principle of cost accounting it adopts. Only in this way can the objective of the Congressional Act, telling the facts, be achieved, and only in this way can the United States be told the economic facts that face us internationally. All costs comprising true economic costs must be defined, even though the definitions may conflict with generally accepted accounting principles, which were not designed to accumulate the economic cost of production.

Accounting principles which recognize true economic costs, so that all segments of the public will be justly treated, is a new and emerging concept and is not fully understood even by the accounting profession. At present it is grossly incomplete. The development of this emerging concept occurred by stages as our economic existence changed over the last twenty years from the nation being the source of most production to merely a "me too" participant nation in international production.

The recitations of shortcomings of accounting principles fifteen years ago were shrugged off by the accounting profession, then scoffed at, and then defended in the name of experimentation, flexibility, management's right to set its own principles, and the avoidance of straitjacket rules. These reactions were made by government and corporate managers alike, but all are red herrings to the real issue of refining our communication so that true costs and revenues are conveyed to the public. True costs as I refer to them mean full economic costs.

I am sorry to say that the members of the accounting profession were in the forefront of resisting a confrontation with inadequate reporting as a result of undefined accounting principles. The reports of the presidents of our professional society make interesting retrospective reading today. It is even more interesting to read the viewpoints of some corporate, academic, and government personnel and to compare those views to some of the present expressions from the same sources. Some of them would lead one to believe that production of goods and services in the nation should be presumed to be sinful—as though production of wealth could be dispensed with without economic damage to the very voice that advocated such economic recklessness.

Such retrospective analysis, however, is not productive except as a method of learning how to approach correction of a deficient accounting product. We need to see what caused deficiencies and why such deficiencies became so deeply entrenched in our year-to-year reporting even though the results communicated to a reader made him believe untruths.

Some find it difficult to understand why the accounting profession can constantly update and refine "auditing standards" but cannot do the same for "accounting principle standards." The answer is simple. Auditing standards have a terminal life without any retrospective effect when changed. Each year stands alone. On the other hand, accounting principles have a life span equal to that of the assets or liabilities recorded by application of such principles of accounting. The roots of today's accounting principles run deep into past history when conditions were very different from today's conditions. Yet some of the accounting principles of fifty or seventy-five years ago are made the basis of today's reports, although they are unrelated to today's economics. Thus, accounting principles carry over from one year to another for many, many years, often overlapping several human life spans. Any change in the definition of accounting principles affects the carried-over assets and liabilities which have been reported upon by both management accountants and government. Each of these authorities reacts in the same way in resisting change, if "change" means change in what was previously reported. The idea of changing yesterday's facts so that they will be honestly reported, consistent with today's conditions, is abhorred by managements, accountants, and Federal agencies alike. The only way to change the accounting within Federal agencies under such conditions is through political changes of the personnel involved.

The ability to change irrespective of prior reports is probably the best test of independent thinking and forthright responsibility to the public segments affected. If one opposes embracing substantively improved facts he lacks the necessary qualifications to use "new accounting" to improve management.

I can illustrate this much more effectively by another situation that has spanned a period of seventy-five years, twenty-five more than the G.A.O. anniversary period. No attention has been given to it as yet, even though the public is today suffering the burdens of ineffective management of the

Railroad Regulatory Commission, the railroad managements, the Treasury Department, and the Congress of the United States.

The industry is that of railroads, probably the oldest and largest industry in this nation, or the world. The roots go back to the days of William Jennings Bryan arguing in behalf of the public against railroads that were allegedly gouging a helpless rural public. Out of that experience came the Interstate Commerce Commission. About the same time the Federal income tax became effective. The cost accounting system created for the railroads was inaugurated at that time, when the principles of depreciating and amortizing plant over the life of the property's usefulness were in their elementary stages, about the time of the Model T Ford.

The depreciation and amortization policies of the railroads were premised on the assumption that railroads would forever continue to be as useful as they then were. There were no roads, no trucks, no airplanes, no power-driven water transportation. The greatest portion of the cost of plant investment was assigned to future users in the belief that under conditions then existing each generation could assign the cost without diminution to the next generation and thus put off the reckoning of cost forever. The government even assessed Federal income taxes on this basis, and as a consequence overcollected taxes in the hundreds of millions from railroads as compared to other businesses. This scheme of avoiding the recognition of the true economic costs of transportation prevailed until 1971, when true economics showed its ugly head. It took as its first major victim the Penn Central. When asked why the Penn Central collapsed, the answer would be that we didn't apply "what was new in accounting" since Williams Jennings Bryan and his famous court cases at the beginning of the century.

Had the railroad industry and the accounting profession recognized "what was

new in accounting," the economic cost of transportation would have demanded changes in railroad accounting. The failure to recognize underlying railroad economics eventually brought Penn Central to its knees and is about to do the same to all in that industry.

Everything pertaining to the railroads has changed since the Interstate Commerce Commission was formed except its cost accounting for public and tax use. Blatant, ineffective management by everyone concerned—the accounting profession, the Interstate Commerce Commission, the Internal Revenue Service, the railroad managements and Congress—has brought a needless loss upon all segments of the public.

The alleged basis for the improper accounting was to restrict profits of investors and shippers for the benefit of the public. In effect, these very restrictions resulted in serious detriment to all segments of the public. To starve the horse that pulls the plow will also starve you. The same conditions applied to the utilities of this nation only a few years later, but with the 1932 depression, the Roosevelt government and regulatory commissions immediately invoked needed improvements, recognizing economic costs in accounting in the 1930's and converting inadequate accounting to what was new. Generally, the utilities have continued to have modern accounting in all respects except one since that time.

The newest problem—accounting for inflation

The greatest advance in modern accounting is now waiting on our threshold—waiting for proper implementation. On it depends the continued productiveness of every institution upon which all segments of the public now depend. It will tell us truths we never dreamed existed. They won't be pleasant but will be honest and from them we will take actions that will save us from further disasters. These actions will include the effectiveness of our representative government, the corporations, and institutions of every description.

This "newness" in accounting consideration is the recognition of "cost of living" in terms of present-day, price-leveled costs. In a manner, we have a mammoth reproduction of railroad economics now applying to every activity in which we are engaged. We are consuming the buildup of values of yesterday in today's living and making no accounting for the costs being consumed. This results from inflation—paying for yesterday's assets in today's diluted dollars and believing that the dollars we pay are true economic costs when they are not. We thus are misleading the public by showing them an understatement of the costs they are presently consuming to live.

The public is being misled into the belief that they are consuming no more than they are paying for. This is an untruth, and new accounting procedures require these facts to be shown if we are to have effective management of our economy at all levels. We are understating the "economic costs of corporation production," and this is beginning to reflect itself in such incidents as Lockheed, Penn Central, Rolls-Royce, and thousands of comparable situations of lesser size. But we must emphasize this is just the beginning of the problems that can become commonplace if costs are not adjusted for inflation.

Other reflections of improper accounting for inflation appear in the deterioration and pitiful condition of primary schools and a resultant cheating of the children of America; the colleges which are shortchanging the young adults; the hospitals which are losing ground in maintaining health service; the poor who cannot survive the diluted dollar; the cities and states that cannot maintain decent living conditions with the diluted dollar; the retired social security worker who cannot stand still even with continued increases, in face of the diluted dollar; every Federal government depart-

ment, the defense structure of the nation and our balance of international payments, which is constantly unbalanced by the diluted dollar resulting from inflation.

Today it is new in our accounting systems to reflect the cost of inflation or to issue reports on cost in price-leveled dollars. Reporting for the effects of inflation should have been done years ago to forewarn of these coming conditions. That timing is now too late, but the use of such newness in accounting can warn of coming further catastrophes and the costs which must be met to avoid them. Without utilizing this new accounting in our reporting practices to the public, we provide a blindfold for that public so it cannot see the destruction occurring to this nation's economy and its people. Even our growing joblessness is a consequence of the economic facts not getting to the public.

If we were to build a computer model of the effect of these forces in the future, the computer would print out a replica of Penn Central or Lockheed, but a billion times as great. On a band-aid basis, we might provide for a slow collapse of Penn Central and Lockheed, but where would we find a pair of big arms strong enough to hold up a nation in that condition? Throughout our society, both in the private sector and in government at all levels, we are using up the warehouse of values built up in the past, but never costed into current living. Now we often hear that the public will not pay for replenishing the warehouses with living conditions that it has enjoyed in the past. If true economic cost had been reported, the seed corn would not have been eaten and we would have been less wasteful of resources in other respects. The use of resources would have been far more frugal and replenishment far less costly and we would have had a far stronger nation to exhibit to the young.

A new accounting based on "economic costs" will provide the facts, so that "effective management of government" can exist, as well as effective management of all the other entities of this nation. Effective management at all levels is a prerequisite to the need for any government at all.

While addressing ourselves seriously to accounting for inflation as a new procedure, we must not lose sight of the fact that inflation has been with us since the beginning of time. Those responsible for reporting to the public who refused to report on inflation costs must bear the negligence for not acting early enough to provide proper warnings to the public of Penn Centrals, Lockheeds, and even New York and other big cities. Those who must be first charged are the accounting profession, Federal and state government regulatory bodies and the Defense Department. The reasons why this delinquency has occurred in reporting true "economic costs" are several:

(a) First, the failure of the accounting profession to adopt price-leveled accounting as a required accounting principle so that all entities would report true "economic costs" in stating their financial position and results of operations.

(b) Second, in addition to the foregoing failure, the profession was far too subservient to managements of all entities, corporate and government, and failed to press for reports on "true economic costs" consumed. Cities and governments never reported consumption of assets as a current depreciation charge. Corporate management never reported price-leveled dollars, but reported only increases in profits based on dollars that were not leveled. These managements, like those of the railroads, at any particular moment were interested primarily in the short-term period of their remaining administrations. Bad news that would accrue over a long-term period was to be avoided in the short run, even though eventually the day of reckoning must come, hopefully as a responsibility of another management. This is a clear illustration of collective ineffective management by the accounting profession, government regulatory bodies and corporate management. None can have a valid excuse for their negligence in reporting the "true costs" of an obvious condition, of which they were well aware.

(c) The third reason is "politics" and here the full responsibility falls on government personnel and management. Its representatives coerced those in the accounting profession to prevent their use of the newest accounting to report the "true economic costs" to the public. In addition, these same government managers would not initiate actions of their own to tell these basic truths to the public. It reminds me of the recent public reaction to the exposé by the *New York Times* on the report on managing the Vietnam War. In our case, not reporting proper "economic cost," no international diplomatic relations could be involved— only a malicious desire to deny the obvious could be charged to government for withholding true cost reports to its own citizens. The Federal agencies went further than "classifying" such "economic cost" facts; they did not even allow a record to be made of them. Without a complete repudiation of past policies in this regard in the use of new accounting techniques, government will be turning its back on "new accounting" reports of truthful facts that would contribute significantly to effective management of government.

The paper tiger

Before the Fibre Box Association,
New York, October 13, 1971

We must keep in mind that decision-making by readers, whether they be corporate management or the investing public, is the end use of all accounting products.

I HAVE BEEN ASKED to speak on management problems. Gentlemen, management in your industry has a real tiger by the tail. While the Fibre Box Association is primarily concerned with the converting segment of your industry, you also must be deeply concerned with the overall performance of the entire paper industry. In this industry there are basically four manufacturing segments and four interrelated management decision-making levels; timber, pulp mill, Kraft board mill, and container plant. For the most part you are a highly integrated industry, and, therefore, management decisions made at any one level of the productive flow have a significant effect on all other decisions. While the dollars received for corrugated boxes will primarily determine the overall profit of the integrated company, the magnitude of those profits is dependent on decisions made at the various levels of the integrated process. Therefore, I believe we must focus today on management problems at all levels of the integrated process in order to fully appreciate the magnitude of the tiger you are wrestling with.

Let us summarize some of the basic characteristics of the paper industry which also represent basic management problems.

Low profits and return on investment

An article in the *Paper Trade Journal* stated that for the first quarter of 1971, thirty-one paper companies representing $2.6 billion in sales reported a 32% decline in earnings from the prior year on increased sales volume. A recent financial study compiled by my firm for the Fibre Box Association covering the year 1970 indicates that the composite return on investment (i.e., net property, receivables and inventory) for 65% of your total industry

101

is less than 2%, and your pretax and pre-interest profits as a percent of sales were less than 1%.

It is not difficult to see some of the factors which contribute to this situation. The Bureau of Census reported that the average sales price per ton of paperboard is less today than in 1960, while raw material and payroll costs have increased substantially in the last decade. While productivity has also increased dramatically in your industry over the last ten years, it still has not kept pace with the nation's inflation spiral. Phil Brockington's report to you this spring indicated that the basic corrugated price trend is far behind increases experienced in other industries during the past decade and generally has not increased significantly since 1960.

Your profit problems are further complicated by the fact that pricing decisions are being made at relatively low management levels. Think of the number of plants and mills in your industry and multiply that times the number of local personnel authorized to make pricing decisions and multiply that answer again by the number of orders being processed. The number of individual pricing decisions being made each day in your industry must be staggering.

To further add to your woes, there is the additional problem of establishing proper transfer prices at the timber and mill levels. These transfer prices become the cost of raw materials at the converting level and, accordingly, have a direct impact on the reliability of your profits if not reasonably determined. Cost estimating techniques vary from company to company. For example, "board cost" in your cost estimating system varies from mill cost at the low level to something higher than the official board market at the high level. Not all costs and, in some cases, not all assets (i.e., goodwill) are presently allocated to the lowest decision-making level and, accordingly, may not be considered by those individuals who are responsible for pricing

decisions. In too many cases, prices established at the plant and mill levels are not being monitored and controlled by corporate management.

Your entire industry is volume oriented. The pressure to consume mill tonnage is great. The huge capital investment in mills requires volume production to reasonably amortize the high-fixed costs. This production is forced to the converting plants, which also have significant fixed costs, particularly related to the corrugator. In many cases your salesmen are compensated according to volume only. This extreme volume consciousness, together with the fact that your customers consider your product a commodity without significant differences from your competitors' product, combine to keep your selling prices under constant pressure.

I know I am not telling you anything new when I say that the past performance and trends of profit and return on investment in your industry are presently, and continue to be, gloomy. I will tell you, however, that the picture is actually worse than it may appear on the surface, because the failure of your industry and the nation to account for "true economic costs." I will elaborate on this later.

Significant capital investments

Historical cost investments in timber, mill, and conversion facilities are enormous. In the conversion segment alone your industry has been adding one plant to the total productive capability every eight days since 1957. However, your real investment in terms of true economic cost is actually far greater. For example, some companies have estimated that the stumpage value of woodlands which have been held for a long period of time may be 15 to 30 times the cost amount at which these assets are shown in the financial statements, due primarily to severe inflation, and this is in addition to land which may be appreciating in value. Also the impact of inflation has had a significant effect on your investments in mills and conversion plants. Based on the increase in the Consumer Price Index over the past decade (1958 = 100; 1970 = 138.5), a 350,000 ton per year Kraft linerboard mill, exclusive of timber, would have cost about $54 million to build and equip in 1958; today the same facility will cost $75 million. A semichemical corrugating mill in 1958 cost $14 million; today it costs $20 million. In terms of today's dollars, a $3.6 million 1958 box plant will cost $5 million. The ominous effects of inflation on the capital recovery process become readily apparent. Your overall investment at this time is far greater in terms of true economic costs than it would appear from an historical cost standpoint. From an income statement standpoint the cost of capital consumed using these historical costs results in an overstatement of past profits, due to a failure to recognize changes in the purchasing power of the dollar and price-level depreciation. In simple terms, both your industry's return on investment and profitability are, in fact, worse than your accountants have reported, because recognition has not been given to the real value of investments in terms of today's inflated dollars and changing technology. We are consuming the buildup of yesterday's values in today's living and are making no accounting for the real costs being consumed. We are paying for yesterday's assets in today's diluted dollars and have convinced ourselves that these dollars we pay are the true economic costs, when they are not. In understanding the economic costs of our corporate production we have recently begun to see the beginning of major problems in such incidents as Lockheed, Penn Central and Rolls-Royce; these can become commonplace if costs are not adjusted for inflation.

Industry future

What does the future look like? Your industry estimates an 80% increase in production volume (unadjusted for effects of inflation) in the next decade if trends estab-

lished during the last few years continue. Breakeven points may soon be set at capacity volume levels. To achieve this growth, present mill capacity must be increased by 50% in the next ten years. An industry investment of $4.7 billion (in both mills and box plants) may be required to meet anticipated demand; 150,000 additional employees could be necessary to man your forests, mills, and plants. In another way of looking at the future, it is estimated that the thirty companies which supply 75% of the industry volume will need $350 million per year, in terms of today's dollars, in the next decade to expand their capacity to meet the expected demand. Based on the present and expected future sales dollar volume of these companies, they will need a 16% pretax return on sales in order to generate sufficient funds internally to finance such expansion without having to resort to costly debt or equity financing.

The new buzz words of the '70's are pollution and environmental control. Mr. Merrill Robison, at the spring meeting of the Paperboard Group of the American Paper Institute, summed up present and future industry problems well when he commented that at a time when the industry is facing the toughest economic problems it has faced in thirteen years, with no signs of improvement, they have the additional headache of coping with the solid waste problem. This, coupled with air pollution and continuing conservation problems, will necessitate the expenditure of vast funds in the future in all of the nation's industries to correct or reduce the magnitude of this very real American nightmare. Unfortunately, in most cases this investment in the future will not increase productivity and will serve to further dilute your present level of earnings and return on investment.

Another major problem which must be weighed is the potential for overcapacity in your industry. From a volume standpoint, you have had dynamic past growth, and experts indicate an excellent future potential. Statistics prepared by Phil Brockington for your spring meeting indicate that your volume has increased in the past decade by 68%. Although container converting profits are not available to the public, the basic price trend of containerboard is practically level for the same period (a 4.3% increase). If current trends continue in the future, you can expect significant increases in production volume and capacity, accompanied by major increases in raw material and payroll costs and in the overall costs of obtaining capital. If such dynamic growth continues to result in overcapacity within the industry, it is reasonable to assume that basic pricing trends will continue at a level which will not result in adequate profits and return on investment. Faced with the problems of potential overcapacity and related poor economic return, management must be prepared to make wise decisions in regard to future expansion. What will your potential capital investment be and how will it be financed? What kind of return on this investment do you require and how will it be achieved? Are other alternatives available to you? These are very important questions you must be able to answer in the '70's.

To summarize major problems briefly at this point, I can sum it up in a few words: industry profits and return on investment are extremely low now, lower than what your accountants would lead you to believe if we look at true economic costs; present and future capital requirements are enormous; and, if present trends in pricing, costs, and interest rates continue, the future looks rather dismal.

What can be done?

As executives you are concerned with planning for future growth, making decisions as to alternative uses of funds and other decisions affecting the profitability of your enterprises. In planning for future growth, you necessarily have to be concerned about the funds required for that growth and the cost of these funds. Often these funds cannot be generated internally and, consequently, must be obtained in the capital markets. The ability to obtain funds and their cost is directly dependent on how well a company can demonstrate that it can utilize additional funds profitably. The remainder of my presentation will be primarily devoted to a discussion of the information management needs in order to employ capital funds for maximum profitability. Two key questions are:

1. Do managements have the information necessary to make proper decisions in attempting to maximize profits and obtain optimum use of their assets?

2. Are present-day accounting concepts and information systems responsive to management's needs and are they assisting them in future planning?

To begin with, management must understand the cost estimating system being used by your companies and be familiar with it in a reasonable amount of detail. This will enable you to determine the extent of deficiencies in your present system and what output you actually need from your system to make the necessary management decisions for the future. We must keep in mind that decision-making by readers, whether they be corporate management or the investing public, is the end use of all accounting products. The facts in business are the same regardless of how they are reported; and true economic conditions and circumstances cannot be misrepresented or perverted without a day of reckoning.

Although I realize that some of you are independent converters, the majority of your industry is integrated from the forest to the container plant, and the decisions of the large integrated companies have a significant impact on independent converters. True and complete cost accountability is necessary at all levels of an integrated operation if proper decisions are to be made.

At the forest level, decisions must be made as to several alternatives: should the timber be sold at that level, harvested for use in plywood or pulp mills, or should land development be considered? Should timber for the mills be purchased rather than produced? The true economic cost of this segment, including proper allocation of corporate overhead and interest costs and adjustments for inflation, must be determined before a sound management decision can be made. Reasonable transfer prices must be established which will not result in an arbitrary allocation of profits to any one segment.

At the mill levels, decisions as to the further processing of timber also require a full recognition of today's costs before management can decide to process the products further as Kraft board, plywood, fine paper or lumber. Or should the product be marketed at the mill level? Or would it be more economical to purchase materials for the Kraft board mills and container plants from outside sources? Problems with proper allocation of costs and establishment of reasonable transfer prices again need to be resolved.

At the container plant level, decisions must be made as to whether high volume and low margins are desirable or should products be oriented to low volume and high margin lines.

As you can easily see, cost decisions made at all of the preceding processing levels now come to rest with you. If improper recognition to costs is given at other stages in the integrated process, you cannot possibly make intelligent pricing decisions at the conversion stage.

To specifically elaborate on examples of the magnitude of your costing problems, our study of twenty-six companies, representing 65% of your industry, prepared for the Fibre Box Association, indicated that the cost systems used by the companies in

your industry have numerous and significant differences. Board costs vary all over the ball park. Overhead factors vary from zero to something in excess of actual overhead costs. Labor allocation methods also varied greatly. Frequently costing decisions are based on the concept of full utilization of assets. In an industry which has been plagued by overcapacity in the past, cost estimating should be based on volumes which are realistically obtainable and not those which are theoretically possible. Since pricing decisions are presently being made on the basis of a variety of costing techniques and theories, the risk of management error is vastly increased.

All costs should be allocated, down to the lowest decision-making level where someone might be using the costs. Local plant level cost and pricing decisions should be reviewed by corporate management, at least on an exception basis within predetermined guidelines, to insure that corporate pricing policies are being followed throughout the integrated system.

Although strategy in profit planning is an individual company matter, adequate sales prices cannot be developed without full recognition of all costs. Because you are a highly competitive industry, individual company pricing decisions have an important impact on the total industry's pricing structure. Considering the high volume and low profits presently generated by your industry, your margin for error in pricing decisions is minimal.

With the use of modern computers, the end results of any number of possible combinations of sales probabilities, changes in products and production methods, variations in inventory levels and inventory mix can quickly be developed in the form of computer-based goals or mathematical models of operating and financial information. Such information, properly prepared and utilized, affords management the most comprehensive insight into possible courses of action for use in the decision-making process.

The information now readily obtainable with modern electronic equipment permits advance assessment of the probable effect of the contemplated changes in all segments of the company, without waiting until after-the-fact operating reports give the results. It allows for consideration of a variety of investment alternatives. Furthermore, this enables management to place step-by-step responsibility on each area of operation, so as to accomplish the planning and control that is important in every successful undertaking. It permits management to measure the results achieved against the advance plans, thereby determining the extent of the variation experienced in carrying out the plans, and, most important of all, to identify and determine the effect and permanence of any error found in the plans or the execution thereof.

Financial modeling is one of the most effective but, unfortunately, least utilized areas in the field of modern management techniques. With respect to your industry, some specific areas for potential use of modeling might be as follows:

1. Product, plant and mill analyses to determine economies of further capital investment.

2. Process further or sell decisions and make or buy decisions at various points, particularly timber stumpage and board production.

3. Pricing decisions.

4. Projections of the effects of increased costs and inflation.

5. Computation of future return on investment and sales if certain decisions are made.

6. Effects of expansion or closing existing facilities.

7. Impact of diversification.

In your industry, the continuance of decentralized pricing and cost decisions is probably necessary. One of the reasons for this is that the lines of communication are shorter and the results of operations are more quickly available. There is closer coordination between those concerned with the production, the sales, and the accounting, enabling plant and mill management to function quickly and efficiently. Another reason is the fact that each container order is different and the variety of products makes establishing overall corporate pricing difficult. Decentralized pricing, however, should be within predetermined corporate policies and the adherence to these policies should be monitored. With today's computers, decentralized management can and should be able to obtain all necessary accounting and financial data through a centralized accounting information system if the accounting organization is dedicated to the service of the decentralized management. Local management must become profit oriented as well as volume conscious and can only do so with good accounting tools.

The competitive race is becoming faster and faster, and success is dependent more and more on accounting information and controls. Both corporate and local management must rely to a greater extent than ever upon accounting information to flag the problem areas in advance, not after the fact.

Today it is new in our accounting system to reflect the cost of inflation or to issue management reports on costs in price-level dollars. Reporting for the effects of inflation should have been done years ago to forewarn of these coming conditions. That timing is now impossible, but the present use of this idea in accounting can warn of further catastrophes and the costs which must be met to avoid them. If we were to build a computer model of the effect of these inflationary forces on the nation in the future, the computer would print out a replica of Penn Central or Lockheed, but a billion times greater.

I believe that a new accounting based on economic costs will provide you with the facts, so that effective management can exist. If the pricing decisions of some companies in an industry are being made using unrealistically low costs for depreciation, that is ignoring the impact of real price-level depreciation, this affects the ability of all companies within the industry to recover capital in an appropriate and timely fashion, since competition usually results in low bidders obtaining the business regardless of the reason. As I indicated before, a 1958 converting plant costing $3.6 million is being depreciated on the basis of that 1958 historical cost. Yet today, in terms of 1970 dollars, it would cost you $5 million to replace that plant without regard to any technological improvements in the interim. The cost of capital consumed at the end of the plant's economic life is computed to be only $3.6 million while the true economic cost is $5 million. Multiply this problem by the number of plants, mills and forests in your industry and perhaps you will see the magnitude of this failure to recognize the true cost of capital in making pricing decisions. Often the replacement of equipment is deferred, due to poor operating results or high costs of capital. The deferred decisions merely postpone the day of reckoning because true economic costs may be increased rather than decreased by such deferral.

Neither generally accepted accounting principles for financial reporting to shareholders or income tax laws and regulations presently permit recording the real capital costs, and therefore your past profits, in terms of current purchasing power, have been overstated. However, there is no reason that this proper accounting for the real costs cannot be used internally. In addition, income tax laws are discriminatory toward capital intensive industries. For example, in addition to being taxed on profits unadjusted for the decline in purchasing power, you may also be taxed on the gains on the disposition of equipment, based on historical cost without consideration of subsequent changes in dollar purchasing power. Much of the taxable gain on property held for any significant period of time is likely not to be an economic gain at all and, in effect, taxing such a fictitious gain represents a tax on capital.

I have been an advocate of true economic cost and price-level accounting for a number of years now. While the accounting profession, taxing authorities and the SEC continue to resist acceptance of this concept, more and more managements, particularly those in regulated industries, have seen the light and have revised their internal management reporting system to account for changing price levels. It seems inconceivable to me that this principle should be relevant for corporate management and not for prospective and present shareholders; however, if it is at least utilized as an internal management tool, you will have the proper cost information on which to make intelligent pricing decisions.

Corporate managements are in almost the same position as football coaches at the big universities. Either they have a winning team in terms of profitability or they are taken out in one way or another. The responsibility for not achieving a winning performance tends to be automatically assessed against the management regardless of the causative conditions, be they strikes, lack of natural resources, imbalance of gold payments, lack of credit, or whatnot. You need all of the sound management tools currently available to the business community, and they must be individually tailored to your specific needs. The best test of the forthright responsibility and independent thinking of management is its ability to change when conditions change, irrespective of prior policies, objectives, or procedures. This statement is illustrated by a favorite story of mine attributed to Abraham Lincoln. In the morning he argued a legal case from his offhand reactions to the issues, and won the case. That afternoon he had another case involving the same point before the same judge, but argued the opposite position. When asked to reconcile his viewpoint with that of the morning, he said he had thought he was right then, but in his afternoon case he dug further into the facts and, on that basis, he knew he was right in his second viewpoint.

Gentlemen, your industry's management problems are really the same as those being experienced by many other high-volume, capital intensive companies. Your profits and return on investment are unacceptable. What now? You can't change decisions made in prior years, but you can make changes for the future. You must develop the proper financial planning and reporting tools you need to make sound decisions on problems such as pricing, expansion, diversification and capital utilization. These tools must be based on factual cost data which reflects the true economic costs of doing business. The tools must be flexible. They must be able to consider and compute the effects of various alternatives. Tools which can only be used to report on the results of past decisions are not unlike the instruments used to dig graves.

If we take a real, hard look at your problems, the facts indicate one sound approach towards a solution. Management must establish realistic goals for future profitability and return on investment. Only full utilization of your present capacity will generate adequate sales prices and acceptable returns. Your future capital investments must provide an earnings return in terms of today's dollars which is, at least, equal to the current rate on borrowed money. If your projections on any expansion project indicate anything less than this level of return, the project should be scrapped and other alternatives for capital employment should be explored. This need for alternate uses of capital is one good business reason for the combination of two companies in different industries. Such a combination in your industry would provide you with increased alternatives for capital employment and generate competition for capital based on profitability and rate of return within the combined entity.

Accountancy as an international language of the business world—improving the credibility of financial statements

Before The Jerusalem Conference on Accountancy,
Jerusalem, Israel, October 26, 1971

Until we define the objectives of financial statement presentations to the public, we cannot communicate effectively with each other or the public on financial results.

I AM HIGHLY COMPLIMENTED to be with you today and to participate in The Jerusalem Conference on Accountancy.

I accept speaking engagements outside of the confines of my country with hesitation. Until the profession in my own country is responsive to the public demand for proper performance, I feel I should confine my efforts to the deficiencies nearest my own responsibilities. In other words, until my responsibilities in my own country are met, I probably should work at home.

However, business, no matter where domiciled, recognizes no international boundaries. Thus, accounting principles and financial statements must communicate across political borders. Sooner or later business interests will penetrate all national boundaries, regardless of the barriers which politicians may impose. In the end, the broad interests of the public will always prevail. Certainly Israel is among the leaders of those who have an international interest in other countries, both in business and politically.

I feel certain, therefore, that any discussion of problems in accounting and financial statements in the United States should be of as much concern to you as to us.

A need for a philosophical premise

As I look back over forty-six years of experience in accounting and the accounting problems we have had through those years, and then contemplate the comments of those who have held views contrary to mine, it becomes increasingly clear to me that our differences arose and continue to exist because our thinking has evolved from differing premises. It has been universally recognized that before debate on any subject can be fruitful, there must first be a "definition of terms." In the accounting profession we

109

have failed to establish and fulfill this pre-requisite in any meaningful way. Rather, we have spent our time in a fruitless endeavor, discussing procedures of accounting and not what balance sheets, income accounts, or footnotes should state or show. We have truly been like the blind men arguing about the appearance of an elephant, based on each of our own separate experiences.

Each major experience that we have as individuals or as a nation leads us to a rationalization of that experience. This is the so-called "moral imperative" that exists in each individual, which forces him to justify his actions, no matter how good or bad. Our profession has latched onto "generally accepted accounting principles" to justify its actions, and clings to them for security much as a child hugs a stuffed animal.

The best illustration of this situation is our profession's desperate attachment to using the "cost" of an asset in financial statements in preference to an estimate of its real value. This distorted view of the usefulness of cost to communicate financial data was fostered by our experiences in the depression years of 1929-1932.

Cost is also the sacred cow that controls practically every decision and policy of our Securities and Exchange Commission. All of the SEC's chief accountants lived through that horrible depression period and have needed a "stuffed animal" security to perform their work in recent years, in the absence of a more basic test of usability. This need for comfort was caused by abuse of property value estimates prior to 1929, an abuse that has subsequently been eliminated. Our stubborn attachment to cost is like a person insisting on turning left until he runs off the mountain because at one time he almost ran off on the road turning right.

When we come to circumstances where we are confronted with the realism of loss in value below cost, such as in accounting for a current asset, we quickly abandon our obsession with cost and adopt current value. Why should current value data be important only when it is lower than cost? This contradictory approach to communicating information to the public destroys the basis for its reliability.

We have been guided by custom and superstition in financial reporting rather than by good judgment based on objectives of what financial statements ought to show. We must define our objectives. Defining objectives in performing accounting is as necessary as defining terms in a debate. Without such definitions our efforts are bound to miss their target. I feel that a great share of my professional life has been wasted because our profession has failed to define the objectives by which our work could have been properly performed and communicated to our customer, the public. It would have been far more profitable for me to have dwelt entirely on these objectives rather than on the contradictory means of achieving ambiguous objectives.

Disclosure vs. performance

Our profession, rather than courageously defining its objectives, has retreated to a habit of "disclosure"—that is, stating what was done without regard to whether it should have been done.

There are many examples of this retreat from the search for objectives and the substitution of disclosure. Your Institute's Booklet 1, "Professional Recommendations and Guidelines," is one example of this. Our Regulations (S-X) used in the implementation of our Securities Acts is another. Our system of accounts for railroads promulgated by our Interstate Commerce Commission which, in my opinion, contributed to the bankruptcy of the Penn Central Railroad, is still another example. Recent opinions of the APB calling for incredibly extensive disclosures are perhaps the best illustration of burying the reader of financial statements in a mass of incomprehensible data. All of these instructions lead to communications with the public through disclosures of what was done. At best, the public will not understand these communications and, at worst, they will be misled.

What purpose is there in such disclosures? Is the public supposed to compare what was done with what should have been done? How can the public do this? When we accept disclosure as the answer to accounting problems, we have not solved the problem at all.

Of course, certain disclosures in accounting are helpful. Disclosures to further describe an asset, a liability or an income item are valid and useful to readers of financial statements. But if that is the purpose, the label, "footnotes" or "notes," should be changed to "further detailed descriptions."

However, disclosures of "procedures" followed in arriving at the balance of an item, without any indication of whether or how the end result conforms to an objective for stating that item, is often a booby trap to the reader. He must analyze such disclosures, a function for which he is poorly equipped, to determine in what respect the accounting is deficient or the result is inadequate or otherwise qualified.

Without objectives and standards, the accountant is trapped

Booby-trap disclosures represent a failure of the accounting profession. The failure of the profession imposes failure of performance on the practicing accountant, because he has no alternative but to follow the disclosure rules established by his profession as he goes about doing his work. Such performance translates itself into mediocre service to the public. Yet the accountant cannot avoid this predicament or improve on his service. He is trapped by his own profession.

Those in the profession who have tried to avoid this failure in performance by call-

ing for a statement of objectives and for standards which would result in a true professional quality of financial communication, have been thwarted by the profession, by the SEC and by many other governmental bodies. The resulting failure to meet our responsibilities has led the public to criticize us. Should we not, therefore, expect the public to make up its own definitions of financial statement objectives and hold us responsible for performance under those standards?

The public has no effective alternative if the profession doesn't do the job. Further, it will exhibit its frustration in lawsuits and indictments against members of the profession, even when it can be demonstrated that the given member's deficiencies are not responsible for the problem.

Deeper consequences of ineffective communication

The consequences go even deeper and extend into our personal lives. Not only does the absence of defined objectives prevent us from communicating properly with each other within the profession, but it results in ineffective communication within our respective firms, among the partners of a firm, and between partners and staff. This lack of effective communication leads to ineffective training, ineffective instruction and ineffective work. All of this in turn creates a waste of money and fees, a cost which is ultimately borne by the users of financial statements.

We cannot exempt ourselves from the pressures to decrease costs by achieving greater efficiency. To this end, definitions of objectives for each item in the financial statements are an absolute necessity. We cannot expect government to do this job for us, any more than the medical profession or the legal profession can delegate their professional responsibilities to government. Government can only be called in to settle arguments arbitrarily if a profession does not have the maturity to do a responsible job itself. Our profession suffers from a lack of professional maturity in this regard, a lack that not only damages individual practitioners but, what is more important, causes major injury to the public.

Until we define the objectives of financial statement presentations to the public, we cannot communicate effectively with each other or the public on financial results. Without such definitions we cannot hope to establish reliability in financial reports.

Assessment of professional responsibilities as related to objectives

My personality is new to you and requires some explanation. My objective in life has not included a desire to lead or participate deeply in the guidance of our profession through its institutional framework. I have always felt that our Institute should confine itself to establishing objectives and standards for its members rather than laying down detailed procedures. My concern has been for the quality of the basic services that I render to my clients and to the public under those standards. I regard this as the most effective and rewarding type of professional work. This work and the quality of our service have given us special status to do a job that the public could not do for itself, a job which it should not entrust to its government.

Removal of frustrations of staff accountants

The need for objective standards should be the first order of business for the practitioner, even if the only results were the elimination of staff accountants' frustrations in performing their field work.

We have seen staffmen questioned and cross-examined extensively as to the adequacy of their work as though the objectives of their work were certain and well defined. They have been questioned as in an inquisition, all because we, the leaders and the regulatory authorities, have neglected and resisted their elementary need of objective standards. Putting zest and zeal in a staffman's work, so that every audit and every report is a monument to his creativeness, is just as much a necessity to high quality performance as any other. Let us not forget the payoff to the public that can be obtained from staffmen.

Subjective facts and objective standards

To render service in this fashion requires that the accountant get close to and understand the economic results of the events and transactions relating to the entity on which he is reporting. The accountant's job is to assess and make judgments of highly subjective facts and conditions, and account for these conditions and communicate them to the reader in accordance with stated objectives. However, these objectives are undefined to the accountant and unknown to the reader of financial statements.

If the objectives are unknown to the reader of financial statements, how can he possibly comprehend what is being told him in financial statements? Yet the professional accountant, who also has no definition of the objectives to guide him, continues to verify the reliability of statements which have no defined purpose. The undefined objectives are the missing tools of the accounting profession.

Fixed objectives can be achieved by varying procedures

An assessment of facts and objectives by the individual practicing accountant gives him very specific convictions on financial statement deficiencies. These specific convictions lead the accountant to specific conclusions on the accounting principles needed to meet definite objectives. But objectives cannot be moving targets, varying with the views of individual accountants; objectives must be specific for all accountants and for the entire public. Procedures, however, to meet these objectives can be varied. Many alternative ways may be used to reach an objective. Alternative accounting procedures are not an evil in themselves, and may be necessary to achieve an objective efficiently. But as long as objectives are not stated or defined, criticism will abound, because our financial communications will then rest only on the procedures we use and not on what end result we are seeking to achieve. Unfortunately, that is where we are today.

It is dishonest for us to hide behind a sophisticated phrase such as "generally accepted accounting principles" to justify the procedure we use to present an item when an alternative procedure would lead to substantially different amounts. Only if we define the result we seek to achieve can one evaluate the procedure we use. Without such clear definition, a practicing accountant will invariably find himself confronted with the need to accept improper presentations because of professional tolerance of accounting procedures that have no relevance to honest economic measurement of the particular asset, liability, or income item. Objectives of financial statements **must** be stated if the practicing accountant is to be in a position to endorse an accounting principle.

The profession prescribes procedures like pills and gives them false authority by calling them generally accepted accounting principles. These practices produce results in financial statements that have no common definition and must be blindly accepted, a disservice to the reader. The reader should be put in a position to judge the results in terms of an objective.

Unless we reach this type of communication, the discrepancy to a reader, between his concepts and the economic facts, can lead to disastrous controversy. The Penn Central Railroad collapse in the United States is an example of the cumulative effect that this process of miscommunication can have. Deterioration accumulates to the point of breakdown.

Accounting's purpose— protect or inform?

To compound the misunderstanding by the readers of financial statements, many leaders in our country, including personnel serving our Securities and Exchange Commission, state that the Securities Acts "protect" the public. Such assertions lead the public to believe that balance-sheet amounts have the preciseness of a cash balance in the bank.

Such assertions are not only mischievous, they are misleading and cruel to the investing public. While the public may be protected from some misinformation, financial statements cannot free the public from the burdens of interpretation or assessing the risks of business, or of judging the quality of management. Since the investor must assess and evaluate the facts, no law and no financial statements can or should protect the investor against the risks of investment. Otherwise the investor would be entitled to no profits.

The government's attempts to make political capital by using the word "protect" instead of "inform" are confusing. Further, the confusion adds tremendous negative leverage to the deficiencies that exist in accounting reports due to the absence of defined objectives. In tolerating the deficiencies in present accounting practice in the United States, the public is unaware of the creeping deterioration in the accounting followed by railroads, of the failure to record properly leased properties, of the failure to record properly deferred taxes, of the failure to recognize inflation losses, or of the failure of oil and gas companies to account for natural resource discoveries in their financial statements. Nor is the public aware of the misstatements created by the recognition as intangible assets of the emotional and exaggerated value expectations of investors in connection with mergers and business acquisitions. Yet our own APB Opinions on the accounting for mergers and intangibles arising therefrom compel one merger to be accounted for differently from another. How can the public understand such procedures that defy any common objectivity?

Generally accepted accounting principles— bridge between fact and fiction

Every breach between economic fact and the measurement reported in financial statements is bridged by a generally accepted accounting principle. By custom that principle validates the measurement reported, irrespective of whether the amount is defined or is proper to a reader in any economic sense.

This acceptance of principles, that arrive at nondescript end results, is given further authority by acceptance of the Securities and Exchange Commission and other regulatory bodies—all without any reasoning to define for the reader the meaning underlying the principle or the objective it is intended to achieve.

To call attention to the gap between economic reality and the measurements reported to the public when those measurements rest on the authority conveyed by generally accepted accounting principles has been called unfair by members of the accounting profession. Many in the profession appear to regard the defense of convention more important than the search for truth. Such a concept violates the basic responsibilities inherent in self-regulation. Consequently, the only recourse available to those who would not be blind to realities has been to practice under protest.

Our profession has repeatedly drawn red herrings across the path to improvement of accounting reports to the public. Speeches, committee pronouncements, meaningless and useless rhetoric, such as Statement No. 4 by the APB entitled "Basic Concepts and Accounting Principles Underlying Financial Statements of Business Enterprises," have all been part of a process of self-delusion and delay in facing up to reality.

Simplicity and understandability

The crucial test of establishing objectives for financial statements must be simplicity. Objectives must be capable of being understood by all who possess reasonable intelligence and some understanding of economics and business.

The profession has recently set up a committee to define these objectives. On its work rests the value to the public of the accounting profession in the future. If its product is a repetition of something like Statement No. 4, the profession might just as well be replaced by robot inspectors from the government, concerned only with compliance with procedures irrespective of the results. The U. S. investing public would then have a replay for all of business of a half century of experience with the inefficient Interstate Commerce Commission. Should all of business be saddled with that type of regulation which has contributed so greatly to the disaster in the railroad industry?

Who should be involved in establishing financial statement objectives?

In the criticism of accounting over the last several years, many segments of the public have claimed jurisdiction over the standards that should be observed. Financial officers of business have put in a claim to participate because the standards affect their reports. This is true. The security analyst has claimed part jurisdiction because he must use the accounting results in making his analyses and recommendations. This is true. The academician has put in a claim because he is devoting his life to research and teaching the subject. This is true. Governmental agencies have made a claim for part jurisdiction through the regulatory authority delegated to them by our Congress.

Labor has not made such a claim, but if the other claimants are entitled to participation, then certainly labor is also. Most public investors to whom financial reports are issued are members of labor. No organization of the consumers of financial reports has claimed jurisdiction over financial statement objectives, probably because there is no well-organized "consumer" or "individual investor" organization. But these consumers must be represented because the reports are primarily for them. The use of the investor's money is what is being reported upon. However, every other party claiming jurisdiction feels that he represents the consumers of financial statements in some degree.

In spite of these jurisdictional claims of various interested users, the jurisdiction over standards of accounting and objectives of financial statements should be the charge of the public accounting profession, whose sole responsibility is to the public consumer. Business management, government, political segments, and labor all have a particular self-interest, a bias. Each has been grinding its particular ax constantly. Since the accounting profession has not emphatically established the public as its boss, these various segments have been encouraged to try to assert their dominance over the profession. Yet each constituency claiming part jurisdiction in defining accounting standards is part of the constituency of the public accountant. The profession is admirably fitted to establish equitable standards and objectives for financial statements for all segments involved.

Need for public endorsement of objectives

The objectives must be set in such a manner that public endorsement of the objectives will have recognized standing before the courts in which the issuer of financial statements and the performance of public accountants will be challenged. The reasoning underlying the objectives must be clearly stated so that the courts will be able to conduct fair trials of performance. In fact, when the objectives are finally determined, their acceptance in behalf of the public should be authenticated by approval by both houses of Congress.

Provisions for future improvements of objectives

These objectives, no matter how well determined, will be subject to improvement in the future. Provision should be made now for effecting such improvements. This can be done by establishing today a framework for determining objectives that can be repeated at the end of each five-year period. In this way all segments of society affected will be assured that there will be continued pressure to consider new directions and definitions as business and social goals change. Continued pressure from one or another segment of society for reform is the best cleanser of outdated practices.

There is precedent for such a broad plan. It is the machinery already established by law in the United States for determining "Cost Accounting Standards."

Pitfalls to be avoided by the newly appointed "study group for objectives of corporate financial statements"

The work of this study group can bring to the public a completely new quality in financial reports of all institutions and businesses in the United States. Conversely, its report could be so general as to be useless to the public, to the issuer of financial statements and to the public accountant. If the end product takes a form comparable to Statement No. 4, "Basic Concepts and Accounting Principles Underlying Financial Statements of Business Enterprises," issued by the Accounting Principles Board in October 1970, the group's work will be wasted.

If the objectives are not crystal clear as to what each principal item in the financial statement represents, they will not serve their purpose. If the objectives cannot be read by the public with a reasonable degree of understanding and cannot be reprinted in handbooks for investors by brokerage and investment firms, they will have missed their mark, regardless of how sound they might otherwise be.

I should digress here to answer those who feel that financial statements cannot be made meaningful to the man on the street. No communication, of course, can be made understandable to a person who will not put forth reasonable effort to understand what he reads. The person who does not do this must likewise assume responsibility for his own shortcomings in interpretation. But to state that a reader of financial statements must know the intricacies of accounting processes is no more valid than to say that only those should drive a car who understand the workings of an internal combustion engine, a carburetor, a transmission gear box and a swivel joint.

In making a clear statement of objectives, no purpose will be served by including the various aspects of accounting theory we might use in reaching the objectives. A prospective driver does not need a complete description in an automobile manual of how a gas tank and carburetor function in order to use the gas pedal.

Accounting jargon needs modification

We should change financial statement captions so that they are more accurate and informative, and we should remove the aura of certainty conveyed by terms such as "Financial Position" and "Statement of Income." Why should we not use words that describe financial statements as they actually are?

The dictionary definition of "approximate" is "to approach closely without exact coincidence—nearly, but not exactly accurate or complete." Why shouldn't "Balance Sheet" be changed to "Approximate Balance Sheet," "Income Statement" to "Approximate Income Statement," and "Financial Position" to "Approximate Financial Position?" This will remind all readers at all times that amounts shown are not exact but in almost every case involve judgment and estimates. This would be the best manner in which to define materiality. Approximations of all facts should be left to the practicing accountant, but to do so requires a proper statement of objectives.

What should objectives include?

The objectives, in order to be useful to the public, must state what the financial statements are to achieve. They might well require a definition of assets, followed by specific illustrations, such as an "inventory" of all assets owned on the one hand, offset by specific liabilities and encumbrances on the other. The objective for plant and property might state that items should be segregated between those in regular use and those useful but not in use. It should also state the basis on which the plant and property should appear in the balance sheet and why, and the supplementary data required, such as original cost or the price-level adjusted original cost.

The objective standards might well require, if the balance sheet is to have meaning to the public in terms of present monetary units, that assets be shown at the "cost of an asset in original monetary units spent," as well as that same cost in "present monetary units." They might further state that either could be shown on the balance sheet, with the other disclosed in descriptive captions.

Benefits to the practitioner and the public

Such objectives stated clearly would leave the Accounting Principles Board with the task of providing minimum standards of achieving those objectives. These standards would continue to be called "generally accepted accounting principles," and there would be no objection to illustrating how different methods or procedures might be followed in reaching the same standard.

Such a base would give each practitioner the opportunity to demand higher standards in achieving the "objectives" than might be demanded by other practitioners. Thus, an individual practitioner would have an incentive to strive for a unique professional reputation for himself rather than just to observe minimum rules. Each practicing public accountant would have room to attain a high standard of performance.

Such objectives would provide all practicing accountants and their personnel with a greatly improved base for training in the methods of verification. They would give the profession for the first time an opportunity to increase its productiveness by delivering a more reliable product at a lower cost to the public.

Many people today try to compare the results achieved by the profession's productive efforts to establish auditing standards with the comparable results from efforts to establish accounting principles. At the same time these people are unable to agree on what generally accepted accounting principles should be. Comparisons of this nature are not meaningful because the objective of all auditing standards is verification at one particular date, and the audit specifications can be readily changed at the next date of verification. Establishing the objectives of financial statements, on the other hand, will require the restatement of balances carried over from prior years if current balances are to be acceptable.

The study group on objectives has the opportunity and responsibility to state the objectives to be achieved by all accounting principles. Once these objectives are established for each major financial statement account, the establishment of alternative generally accepted accounting principles to achieve such objectives will be comparable to the present situation of agreeing on generally accepted auditing standards.

We will then have transferred the emphasis from the means to the objectives in both auditing standards and accounting principles.

This is the heavy burden of the study group under the chairmanship of Robert M. Trueblood. In the hands of this group lies the great responsibility for finding the posi-

tive and simple answer that spells out the public accountants' responsibility in achieving credibility in financial statements in behalf of the public.

*The public accountant and his
public responsibility*

It has become popular in the United States to proclaim one's concern for the public interest. This is like being for motherhood and apple pie. Some of those in our country, and there are many, proclaim this concern but are beyond the reach of the public. In many cases they are self-serving and hypocritical and their utterances are hollow.

In the United States, particularly, the accounting profession is within the reach of public accountability at all times. Members of our profession have been hailed into court for general or conspiratorial misconduct by public officials, by individual investors, by corporate investors, and by the Securities and Exchange Commission. Many of those I cited before as claiming to have part jurisdiction over the determination of financial statement objectives, and who have been loud in their public interest rhetoric, have never appeared in a court to shoulder any responsibilities. The public accountant, on the other hand, has shouldered his responsibilities by weathering the fire of public trial; few others have appeared beside him, nor is it possible for them to do so.

It must, therefore, be primarily the charge of the public accountant to take the lead in bringing stability to this area, and to assure that financial statement objectives are formulated that serve the public and are endorsed by that public through its Congressional representatives. This cannot be done by gimmicks, by self-serving declarations, by paternalism, or by prescribed rules of procedure which do no more than set up a series of hoops through which one must jump with no definite end result established.

The public accountant must furnish the public a statement of objectives that is clear and that states what each financial statement caption and amount represents. The public accountant must give his opinion that the financial statements are prepared in accordance with such objectives by the use of generally accepted accounting principles that were considered proper in the circumstances.

Those who say that the general public is not able to understand financial statements and that the public, therefore, should be disregarded in establishing financial statement objectives are in effect saying that:

(a) The general public should not invest in equity ownership of corporations.

(b) The general public need not understand the reports on the use of monies furnished by it to maintain our corporate, civic, and government institutions.

(c) The general public need not be given the tools by which it can understand the economics that control their living conditions and, therefore, their income.

No one who states that the man on the street cannot be served by properly and adequately prepared financial statements will subscribe to the presumptions of the above corollaries of that position. Certainly the profession will not.

More often today we see statements implying that it is too bad that accounting standards involve politics. The fact is that public accounting must involve politics. Issuers of financial reports often subject their public accountants to pressures to make accounting in such reports serve the political bias of one segment of the public or another, but accounting must have well-grounded objectives that serve every segment simultaneously without bias, and thus resist such pressures. Then the accounting profession can explain criticism of its work.

As long as accounting is the means by which collective wealth is accounted for by constantly changing managements to a multitude of owners who, in turn, derive their income from a multitude of consumers through the employment of a multitude of hands, accounting must constantly prove its independent status to each. The public accountant must accept as part of his way of life the constant demands upon him to prove and reprove his work. To serve one segment of the public properly, it must serve all with an even hand, and, to provide service to one, the profession must demonstrate that its service is proper to all.

Yet accounting does nothing but report back in monetary terms those conditions which that public has allowed to occur. Accounting cannot change the assets, the liabilities, the loss or the profit arising from such conditions, and it cannot change the conditions on which it reports. It can only measure them according to standards accepted by the public.

New paths for continuance of private ownership and operation of public utilities

Conference on Public Utility Valuation and the Rate-Making Process, Iowa State University, Ames, Iowa, May 16, 1972

Pragmatic adjustments of rates must recapture, in behalf of equity capital, some of the protection against inflation in order to increase the flow of such capital into utilities.

I AM HAPPY TO BE HERE today to discuss what I think is the one most important factor underlying adequate utility service to the citizens of this country. That subject is the need for the providers of capital funds to be properly compensated for the use of these funds. Today that is not done and, as a result, an accrual of deferred costs is accumulating what could well cause a financial breakdown in utilities. If the financial conditions of utilities do not improve or if they get worse, it appears reasonable that the public will receive a rude shock, a shock that will be far more costly in terms of both cost and service than corrective action would be now.

Retraction

In May 1962, when I was honored to appear on this platform at the first Conference, I made the following statement:

"The value of these conferences must be greater because no pressing and immediate economic objective will be sought, thus enabling us to look beyond the urgencies of a specific case under trial."

Now, ten years later, I must say that the present urgency is such that we must address ourselves to it directly and immediately.

I also stated at the first Conference:

"People invest capital, people manage efficiently, people innovate, improvise, eliminate and do all of the other things that can add up to a better job of utility service at lower costs. In short, let us not allow the gas and electric utilities to take the same route to deterioration that regulation has brought to the railroads."

That was ten years ago and, at that time,

public utility common stocks were selling at 20 times earnings. This price-earnings ratio required $5.00 of earnings to justify $100 of market value. Since that time, the price-earnings ratio has fallen until $5.00 of earnings commands only $50.00 of market value investment. Stated another way, the cost of equity money included in the cost of utility service has doubled in ten years but the utility user is not paying this cost; it is, in part, coming out of the hides of investors. This common equity cost of money is a significant part of the cost of total utility service; typically (with Federal tax thereon), this cost represents about one quarter of the total of a customer's bill, but a much lower proportion than it was ten years ago.

Lest you misinterpret my comments and attribute bias to me because of them, I have neither love nor crocodile tears for the people with money. They and the utility consumer sit at either end of the teeter-totter. Often they are the same person. Each needs the other, but while utility consumers have no option but to attract investors, investors have many options other than utilities. My position, as a fact finder, is that the facts should balance these two ends of the teeter-totter to a level position—not leave one end in the air and the other on the ground until the one on the ground walks off and lets the consumer on the other end crash down. Right now, the consumer is held high in the air and the investor is sitting on the ground holding him up, and the game is becoming boring to the investor. The investor is showing signs of getting up and leaving, letting the consumer crash.

My interest and comments lead to a conclusion that both the consumer and the investor are in dire need of each other. Emotional bias toward one or the other is a disservice to both; therefore, I want no part of it.

Since 1962, we have also run the predictable course caused by the absurdity of railroad accounting and regulation of that accounting which, in my opinion, took its first big toll in the bankruptcy of the Penn Central Railroad; others are bound to follow as long as present accounting is followed. The true economic cost of railroad service in the United States has never been known and could not be known from the accounting which was and is now followed. The coordination of pricing of railroad service in relation to the economic cost of that service is the only manner in which the Penn Central debacle could have been avoided; and it can now be corrected so that the experience of Penn Central will not be repeated by other railroads. The same comments can be made for utility companies and the services they provide.

I said in 1962 that we should not allow the electric and gas utilities to take the same route and have the same result that poor regulation has brought to the railroads. Yet we are doing exactly this. Cost of service is outrunning customer payments for those services. A financial breakdown of a utility has not yet taken place in a manner such as Penn Central, but we are allowing utilities to go down the same "railroad track" and the final comparable result is rather easy to predict if corrective action is not taken.

Neither operators of public utility property, managements, regulators, nor politicians can save the public from paying the whole cost of utility service used. Avoidance of that cost by the public is impossible. The public will pay for this service in one way or another—either in utility rates, in the erosion (now well along) of market prices of utility capital which the public owns or, lastly, out of the national treasury, as is now done for Amtrak and Penn Central. How much less might have been the total cost to the public if the cost of railroad service had been properly coordinated with the price of service rendered?

Even more important, the public could now have a continued viable nationwide rail service, which our existence demands, instead of limited service by an industry plagued with bankruptcy. The Penn Central debacle has had a backlash that affects every other railroad. Visualize, if you will, the consequence of just one large utility in bankruptcy or under the custody of the courts. That circumstance would have the same catastrophic effect on all utility companies and their capital providers as now exists for railroads. Therefore, the full impact to the public of not providing for the total cost of utility capital requirements must be carried to the doorstep of each of us whose inaction could trigger such a development.

In addition, the public is too frustrated and angry to suffer again the depressive shock of such miscarriages as Penn Central and Lockheed that, in the opinion of the public, could have been avoided by proper management concern and action. The public simply cannot understand why managements and regulators cannot devise proper preventive action before a breakdown occurs, and its views in this respect are unanswerable. No one can quarrel with the reasonableness of this view. Managements and regulators must be hard-nosed and honest in everything they do, and they must take the hard knocks in the process of instituting corrective action. That is leadership responsibility. The public calls such lack of preventive action dishonesty of leadership and management. While most of us would dispute this characterization, the public's mood takes an extreme position when those who should know, such as ourselves, do not act up to our full analytical capacity and responsibility. No one can make restitution to the public for the enormous costs that are inflicted on it when these breakdowns occur. Communication is then blocked, just when it is most needed for corrective action.

Let us not forget that this condition could again prevail for utilities as it existed in the 1930's. In other words, there is no escape from the damage caused by not anticipating the lack of revenue coverage for the full cost of utility service. In these times, when the seriousness of inflation and the avoidance of price increases take first priority, the corrective action needed to maintain viable utility service must be so structured that it guarantees no windfall profit accrual to anyone. The public must have reliable confidence in such a result.

What has happened since 1962?

In the last ten years one can say that there has been no general change in the method of rate regulation. Why, then, should conditions now be so much different from what they were in 1962, irrespective of the demand for capital? The answer is that, while conditions changed, regulations did not. Conditions and regulations have moved in opposite directions. Irrespective of the same method of regulating rates, the compensation that can be obtained by investors from other sources of investment and past imperfections of original cost regulation have badly misled investors. Investors, therefore, have turned to other industries to secure an adequate compensation on their capital.

Thus, utility regulation, as it has worked for the last ten years, has not been adequate to maintain intact the one main criterion of fair rates established by the Supreme Court. That criterion was, and is, and must be in the future, sufficient earnings to attract new capital with the same fair compensation to the embedded capital. To attract new capital the utilities must provide a compensation on capital equivalent to that obtainable where risks are comparable. Today the greatest risk is inflation. And the impact of inflation on capital cost is greater in utilities than in practically any other industry.

Where we stand

Let me pause here, however, to emphasize some of the present conditions that affect the economic cost and the acceptance of that cost as a part of utility service to the public:

1. The demand for capital in the electric field alone is estimated to be in the area of $400 billion over the next twenty years. This is in the dimensions that we usually speak of in relation to the national debt. This capital demand does not include the gas or the telephone utilities; if you include these two, I estimate a total demand for capital by utilities to be twice that amount or more in the next twenty years. And, of course, this demand will be an ascending one from a present annual capital requirement about one half the average annual demand over the next twenty years. This is a much greater requirement for capital than the utilities have ever needed in the past, even with adjustment for price level. And it comes at a time when the cost of capital is higher than it has been at any time since utilities were first developed prior to the 1930's. The cost of capital requirements in relationship to the other costs of service has always been a very significant part of the total cost of service. Nevertheless, while the cost of capital has increased in the same (or greater) degree as all other operating costs, the portion of the utility bill for these capital costs has decreased. It is not difficult to foresee the ultimate effect of these two irreconcilable conditions.

2. Long-term investment requires long-term payoff; therefore, very high carrying costs are a fact of life in the early years of investment.

3. There is a constant increase in demand for all utility services. This differentiates utility service from practically every other product. Yet the lack of production capacity does not automatically increase the price of utility service. In fact, under orthodox rate making, the opposite, price de-creases, would occur if increased capacity were not installed.

4. Investment in utilities is at the lowest point of attraction in the last several years. This condition is to be compared to the relatively high attractiveness to the investor of practically every other industry where capital needs are of a much lesser magnitude. This lesser attractiveness is caused by one factor—the probability of greater compensation from investment in other industries.

5. The utility industry has two factors in its favor which practically no other business enjoys. These factors are an assured future increase in demand, and customers who, on the whole, believe that more relative value is received from their utility services than from any other services or products they buy.

With the contradictory conditions of high attraction to customers and low attraction to investors, what is to be done to make the service available? Technology and the physical resources are all available to provide the required producing facilities. The big hurdle, and the only important hurdle, is providing adequate incentive to the providers of capital, so that production of these facilities can become a reality. When other industries cannot command capital to provide additional capacity, they have the option not to build such capacity. Utilities are not in that position. Their first responsibility is to meet the demand for service, because the customer has nowhere else to go.

There are those who desire to capitalize on these conditions by using them to divert attention and fuel political controversy. The latest book to do this is *A Populist Manifesto*. It digs up the old proposal of government ownership, based on the false declaration that utility capital is receiving excess profits. Such commentaries cause the public to be suspicious of the credibility of industry communications as to the real facts affecting their utility service. Because of these suspicions and the shock of Penn Central, the required restructuring of utility rate regulations today to meet the high cost of capital must, if it is to be successful, be done on a basis which assures the public that only the actual present cost of operations will be covered by billings for service.

I often wonder how naive the authors of such books are, or if they are naive at all. Is it possible that their principal objective is to falsify and mislead so that disaster cannot be avoided? Do they know and wish to ignore that our governmental staffs themselves have a lower credibility than most segments of society? Why else would competitive management be sought for such operations as the Post Office or for COMSAT? In the face of this observation, however, there was a recent editorial in *Newsweek* stating that corporations were at the crossroads in satisfying the public in their ability to furnish the necessary services at the lowest cost.

Our urgent problem now

How can communication be established by utilities with the public to bridge such a gap and earn the public's confidence in the economic facts of providing utility service at the lowest costs under today's conditions? How can a method of communication be constructed to assure the public that a particular method of regulation will provide this lowest economic cost? This, I think, is our job and its need is immediate. We, as businessmen, government, and others constantly throw general figures before the public, but we do not adequately explain such costs in a manner that an individual can understand and relate to his own pocketbook and welfare. This must be done.

Each of us could comment at length on the many problems we have today; unemployment, poverty, health, inflation, cost of living, higher incomes, ad infinitum. Yet,

prerequisite to meeting all of these problems is obtaining the means to provide an adequate, but lowest possible, return to the investor which will result in adequate utility service.

What is increasing the cost of utility service?

I am not competent to comment on the scientific techniques of furnishing utility service, but it is interesting to note that no significant charges have been made as to the utilities having wasted money in the technical or scientific areas. In fact, the opposite is true. The charges made are that utilities have not made timely capital investments to minimize destruction of ecology and the environment. Criticisms have also been made that the utilities should do more in research and development, independently of utility equipment suppliers.

The increases in operating costs of utilities include those increases that affect all businesses and individuals. For example, in other industries total operating costs are related very closely to labor costs, and labor costs affect utilities in the same way. However, unlike most other industries, an almost equal impact on utilities is imposed by greater capital costs. In the final analysis, these capital costs are also the result of labor costs that are passed on and recognized in setting prices in other industries. First, and most obvious, is inflation; but there are others, such as the scarcity of different fuels, higher costs due to ecology, preservation and improvement of environment, etc.

These are costs with which the whole of our economy is grappling in stabilizing prices. As the costs of meeting such conditions become effective, we create a spiraling effect as the cost of each justified correction comes into the cost of service stream. The base on which to stabilize all prices is the cost of labor. But to stabilize labor cost, the cost of living must be stabilized and, while utility service is a relatively small portion of the cost of living when compared to food, it is probably the next most important essential service and, thus, its cost cannot be avoided by the consumer.

The price freeze

In order to halt pyramiding and spiraling costs, which compound with each changed condition affecting the cost of living, the President, under the powers given him, adopted the price freeze, with which we are all familiar, and then started lifting it by phases, thinking that uniform rules of price correction for use-justified costs would halt runaway prices occurring before the freeze. Yet the freeze itself has probably been responsible for a greater part of the increased capital costs affecting utilities. While these spiraling prices in all unregulated industries were occurring and were caused by increased price levels for each industry at or, say, within a year of the date of the freeze, this same condition did not exist for any regulated utility.

I have never seen a presentation made to the Price Commission that explained why the average price-level base for the computation of about 40% of the cost of utility service was, say, reflected not at the prefreeze price level, but at the price level existing at the time the plant was built, say, on the average of ten or fifteen years ago. These costs consisted of depreciation, Federal taxes, interest and compensation to equity capital and, therefore, as they go up for new plant construction, they should constitute justified costs for increasing rates, as do labor costs. In nonregulated industries, these costs for older plants could be reflected in current prefreeze prices, while in utilities they could not. Yet, the Price Commission has not publicly recognized, nor in my opinion does it understand, this difference in pricing between regulated and nonregulated businesses. It is well that price regulation for utilities was delegated to utility regulatory commissions, but these facts of life

must still be explained to the public if they are to be understood.

Imperfect original cost regulation provided false incentives to equity capital

Ten years ago, original cost-based rate regulation was in effect; however, the rate of return on original cost base of around 6% after deducting the cost of borrowed capital, left compensation for common capital in the neighborhood of 10% or more, even though the market cost of that capital, based on the price-earnings ratio, was one half of that rate. This differential was considered by investors to be evidence that regulators were recognizing that more than a market price-earnings ratio cost return on original cost of capital was being allowed on common stock equity because of inflation. This conclusion was sufficient to classify utility equity capital as growth capital and, thus, gave a low cost for new equity capital.

After 1962, as debt interest cost moved up and closed this gap between market cost of capital and allowable return, it was evident that regulation would hold to cost of capital return on original cost, leaving nothing for inflation. That is where the utilities are today and, if this is to be accepted, utility capital is a nongrowth stock. A nongrowth stock demands a much higher compensation than a capital stock that possesses growth possibilities which will compensate for inflation dilution. Thus, today, investors demand utility earnings of much more than 10% of stock market values, just double that of 1962. The Dow Jones averages today for utilities are less than in 1962, while the industrial average has increased 47%. If utilities were to compete with this "other industry" average attraction, the allowance on equity capital must be 50% greater than it was in 1962, or 15% on the average. The utilities are paying the price for imposed nongrowth probabilities that double the 1962 carrying cost of equity capital at the very time the load of such costs is the heaviest.

Can regulatory pricing be modified to meet the equity capital problem?

In 1962, we could study regulatory methods of setting rates and consider prophesies of the future. Now the utilities are in the dilemma of having high demands for capital and the realization by investors that utility equities are nongrowth. Therefore, annual costs of capital are the highest that they have been in over forty years. It could have been prophesied in 1962 that this condition would exist under today's conditions. However, the specter of inflation difficulties was met with indifference over a long period of years, and now the effects of inflation have accumulated to the point that the problem can no longer be ignored.

Utility management was indifferent because they believed that inflation trouble, if it occurred, would be after they, as individuals, were gone. Regulators were indifferent because the whole political buildup of original cost regulation would tumble if the effects of inflation were to be provided for. Efficiencies in fuel cost, billing procedures, etc., then provided some relief but now cannot be expected to make up for inflation costs, although there certainly is always room for effecting lower costs.

I am, in retrospect, impressed by the foresight of the decision of the United States Supreme Court in the Hope Case in 1944, that original cost regulation had to presume that pragmatic adjustments would be necessary under changed conditions.

Pragmatic adjustments in rate regulation are necessary right now. Such adjustments must be in cooperation with the objectives of price stabilization because inflation is the disease that everyone suffers from and it must be put under control. But pragmatic adjustment must recapture, in behalf of equity capital, some of the protection against inflation, in order to increase the flow of such capital into utilities. Such a provision could trigger a desire on the part of the public to invest in equity securities of utilities once again, and thus permit utilities a lower total carrying cost of capital. How can this be done?

Action along this line should demand the greatest cooperation of public regulators, government, and management personnel. No matter how such adjustments are pragmatically made, they cannot be expected to exist longer than our present emergencies. Hopefully, something will be learned from this experience that will permit a change in long-term regulatory procedures, and thus avoid some of the present burden of high costs that could have been prevented by earlier changes.

I would like to advance for discussion the following pragmatic adjustments of regulatory procedures that I believe would, in part, meet the objectives sought:

1. Individual utilities should present to regulatory commissions and the Price Commission proposals to presently allow increased rates based on a pro forma rate base and operating costs, after allowance for acceptable inflation goals, based on annual operations expected five years hence. However, this would be done with the limitation that such increased rates would be no greater than a determination of rates based on a historical rate base and operating costs, adjusted to reflect today's price level. This latter provision would constitutionally protect consumers from being charged an amount greater than the current value of service, based on today's costs.

2. At the same time, all net earnings in excess of an amount equal to the application of regular rate-making procedures, as determined by the regulatory commissions, allowing for the full cost of capital in the marketplace, should be set aside at the end of each year as a reserve, thus delaying any further rate increase until such reserve is used up. Hopefully, by then

prices would be stabilized and we could return to orthodox rate making.

3. All increases in cash dividends should be stopped and stock dividends substituted so that small stockholders, who pay very little in Federal taxes, could have their stock dividends sold in their behalf for cash while larger stockholders would not sell. Such a program would permit a reduction in the high dividend payouts with concurrent increases in stock dividends. Such a procedure would eliminate Federal income taxes paid on most dividends by most stockholders, would encourage larger investors to increase equity investments in utilities, would increase cash retention by the utilities, and would increase equity capital without selling new securities, thus increasing interest coverage and increasing attractiveness to investors of utility debt.

Conclusion

In conclusion, such a program would:

1. Guarantee that no windfall profits or income would accrue to anyone, but would guarantee fair compensation on the original cost of capital adjusted for inflation. This alone might increase the attractiveness of investing in utility equities but, admittedly, it would not be great.

If the government theory is that required cost increases justify increases in prices in Phase II and if, in the case of utilities, this required cost increase consists of cost of equity capital, the government should exempt utilities from piggybacking Federal income taxes on such justifiable costs. The government could do this by exempting the cost of new equity capital from taxation during the period of Phase II. This would eliminate price increases of double the annual cost of equity capital.

2. Stabilize utility rate increases to four-to-five year intervals, thus arresting spiraling utility costs. This condition should make a material contribution to price stabilization sought by the price freeze.

3. Guarantee the retention of greater earnings, which is the cheapest source of capital. Through the use of stock dividends this retention would be compatible with the best interests of both small and large stockholders and the utility consumer. This procedure would also tend to change the relative position of large and small utility investors by encouraging large investors to become equity investors instead of creditors, and by encouraging small investors to become debt holders instead of equity owners.

4. Increase the attraction of capital by eliminating the lag in providing fair compensation to the equity stockholder, stimulate new investors' interest, hopefully create a sufficient investor demand for utility securities to reduce the cost of capital, and reestablish utility equity securities as growth securities with a concurrent lower cost.

Further thoughts on what is endowment income

Donaldson, Lufkin & Jenrette, Inc.,
Fourth Annual Endowment Conference,
University Club, New York, May 25, 1972

Proper investment decisions cannot be made on the basis of financial reports that reflect a ten or twenty-year old dollar and today's dollar as having the same purchasing power and value.

I HAVE BENEFITED very much from reading the presentations that have been made at these Conferences in the last three years. I hope that this year I can make some contribution to others in return.

Battle scars of last three years from "total-income" concept

The experience of the last three years has made many of us who were advocates of the "total-income" concept of accounting for income from endowment funds feel like the six blind men describing an elephant. While our advocacy was motivated by our own experience in relation to increasing total income, we did not comprehend that others would embrace this concept as a method of dipping into reserve funds to enlarge the expenditure programs of a fund beyond the ability of the fund or its institution to maintain such programs from year to year. We now recognize that proper controls over the total-income concept were never properly conceived or developed so as to inform trustees of the consequences of the programs they approved.

The controls were underdeveloped because of legal problems in distinguishing between capital and income and restrictions on funds by donors. Also, a conflict has existed between trustees who have desired to build the principal of funds and trustees who have desired to spend greater income to accelerate the achieving of the purposes for which the funds were given, but which could not be afforded under a more limited concept of income. In brief, we had not thought out our problems well enough.

The conflicting influence of these factors on the total-income concept, together with the gyrations in stock market prices since 1968, has left many of us battle scarred in the eyes of those who were wedded to the

127

orthodox interest-dividend income concept. Since then, many of us have tried to use this unsatisfactory experience to repair the total-income concept so as to avoid the failures of the past and to attain its objectives of greater overall return to the funds, as compared to the obsolete dividend-interest concept and its depressing effect on total return to the funds.

Causes of stock market gyrations

One difficult problem of the total-income concept is to develop a method of bridging stock market price gyrations. One of the important artificial causes of such gyrations is the form of reporting profit achievements by corporations in our standardized reporting system.

Being an accountant, I have spent a lifetime witnessing the misuse of financial reports in stock market pricing in times of inflation. Such reports were not and are not now prepared to be informational under such conditions. I have seen investment decisions made from financial reports that reflected a ten-year old dollar, a twenty-year old dollar and today's dollar as all having the same purchasing power and value. This results in a misrepresentation of the risks and earnings of the business being reported upon.

The deficiencies in accounting reports are compounded during times of inflation because the dollar understatement of assets consumed is amortized into reported earnings, so that the resulting income is inflated and is misrepresented as "earnings" in all investment statistics, such as annual percentage of growth, return on capital and cash flow. These statistics are all based on erroneous inputs of earnings data. During inflationary periods, therefore, the structure of accounting reports overstate and misrepresent true economic earnings. Since these exaggerated earnings are used by many for their stock market value measurements, stock market values are exaggerated and this is bound to cause market price gyra-

tions. Since the exaggerated earnings from inflation have a rather short life during periods of expansion, corrections of earnings and stock market prices must take place during that life. Thus, market price gyrations are inherent in our system of bookkeeping and statistical computations. The only way to measure the extent of the exaggeration is to compare reported income with the same income computed on a constant dollar basis. When this is done, a substantial portion of reported income is identified as inflation and, therefore, unreal.

As a consequence, in times of inflation value measurement statistics include inflation, and thus they are not effective as measures of value increases that exceed inflation price increases. The only time our statistics honestly recognize this point is in the computation of Gross National Product. Those who point with pride to the Dow Jones Index going up 45% over a ten-year period should be reminded that this is not an increase in values. Part of this increase represents a loss in purchasing power resulting from inflationary price increases. In the last ten years, that price increase has been 33⅓%. Therefore, average investment value increases indicated by Dow Jones have been about 10% or 12% over the last ten years, or about 1% per year.

We see natural resource companies reflecting revenues at today's inflated sales price and from that amount deducting the cost of discovery of those resources in prices of ten, twenty or thirty years ago, rather than in today's dollar equivalent. The resulting difference is reported as net earnings, and then these are converted into stock market prices of 10 to 20 times that misconceived income. It is easy to see why the gyrations in the stock market take place. Discovery costs incurred today and paid for in today's dollars partially correct this overstatement of income and result in a downward influence on market prices. Analysts and investors alike are investing blindly in such instances insofar as the effect of inflation is concerned. Full-cost accounting for natural resource companies provides some degree of proper measurement but, for those not on full-cost accounting, the reporting of earnings can be grossly misrepresented.

Railroads, for instance, have accounting systems that misstate cost of service and distort the basis of cost of service. No railroad company director has a right to rely on accounting reports of operation of the railroads unless they are adjusted for such misstatements, a correction which would require major surgery. Imagine in such cases how much the investor is misled even while he is enjoying the peace of mind that he attributes to his accounting reports. These are not new observations by me. I made them twenty years ago when inflation growth was rather modest. On railroad accounting, I stated in 1962, that investors were being led to a shearing; a Congressional investigation took place, but nothing was done. Had proper action been taken, the Penn Central debacle would not have happened.

Gyrations of stock market prices are bound to occur because market prices are not based on reliable facts as to earnings or assets, and market prices at any one date are not sound foundations for determining future values. Thus, the total-income concept used in reliance on stock market prices as evidence of value must be equally false as a base for permanent planning. Our difficulties in the use of the total-income concept arise mostly from using stock market prices as a secure spot criterion of value measurement of investment successes. Commonsense knowledge that inflation causes an evaporating rate of earnings used in appraising values, tells us that such stock market prices are not reliable for year-to-year planning. Price-earnings ratios, calculated from earnings and stock market prices so precariously self-supporting, are even more dangerously misstated. In this way, one single error used in reported earnings contaminates almost all statistics of investment measurement. When the error, in the case of inflation, begins to correct itself, every measurement is comparably corrected and market gyrations automatically occur.

Principles controlling "total-income" accountability concept

Those of us who advocated the total-income concept, sold it to our colleagues, and then applied it in practice for those funds on which we serve, must admit we did a poor job in making the concept workable. I find it so easy now to establish the objectives and guides that I wonder why I was not more explicit before. I would, therefore, now like to state these objectives and guides so that the concept can be used to accomplish its true function of maximizing total expendable monies of the funds involved.

First, the objective of the total-income concept was and is to release investment decisions from the artificial restriction imposed by the amount of dividends or interest income. This amount is often a happenstance and yet has been regarded (often with the support of legal opinions) as the only portion of endowment return that could be used to meet the cost of carrying out the purposes of a fund. This definition of income omitted completely the rise or fall in the value of the principal amounts. The total-income concept never was intended to deplete fund balances in a manner that would not occur under the dividend-interest income concept. To the contrary, it was a method of accountability that permitted investment decisions to be based on total income and be free from inherent depletion of principal that existed under the orthodox dividend-interest income concept.

The total-income concept was structured to avoid despoiling the principal of the fund by requiring investment in fixed-income securities in order to qualify income as legal for operations. Forced investment in fixed-income securities, during periods of inflation, resulted in inflicting a loss in principal in order to have income. Thus, the orthodox method of dividend-interest income concept of accountability was, during periods of inflation, no more than a method of depleting principal. Inflation dilution in such cases could be equal to, and in many instances more than, the entire amount of interest received. Thus, under proper economic accountability, the interest should have been applied to restore the depletion in principal before any amount of the interest was available for operations.

For instance, if a bond had an interest coupon of 5%, but that year's inflation was 5%, the percentage of principal loss was equal to the income received. In an economic sense the fund broke even. There was, in fact, no income. The total-income concept would report this transaction as "zero" total income. The orthodox dividend-interest income concept, however, considered the interest received to be spendable income and thereby depleted capital in times of inflation. We are and will be in an inflationary period for at least the next generation. The total-income concept was created to combat this obsolete procedure of endowment fund investment and income recognition by revealing that investment decisions to acquire fixed-income securities resulted in built-in inflation loss of fund principal.

Investments in equity securities could lead to the same result. For example, the record shows that high-dividend payouts (to achieve income) were possible when additional productive investment was not required by expected growth. A great portion of such dividends was a return of capital because of inflation. In other cases, the high payout was motivated, as in the case of utilities, to attract capital that could not otherwise be compensated for inflation loss. Many of the most attractive investments that possessed capability to meet inflation loss and, in addition, to provide an income were those that required dividends to be limited because of the need for capital to enlarge the company and acquire more earning-building opportunities. I need not mention examples

of these; their names are common knowledge. However, such investments would fail to provide income according to the distorted definitions of income under the dividend-interest income concept. As a result, such low dividend-paying stocks were out of bounds in a major degree to funds dependent upon income to meet their operations. Therefore, the orthodox concept of income defeated proper economic management of the fund as well as the purposes of the donor. Yet the probable increase in investment value of such investments could be reasonably anticipated as being sufficient to cover both the inflation dilution of principal and an additional amount equal to a fair return as income. The latter return would then be real economic gain, not a gain offset, or largely offset, by inflation loss in principal.

The total-income concept resolved the paradoxical positions that hamstrung prudent investment decisions. The total-income concept did not release capital for high-flying, long-shot investments of a gambling nature. Nor did the total-income concept permit invasion of endowment principal. These results happened only because the procedure of properly dealing with inflation or purchasing power loss in the dollar was never established. Establishing this procedure, therefore, becomes the first requirement of a proper application of the total-income concept.

The procedural requirement should be that the income account of every endowment fund be charged and the principal of that fund be increased each year by the amount of inflation (purchasing power) loss, as indicated by the Implicit Price Deflator, applied to the amount of the principal for each year. This should be computed and recorded for each year to restate the original principal of the fund in today's diluted dollar. Any invasion of the restated principal or failure of assets to equal such principal would be a failure on the part of the trustees to maintain the principal intact, unless the deficiency related to a specific approved withdrawal of fund principal.

The trustees of private foundations should not be confused by the difference in the definition of income for tax purposes under the Tax Reform Act of 1969 and true economic income to which I refer. Under the Tax Reform Act, the distributions required, even though made from tax-law defined income and short-term gains, may economically be less than the inflation depletion in principal; thus, under the tax law, the required distribution of so-called income might well be capital distributions. The Tax Reform Act as applied to private foundations, however, has an objective of fund distribution completely contrary to endowment fund objectives of principal preservation to meet operating commitments. Furthermore, as a result of the Tax Reform Act, the pressure for distribution from private foundations has already become evident, and will continue to cause private foundation funds to be transferred to public-supported funds. As this occurs, a strict accountability between principal and return is in order for all funds; thus, the total-income concept of accountability should become the applicable standard of proper measurement of fund performance.

Second, the form of income account should also be modified to state clearly to the trustees the economic conditions affecting the fund. Present reports on investments, in most cases, are fragmentary at best. An income account that shows as total portfolio income the amount of interest, dividends and the transfers of principal to adjust expendable income to, say, 5% of total fund market value, is wholly inadequate under the total-income concept. Trustees should know clearly where the principal of the fund stands on an economic basis in order to exercise prudence in making investment decisions or approving the use of fund income in the form of interest or dividends, in the form of capital gains, or any part of the principal.

Therefore the form of income account of the fund should show the following data:

1. The original contribution to the principal of the fund, price indexed or equated to present inflation-diluted dollars, the present principal that trustees are responsible for.

2. The fund income account should show on its face the following factors under the "Results of Investments":

(a) Interest received $

(b) Dividends received

(c) Appreciation or loss on investments realized

(d) Appreciation gain or loss on investments during period—not realized

     Total of above $

(e) Deduct—Inflation loss to maintain fund principal intact $

(f) The amount transferred to, or deducted from, "income equalization account" to restrict use of the above net proceeds of the fund to, say, 5% $

     $

Income equalization account

My own experience confirms that the orthodox view, that all dividends and interest income are available for current expense, has, in fact, resulted in many instances in an invasion of the original purchasing power of the contributions of principal. On the other hand, an unduly conservative result existed when a disproportionate amount of the fund was fortuitously invested in or was received in contributions of low-yield equity securities that appreciated to an amount greatly in excess of what prudent diversification investment might have later demanded.

Even in these exceptional cases, however, after providing for inflation dilution the balance of appreciation, representing income available for operation even under the total-income concept, was far lower than any of us suspected.

The total-income concept requires a plan to build up a substantial income equalization account that will cover the operating requirements during the period in which stock market price fluctuations are at their highest. To do this, the percentage of fund used for operating purposes should be set at a rather low percentage in relation to prevailing interest rates. Investment men can determine this rate from what they would regard as the interest rate demanded under an inflationary protection clause of principal. As successful investments produce greater returns in appreciation, the percentage of the fund used in operations can be increased. Only performance will permit or justify such an increase. The fund will be fortunate if past performance has already built up a substantial "income equalization reserve" from past investment successes.

An invasion of capital of a going fund, beyond the reserve in income equalization, must be considered as either an emergency use of principal to be restored or a partial liquidation of principal.

Accounting for investments under the total-income concept will place great pressure on investment decision makers to make investments in only those companies that keep their capital whole, and that report profitability after making provision to keep their capital whole. Proper accounting by the companies cannot be presumed, for reasons I have already explained. If companies do not maintain financial practices which keep their capital whole through retention of earnings, investors of capital in those companies cannot be kept whole when inflation loss occurs.

Investments in emerging industries and occupations

History and precedent provide all of us with abundant evidence that a prudent investment policy must recognize new industries and new occupations as opportunities for capital investment. Such investment decisions are not based on the usual criterion of established earnings records or assets on hand. Endowment funds must make some allocation for participating in such prospects if, in the long run, the principal of any fund is to be kept whole over long periods of time. It is only necessary to identify the blue-chip investments of the 30's, 40's and 50's, and see what has happened to them to prove that today's blue chip can very well be tomorrow's white chip.

Experience with the total-income concept triggered recognition of this policy in many instances, but experience also shows that the concept was not well enough understood to restrict fund investment in this area to a proper portion of the total fund. Likewise firm requirements that had to be met in making such investments were not established. As a result, far too much investment was made in gambling on highfliers, or new ventures of no particular uniqueness, rather than in new products and services that would have reasonable probabilities of growth.

Several important rules must be observed in "new development investments" for endowment funds. One is that such investments must be categorized as "development investments" and appear as such in all reports of fund investments and condition.

The second rule is that such investments should be restricted to a certain percentage of all investments, and that percentage should never be violated. This will result in an appropriate investment in each project and the holding of a reserve for prospects yet to come.

The third rule is that the downward adjustment of market prices of such investments should be reflected in the "total income" of the fund, but the upside appreciation should not be reflected in "total income." The upside appreciation is so often the result of demand for securities rather than performance. However, as performance is achieved and a sound economic base for stock market prices is established, these investments become matured. At that time, development investment should be transferred to the regular portfolio and accounted for under the total-income concept as are other matured investments. This transfer reopens opportunity for further investments in development projects.

The establishment of endowment fund accountability in this fashion under the total-income concept will provide trustees and those in charge of operations with better information about their own economics and will lead to greater resources for use. Also, the trustees will have the peace of mind which comes from knowing that their administration is based on sound economic facts.

Acquisition/merger accounting artificially discriminates against public investors and small businessmen

Before the Financial Executives Institute, Milwaukee, Wisconsin, December 12, 1972

A representation that goodwill is an asset, when it is incapable of affirmative determination or verification, constitutes misrepresentation of financial position and damage to the extent relied on by the public investor.

Origin and use of present merger/acquisition accounting

PRESENT MERGER/ACQUISITION accounting was determined by the accounting profession under the authority of its Accounting Principles Board (APB) and is expressed in Opinions known as APB Opinions No. 16 and 17, issued in August 1970. The history of how these Opinions came into being is now unimportant except that they were issued during a period of public clamor about mergers and acquisitions that were contributing to corporate bigness, to stock market speculation and to the transfer of companies from local ownership to national and multinational ownership.

In the financial community, the combination of a company having an unjustified and inexplicably high P/E ratio multiple with a company having a low P/E ratio multiple was contemptuously described as leading to "instant earnings" accounting. Many ignored the change in the growth rate created for the high P/E ratio company and the growth dilution involved and thereby failed to see that the results complained of were probably offset in a lower P/E ratio. Thus, by innuendo, accounting was blamed for the Wall Street P/E ratio gyration syndrome. That syndrome still exists.

The accounting profession was not blameless, however, for during the 1950's it had brewed a stew called "pooling of interests" that had no substantive intellectual reasoning to support it. The pooling-of-interests notion rested on arbitrary artificial corporate prerequisites and it permitted wholly erroneous book values of one company to be written on the books of another in an acquisition or merger. The result did, in fact, misrepresent the true earnings capacity of the acquired company. However, pooling also avoided the recording of a fictional

135

goodwill item. Thus, this contrived accounting procedure called "pooling" had mixed blessings.

In the case of merger/acquisitions classified as purchases, i.e., paid for with monetary media other than common stock, an unidentified intangible arose equivalent to the excess of the price paid over the fair value of the identifiable assets acquired. The profession did not require an identification of all the components of the entire purchase price. The unidentified difference was given the name of "goodwill" and was to be recorded as an asset, an asset that had absolutely no meaning because it had no direct identity with any resource belonging to shareholders.

The accounting profession, therefore, with a half-baked notion about this unidentified difference, logically reached half-baked decisions on accounting for it. In the case of purchase/acquisition mergers, goodwill is a consequence of the stock market price of the company acquired, measured and evaluated in terms of P/E ratios at the date just prior to acquisition. The higher the P/E ratio for the acquired company, the higher the cost to acquire the company and, therefore, the higher the so-called unidentifiable intangible called goodwill. The higher goodwill is directly the result of the value placed on the forward growth factor that is an integral element of the higher P/E ratio.

Thus, stock market prices, the greater amount of goodwill, and the P/E ratios go hand in hand, the latter being the common denominator among stocks, irrespective of the price of each stock. It is the P/E ratios that permit comparability of one company's stock price with another's. If the P/E ratio of one company in an industry is high, it is a signal to those companies that have lower P/E ratios that a higher stock market price may be supportable, and this often becomes the sole reason for bidding up the prices of the companies' stocks. Such stocks are even called the investment favorites of the day.

Thus, the P/E ratio is the leveraging rod of one company's stock evaluation against another's and it often creates higher and higher stock market prices as well as higher and higher P/E ratios. Seldom is a high P/E ratio leveraged down by a low one. Yet, *no one* has ever produced any reasonable economic basis or calculation that provided specific economic support for a particular P/E ratio.

The acceptability of P/E ratios by merger candidates is dependent upon the comparability of these multiples by the two companies involved in the merger/acquisition. These P/E ratios are supported in the marketplace by self-serving declarations of analysts and security advisors to the public investors. These sources almost always appraise P/E ratios with generalities, such as stating they fairly discount future growth or that expectations of such and such percentages of growth justify such and such P/E ratios as compared to another stock, etc. There is no end to the **general declaratory opinions** on reasons for a given ratio. However, the components of particular P/E ratios are never produced for the public investors' understanding so that an evaluation can be made of the underlying economics of the stock price.

With P/E ratios becoming the guide for equating stocks among companies for merger or acquisition, it didn't matter how high the ratios were if the ratios of the two involved were each relatively overpriced or underpriced. The gamesmanship in the 1960's was to give a 10% interest in a million dollar dog for a 100% interest in a $100,000 cat. When pooling accounting was used, the P/E ratios would affect only the number of shares of stock (animals) issued in the acquisition/merger. The number of shares did not then and do not now affect any numbers on the balance sheet except the stated value of the stock issued, an amount of little significance in any case.

Under the "pooling loophole" in accounting, neither the value of the dog nor the value of the cat needed to be recorded, since the overall price agreed to in the combination had no accounting significance. But, under "purchase" accounting, the requirements were that one side of the relative value—the cat—must be recorded as an asset even though the acquisition price, as determined through the P/E ratio, included the value of the cat's mouse-catching ability into eternity in relative comparison to the dog's watching ability into eternity. This value represented the forward pricing of future earnings and was an integral part of the P/E ratio. The P/E ratio produced a so-called "goodwill" asset (equivalent to the cat's future mouse-catching value) for the acquired company irrespective of the payment medium in the acquisition/merger. Under pooling accounting the acquiring company was *prohibited from recording* such goodwill (i.e., that related to the $100,000 cat), while under purchase accounting the acquirer was *prohibited from not recording* it.

Thus, "pooling" and "purchase" accounting had vastly different effects on the balance sheet (and future income statements), even though the total consideration for the acquisition/merger was identical, regardless of the method of accounting elected on behalf of the stockholders. It is regarded as strange to the superficial thinker that business could exercise a choice between these two methods of accounting for the same single transaction. Yet, the selection of one method was completely understandable when it was recognized that one method changed the whole face of the balance sheet and income statement as compared to the combined balance sheets and income statements of the two merging companies, while the other method simply combined the financial statements of the two companies as they were. This difference in the image-appearance of balance sheets was very important to managements dedicated to honest presentation of assets to public investors.

Pooling, with all of its defects, was still preferable and a more honest accounting to public stockholders than purchase accounting that watered up assets by tremendous amounts of so-called goodwill, a meaningless misrepresentation of assets to public stockholders. Why should the forward pricing of future earnings created and controlled entirely by stockholders be put on the corporation's balance sheet as a corporate asset when such pricing of the future has absolutely nothing to do with operations?

The exchange values of stock (a function of future earnings) were entirely the creation of stockholders, not the corporations involved, irrespective of rosy predictions on growth by management, analysts or hearsay. Thus, why shouldn't prudent management prefer the "pooling loophole" to avoid meaningless, fictitious goodwill created by pricing speculations on future values totally unrelated to existing assets or income?

The SEC was established to protect investors after Insull and other acquirers prior to the 1929 crash did exactly what our new 1970 purchase accounting prescribed. Insull often purchased companies by assuming debt equal to identifiable net assets and then added an equal amount as an asset for future growth value that was credited to equity capital. The rule-of-thumb measurement he used was different, but the result was the same, i.e., putting speculation on future values on the present balance sheet, masquerading as assets among the good assets, with the probability that the goats would be counted along with the sheep by public investors.

The APB created a fiction in accounting in response to public clamor

As the 1960's came to an end, a frantic public and some congressmen pressed the SEC to do something on the subject of mergers and acquisitions. The SEC zeroed in on the deficiencies in accounting for merger/acquisition, as though that was the place to attack the phenomenon of mergers and acquisitions and all of the alleged environmental ills that bothered the public.

137

The accounting profession, having been caught with its mergers/acquisitions accounting principles pants down during a period of problems in that area, became the culprit of all the ills.

The profession's dual accounting on mergers/acquisitions, therefore, had to be tightened, but neither the profession nor the SEC wanted to face up with full honesty to consistent and proper accounting in all cases. So, they just made the pooling loophole smaller by toughening admission qualifications without removing any of the impurities that were injurious to public investors. But, they also toughened acquisition/merger purchase accounting by adding more accounting improprieties in that area. Thus, the profession gave birth to Opinions No. 16 and 17 that toughened the rules but made no improvement in them. On the contrary, many more accounting improprieties were created for both methods of accounting. These bulletins provided two basic but contradictory accounting procedures for mergers/acquisitions as follows:

(a) Companies that acquire/merge with other companies and use common stock as a medium of payment for 90% or more of the consideration *must use* the "pooling loophole" in accounting and *may not* record in the accounts the so-called "goodwill" paid for in common stock in the acquisition. This accounting, and its consequences, is all wrapped up for public stockholder disclosure with the words "pooling-of-interests" accounting. The definition of this term is found only in Opinion No. 16 in language that even professional accountants find impossible to understand. It is not found in the dictionary used by public stockholders. Thus, the amount of goodwill involved in an acquisition/merger accounted for by pooling is neither disclosed to the public stockholder nor recorded in the accounts. It is bypassed. Under this accounting pronouncement, no corporation is permitted to record the correct amount of "goodwill" acquired. Thus, the choice of doing the accounting correctly is denied all corporations that acquire other companies with only common stock. The directive to record an acquisition/merger by the improper pooling method, when prior to that a company had the choice of making a proper recording, is billed to the public as "tightening up" accounting.

(b) Companies that acquire/merge with other companies when the medium of payment is more than 10% in cash, debt, preferred stock, preference stock, Class A stock, or anything other than common stock *must record* the so-called "goodwill." (This is different goodwill from what correctly defined goodwill might be.) Secondly, the acquiring company must arbitrarily reduce the amount of earnings from the acquired property reported annually to public shareholders by not less than 2½% of this fictitious "goodwill."

These opposing methods of accounting requirements created a structure:

(a) To preserve whatever sensible benefits flowed from the "pooling loophole," irrespective of its unsupportable premises, and

(b) To maintain unsupportable premises for purchase accounting by prescribing rules not supported by the facts involved in order to create an appearance of tightening up on merger/acquisition accounting, irrespective of the unfairness and misrepresentations that result.

To accomplish such a result, some reasoning had to be concocted to sell its incomprehensible complications to the public as having a "conceptual" base. This was done with SEC approval. To have reached a wholly honest and factually responsible basis of accounting would have required public disavowal of a theory that was some twenty-five years old and recognition that assets have real inventoriable identity that is not created by mere presumption and calculation. That, however, would have required straightforward reasoning and simplified accounting principles and an admission that artificiality must go. That was not done.

To establish a conceptual excuse for the "pooling loophole" so that goodwill appeared to be properly accounted for in some cases, complete data on a merger/acquisition had to be sacrificed. In this suppression, the public investor is discriminated against by denying him any identifiable breakdown of the acquisition/merger price. In creating this artificial conceptual base for "pooling," the accounting profession arbitrarily decided that only a common-for-common exchange between each entity (acquirer and acquired) could maintain prospectively the risk elements of the (acquired) former investment holders. The fiction created was that all the stockholders did was to mutually exchange risks and benefits.

Further, the "pooling-of-interests" concept is intended to present as a single interest two or more common stockholder interests which were previously independent so that the combined rights and risks of those interests ". . . neither (acquirer or acquired) withdraw or invest assets but in effect exchange voting common stock in a ratio that determines their respective interests in the combined corporation," etc.

The above rationale provides a jargon of words to artificially conceptualize the make-believe conditions that no purchase or sale of stock takes place when 90% of the consideration of a merger/acquisition is common stock.

This "no sale of securities" or "no purchase of property" was conceptually necessary in a pooling-of-interests acquisition/merger to justify the nonrecognition of "goodwill." This was a proper objective because the so-called goodwill recorded in a purchase acquisition/merger was fiction and a misnomer too. Thus, the objective was to find a reason to avoid recognition of "goodwill," at least *under some* circum-

stances. The decision makers thought this couldn't be done for the purchase accounting method, so this "no-sale" fiction was created when common stock was used to qualify acquisitions/mergers for the "pooling loophole." The accounting profession sacrificed honesty to the public investor and perpetuated the pooling myth that records all net assets at amounts appearing on sellers' books, but nothing more, thus, preserving the make-believe condition that a purchase did not occur.

Artificial base supporting concept
of "pooling" now revealed by
SEC confession of fact

Like all perfect crimes against reality, some honor-bound member of those commissioned to maintain the artificial appearance chickens out and confesses a fact that tumbles the lie. That is what the SEC did in issuing Rule #145 that replaced Rule #133 to support the "no-sale/no-purchase" concept on which the "pooling loophole" accounting rested. The SEC demolished this fictional concept on October 11, 1972, almost exactly two years after Opinions No. 16 and 17 were issued.

The SEC finally reached the point where even it could not stomach the "no-sale" concept of its previous Rule #133. That Rule rested on the idea that a "combination" created in an acquisition/merger ceremony in which one entity issued stock for another *merely* combined risks and benefits of two entities but involved no sale of securities or purchase of property. The following excerpts of Rule #145 recognize securities issued in a merger/acquisition as optional consideration to a seller (because the stockholders can opt for the cash evaluation method for their stock) and face up to the reality that the merger/acquisition ceremony, regardless of what kind of stock or debt is involved, is, in fact, a sale of securities for property acquired (italics supplied):

"Rule 145 is also intended to inhibit the creation of public markets in securities of issuers about which adequate current information is not available to the public. This approach is consistent with the philosophy underlying the Act, that a disclosure law provides the best protection for investors. *If a security holder who is offered a new security in a Rule 145 business combination transaction has available to him the material facts about the transaction, he will be in a position to make an informed investment judgment. In order to provide such information in connection with public offerings of these securities, Rule 145 will require the filing of a registration statement with the Commission and the delivery to security holders of a prospectus containing accurate and current information concerning the proposed business combination transaction."*

Explanation and Analysis

"I. Rescission of Rule 133. Definition for Purposes of Section 5 of 'Sale,' 'Offer to Sell,' and 'Offer for Sale.'

"Rule 133 provides that for purposes only of Section 5 of the Act, the submission to a vote of stockholders of a corporation of a proposal for certain mergers, consolidations, reclassifications of securities or transfers of assets is not deemed to involve a 'sale,' 'offer,' 'offer to sell,' or 'offer for sale' of the securities of the new or surviving corporation to the security holders of the disappearing corporation."

"The 'no-sale' theory embodied in Rule 133 is based on the rationale that the types of transactions specified in the Rule are essentially corporate acts, and the volitional act on the part of the individual stockholder required for a 'sale' was absent. The basis of this theory was that the exchange or alteration of the stockholder's security occurred not because he consented

thereto, but because the corporate action, authorized by a specified majority of the interests affected, converted his security into a different security."

". . . the Commission is of the view that the 'no-sale' approach embodied in Rule 133 overlooks the substance of the transactions specified therein and ignores the fundamental nature of the relationship between the stockholders and the corporation. The fact that such relationships are in part controlled by statutory provisions of the state of incorporation does not preclude as a matter of law the application of the broad concepts of 'sale,' 'offer,' 'offer to sell,' and 'offer for sale' in Section 2(3) of the Act which are broader than the commercial or common law meanings of such terms."

"Transactions of the type described in Rule 133 do not, in the Commission's opinion, occur solely by operation of law without the element of individual stockholder volition. *A stockholder faced with a Rule 133 proposal must decide on his own volition whether or not the proposal is one in his own best interest. The basis on which the 'no-sale' theory is predicated, namely, that the exchange or alteration of the stockholder's security occurs not because he consents thereto but because the corporation by authorized corporate action converts his securities, in the Commission's opinion, is at best only correct in a formalistic sense and overlooks the reality of the transaction.* The corporate action, on which such great emphasis is placed, is derived from the individual consent given by each stockholder in voting on a proposal to merge or consolidate a business or reclassify a security. *In voting, each consenting stockholder is expressing his voluntary and individual acceptance of the new security, and generally the disapproving stockholder is deferring his decision as to whether to accept the new security or, if he exercises his dissenter's rights, a cash payment. The corporate action in these circumstances, therefore, is not some type of independent fiat, but is only the aggregate effect of the voluntary decisions made by the individual stockholders to accept or reject the exchange.* Formalism should no longer deprive investors of the disclosure to which they are entitled.

"The Commission also is aware that Rule 133 has caused anomalous applications of the provisions of the securities laws. For example, transactions which are deemed not to involve 'sales' for purposes of Section 5 of the Act, nevertheless are deemed to be 'purchases' for purposes of Section 16 of the Exchange Act. Moreover, transactions which are not deemed to be 'sales' for purposes of Section 5 of the Act, nevertheless are deemed to be 'sales' for purposes of the anti-fraud provisions of the Act and Exchange Act and 'sales' for purposes of the Public Utility Holding Company Act of 1935, the Trust Indenture Act of 1939, and the Investment Company Act of 1940."

———

"*The Commission recognizes that the 'no-sale' concept has been in existence in one form or another for a long period of time.* Certain persons who commented on the October 9, 1969 and May 2, 1972 proposals have cited this as a reason for retaining the present Rule 133 and others have asserted that the Commission lacks the power to revise the rules. The Commission does not agree with these comments. Administrative agencies as well as courts from time to time change their interpretation of statutory provisions in the light of reexamination, new considerations, or changing conditions

which indicate that earlier interpretations are no longer in keeping with the statutory objectives. The Commission believes, after a thorough reexamination of the studies and proposals cited above, that the interpretation embodied in Rule 133 is no longer consistent with the statutory objectives of the Act. The Commission's judgment is based upon a number of factors, including the observation that Rule 133 has enabled large amounts of securities to be distributed to the public without the protections afforded by the Act's registration provisions.

"In view of the above, the Commission is of the opinion that transactions covered by Rule 133 involve a 'sale,' 'offer,' 'offer to sell,' or 'offer for sale' as those terms are defined in Section 2(3) of the Act. The Commission no longer sees any persuasive reason why, as a matter of statutory construction or policy, in light of the broad remedial purposes of the Act and of public policy which strongly supports registration, this should not be the interpretative meaning."

———

"*Paragraph (a) of Rule 145 provides that the submission to a vote of security holders of a proposal for certain reclassifications of securities, mergers, consolidations, or transfers of assets, is deemed to involve an 'offer,' 'offer to sell,' 'offer for sale,' or 'sale' of the securities to be issued in the transaction.* The effect of the Rule is to require registration of the securities to be issued in connection with such transactions, unless an exemption from registration is available. In this regard, the purpose and effect of the Rule is the same as set forth in the releases of October 9, 1969 and May 2, 1972, to rescind Rule 133 and promulgate a rule requiring registration under the Act of the securities to be offered."

Now the SEC and the New York Stock Exchange, by enforcing Opinions No. 16 and 17 on behalf of the accounting profession, are in the unenviable position of requiring an accounting procedure based on a premise that has been held to be contrary to fact. For both of these bodies to refuse to protect the public stockholder from this discriminatory and misleading accounting defeats the objectives of fair accountability.

Worse yet, however, the accounting profession under present circumstances cannot be honest with itself, with corporations that they audit, with the public investor, or with the SEC and Congress. The accounting profession must abolish "pooling-of-interests" accounting forthwith, preferably retroactively, so that some salvaging of past misleading reporting can be achieved. At the most, this should take knowledgeable, competent and honest men and woman 48 hours to do.

Purchase accounting is even more discriminatory and damaging than pooling to public stockholders and small businessmen

Scuttling the fake foundation supporting "pooling" accounting leaves only "purchase" accounting as a method of recording all mergers/acquisitions. However, "purchase" accounting as prescribed by Opinions No. 16 and 17 is even more diseased with accounting misrepresentation than "pooling" is with all of its conceptual defects. Thus, no advancement toward proper accounting is achieved by discrediting pooling unless the greater misrepresentations to the public investors caused by the alternative "purchase" accounting are removed.

Under "purchase" accounting, Opinion No. 16, paragraph 67, recognizes properly that the values of all net identifiable tangible and intangible assets of a company acquired/merged should be determined and recognized. The diseased root of "purchase" accounting that causes misrepresen-

tation and damage to the public lies in that part of paragraph 68 of APB Opinion No. 16, which is in italics below:

"68. Allocating cost. Acquiring assets in groups requires not only ascertaining the cost of the assets as a group but also allocating the cost to the individual assets which comprise the group. The cost of a group is determined by the principles described in paragraph 67. A portion of the total cost is then assigned to each individual asset acquired on the basis of its fair value. *A difference between the sum of the assigned costs of the tangible and identifiable intangible assets acquired less liabilities assumed and the cost of the group is evidence of unspecified intangible values.*" (italics supplied)

For the APB to prescribe that a determination be made of a supposedly credible amount for accounting disposition based on a residual or "difference" method, without specific knowledge of what element of cost that residual or difference represents, constitutes irresponsibility. To state that the residual cost remaining from a group cost "is evidence of unspecified intangible values" is such a contradiction of elemental accounting principles that it is difficult to envisage what conditions could force even an average accountant to such a conclusion. Is it not more probable, that instead of the unidentified amount being "evidence of unspecified intangibles," one should presume that it is evidence of undelivered property, negligence in determining overall price intended to be paid, or just plain waste? Only evidence can prove otherwise. Where is the "show me" friendly characteristic of a good auditor? Can there be any professional basis for accepting an unidentified "difference" remaining from any group cost as evidence of a specific cost—particularly of an asset?

To illustrate the point involved, one should visualize an invoice from a contractor for $5 million in connection with a specific contract. Against this invoice a detailed inventory of fair value of assets delivered is deducted—and, say, $2 million is a difference left unaccounted for. Assume further that some supervision (comparable to proper goodwill) cannot be inventoried, but a generous estimate of that asset is $100,000. In that case can it be assumed by directive, such as from APB Opinion No. 16, that the remaining "difference" of $1,900,000, because it is a difference, is evidence of "unspecified intangible values?" If not, why not?

Any reasonably competent public accountant that came up with such a conclusion on such a plain-vanilla audit function would be subject to reprimand, loss of repute, to a lecture and would be required to take special training in fundamentals of fact-finding and verification. Yet, the most august body (APB) of the profession performed its job in exactly that unprofessional and irresponsible manner. Worse yet, the SEC and the NYSE blindly enforce this absurdity and may extend it to its logical end to all new entities and to even present entities, if a majority of stock transfers hands.

How does misrepresentation and damage therefrom occur by reason of this conclusion?

First, insofar as the public investor is concerned, when he receives a balance sheet, how is he to know that a variation exists in the quality and vertification of one asset as compared to all the others? No other asset is determined on a residual or difference basis with no specific affirmative verification required.

Every public investor has a right to rely on the fact that cash, receivables, inventories and plant are affirmatively determined and verified. He has a right to expect that the public accountant had affirmative information from various sources that these qualities exist, or, if they did not, that the independent public accountant was negligent in his work. If the SEC and the NYSE had knowledge that these qualities didn't exist, they too would be remiss in their work.

Why should the public investor be expected to think or know that goodwill is an asset not possessing either of these qualities? A representation that goodwill is an asset when it is incapable of affirmative determination or verification constitutes misrepresentation of financial position and damage to the extent relied upon by the public investor.

Amortization of intangibles misstates income

Likewise, the investor has the right to expect and rely on the fact that charges against revenues constitute the cost of services and materials affirmatively used to produce those revenues. This is true of all charges against income except those charges to income directed by APB Opinion No. 17, the amortization of so-called "goodwill." This charge, representing an arbitrary portion of the unspecified difference remaining from a group cost calculation, consists of no affirmatively used services, materials or assets. If management and independent accountants do not know what this difference, dubbed "goodwill," in fact is at the time it first arises, why would they arbitrarily decrease earnings, when presenting earnings to the public investor, by amortization of this fictitious amount? Why would the SEC and the New York Stock Exchange, neither of whom can plead innocence of what is being done, allow such misrepresentations of income to public investors year in and year out?

Such misrepresentation may or may not cause damage to the public investor depending on what action he takes concerning his investment. He may sell his security believing that the earnings per share so indicated is reliable and that the resulting higher P/E ratio is a signal, in his judgment, of the time to sell. Since that P/E ratio he relies on is, in fact, unreliable, the misrepresentation resulting from amortization of the "unknown difference" has damaged him.

This is not all. Most public investors are

143

unsophisticated people (those most in need of protective services of the SEC and the NYSE) and have neither the time nor the knowledge to wade through the jargon of Opinions No. 16 and 17 to be informed that amortization of this so-called goodwill is a dubious charge. Already the number of interpretations of these Opinions issued are enough to make a small book. On the other hand, the wealthy, the big investors and sophisticated investors either know or have advisors who know that the so-called amortization of goodwill results in nothing more than a method to retain more earnings in the company, a function of the surplus account—not the income account. They compute, and should compute, a reliable P/E ratio on earnings before goodwill amortization, thus producing a lower P/E ratio than those determined from EPS served to the unsophisticated public investor in annual reports.

So, the directives of Opinions No. 16 and 17, on purchase accounting, create a misrepresentation that helps the knowledgeable public investor to profit at the expense of the unsophisticated—usually the small investor. This damage to public investors rests on the shoulders of the SEC and any independent public accountant who accepts directives of generally accepted accounting principles established by Opinions No. 16 and 17 without deciding in his own mind the consequences of doing so.

*Public investors are not the only
casualties—the small businessman
is shot down too*

Even the above is not a complete inventory of damage caused by the misrepresentation flowing from amortization of so-called goodwill. The small businessmen suffer more from this misrepresentation than most public investors.

The majority of small businesses are built by men and women over a lifetime. In many cases, these people were personnel spin-offs of creative-idea people from large corporations. Many of these businesses cannot be, or are not, continued at the close of the entrepreneur's life and must be sold to others so that the small businessman can have some enjoyment from his life's work. The small businessman seeks a company to acquire/merge with his that provides his company with a good home and that has the capacity to pay him in cash, or reliable securities, in order to relieve him of as many entrepreneurial burdens as possible.

In all such instances, the small businessman evaluates his business at a P/E ratio applicable to comparable businesses with publicly held securities. With few exceptions, significant future growth value is included in the P/E ratio and on the value he places on his company, just as future growth value is a significant factor in the P/E ratios of other companies. Such valuations in acquisition/mergers produce significant amounts of fictional goodwill difference required under the purchase accounting of Opinion No. 16. Since the buyer is required to amortize this fictional goodwill, he can report earnings to his stockholders only equal to actual earned income less amortization of the fictional goodwill. Therefore, the buyer applies, say, the agreed P/E ratio to the earnings of the proposed acquisition remaining after this amortization. The result is a lower price to the small businessman than he fully expected to receive and was, in fact, entitled to for his company.

The buyer, while sympathetic to the seller, is correctly controlled by the enforced absurdity of amortization of goodwill, which synthetically reduces actual income. The small businessman may try to go to another prospective acquirer but, if he does, he finds the same discounting of the worth of his company for goodwill amortization. The acquirer has no out from the combine put together in Opinion No. 16. The small businessman finds that arbitrary and meaningless accounting rules are holding him captive from receiving a fair price—locked in so that his rights are made subordinate to arbitrary rules that must be observed by all his buyers. In order to realize on his life's work, he has to pay the ransom imposed on him by goodwill amortization rules. He cannot be released from the price reduction caused only by an arbitrary decrease in income capacity of his business. While factually this discounting of income is the result of a misrepresentation, the small businessman must accept the damage caused him by meaningless accounting rules. He must bow to the APB bureaucratic rules enforced by the SEC and give up a significant part of his fair price to a bigger business. He asks himself, "Why is there this partiality in favor of big business when big business resents it as much as I do?"

This loss to the small businessman can be made more clear by an example. Assume a P/E ratio of 15 is agreed to for the acquisition of a business now producing $200,000 net income. The acquisition/merger consideration would be $3 million, of which $1 million is artificially assumed to be goodwill.

Since the buyer must arbitrarily report income of $200,000 less amortization of goodwill of $25,000 (2½% of $1 million), he would report net income as $175,000 instead of $200,000. Since the "goodwill" is a variable of price, the amount the acquirer would actually end up paying the small businessman is $2,727,000, of which $727,000 would be goodwill. The amortization at 2½% is $18,175, and the acquirer reports net income of $181,825 ($200,000 less $18,175) for which the small businessman gets a price of 15 times, or $2,727,000. The arbitrary accounting rule has cheated the small businessman out of $273,000, or 9% of his property. This is a discriminatory damage of major proportions to the small businessman, with an equivalent gain for the acquirer, all because of the bookkeeping for fictional costs imposed by Opinions No. 16 and 17.

This is not a theoretical or academic issue. Such adjustments occur daily in the negotiations of acquisitions/mergers. Thus, artificial accounting obstacles put in the path of mergers/acquisitions have only helped the acquirer at the expense of the small businessman. The greater the achievement of productivity by the small businessman, the greater the damage to him by the amortization accounting rule of Opinion No. 17. This free advantage to the acquirer often more than compensates him for his finding and acquisition costs.

What are the advantages of this exercise in amortization bookkeeping? None to the public stockholder or to the small businessman, but the APB declares (without any proof whatsoever) that such goodwill eventually disappears—an assumption wholly inappropriate because even the APB doesn't know specifically what the so-called goodwill is. How then can the APB assert that it eventually disappears when they do not even know what it is to start with?

Negligence exists in failure to identify and properly account for the components of so-called goodwill

To provide the basis for correct accounting, we must return to an analysis of the "difference" between group cost and the inventory of identifiable properties acquired. The whole of the group cost does not come from thin air—it flows from the application of valuation measurements, and the cost can be broken down among the factors represented. In this way the whole group cost can be related to specifics—and the so-called "difference" that has been arbitrarily named "goodwill" can become identified.

If the group cost is identified as to its specific component costs, proper accounting can then be applied to each of the components according to their characteristics. Goodwill has been so misrepresented in Opinions No. 16 and 17 that its real identity and definition may well be lost, and this should not happen. Properly identified, goodwill is a good asset. Its definition has been stated as the value "of nothing more than the probability that the old customers will resort to the old place."

The origin of the group cost is readily determinable from the actual negotiating discussion and terms that determine the consideration given. The consideration given is usually computed to equal the value of the stock being acquired in the hands of the acquirer. The components that make up the value of the stock being acquired are related to the P/E ratio agreed to as the "long-term growth rate of the company"[1] or to "the present worth of future earnings available to that stock"[2] of the company being acquired or merged. This concept is so universally accepted that its existence does not seem subject to any controversy. Since this is the basis for the group cost of an acquisition/merger, the accounting profession and the SEC should have required a breakdown of that "group cost" before prescribing the accounting for it.

Looking back at the debate that preceded Opinions No. 16 and 17, all parties involved were arguing about accounting for a "difference," the composition of which was un-known. If the APB and the profession had researched the point in specific transactions, the nature of the "difference" could be understood better. Even though this prerequisite was not completed prior to the issuance of Opinions No. 16 and 17, it can now be done. When an analysis of the group cost is completed, the so-called unspecified difference for which Opinions No. 16 and 17 prescribe a disposition disappears and the conclusion reached ceases to be applicable to specific components of the group cost.

Identification of components of
"difference," i.e., so-called goodwill

To determine the components of the group cost, it is helpful to analyze an actual acquisition/merger that has been completed, is in process, or is taking place. The group cost results from the bargained price in the combination and reflects the growth-rate factor used in negotiation and embodied in the P/E ratio of the acquisition/merger consideration. A growth-rate factor of one actual acquisition/merger under review follows:

1. The Boston Company, Inc. Investment Brief —*Risk And Return.*

2. Reiling and Burton, *Harvard Business Review,* November-December 1972.

THE GROWTH-RATE FACTOR OF AN ACTUAL ACQUISITION/MERGER UNDER REVIEW

	Productivity Growth, After Eliminating Minimum Earnings of 10% on All of New Capital Invested During Period	Growth, Including Earnings on New Capital Obtained Through Retained Income
1971—EPS..	$1.08	$1.08
Increased capital—		
Dec. 31, 1971—		
equity................................$80 million		
Dec. 31, 1967—		
equity............................... 50 million		
Increase (all		
retained income)....................$30 million		
10% earnings............................$ 3 million		
Per share (10 million shares).........................	.30	
Balance—EPS, exclusive of earnings on new capital........	$ .78	
1967—EPS..	.68	.68
Compounded annual growth rate including inflation additions....	3.5%	12.0%

SUMMARY

Productivity growth (3.5% ÷ 12%)...................................	29.2%	
Earnings on capital obtained through retained future income (8.5% ÷ 12%).	70.8	
	100.0%	

In negotiation, it was agreed that a growth-rate factor of 12% compounded annually would be used. In addition, a premium of 20% over the market value of the stock to be acquired/merged would also be offered to the shareholders of the company to be acquired. Since the market price of the shares of the company to be acquired was $17.50, the premium brought the total combination price to $21.00 per share. Based upon the earnings per share of $1.08,

a P/E ratio of 19.4x resulted. On 10 million shares outstanding, the exchange price was calculated at a "group cost" of $210 million compared to the original net cost of identified net assets of $80 million. After estimating the present value of all identified tangible and intangible assets, a "difference" remained under the Opinion No. 16 approach of $105 million. However, a breakdown of this "difference" into its components follows:

BREAKDOWN ANALYSIS OF MARKET PRICE OF STOCK OF COMPANY BEING CONSIDERED FOR ACQUISITION BASED ON 12% COMPOUNDED ANNUAL GROWTH IN EARNINGS THAT WAS USED AS BASIS OF NEGOTIATION

Year (1)	Estimated Future Earnings Per Share 12% Compounded Growth (2)	Earnings Increase Each Year (3)	Value of Earnings at Date Achieved on 10% Return Basis (Earnings x 10) (4)	Percentage Representing Present Value (5)	Present Value This Year (Col. 4 x 5) (6)
1971	$1.08	$ —	$10.80	100%	$10.80
Future—					
1	1.21	.13	1.30	91	1.18
2	1.35	.14	1.40	83	1.16
3	1.52	.17	1.70	75	1.28
4	1.70	.18	1.80	68	1.22
5	1.90	.20	2.00	62	1.24
6	2.13	.23	2.30	56	1.29
7	2.39	.26	2.60	51	1.33
8	2.67	.28	2.80	47	1.32
9	3.00	.33	3.30	42	1.39

Market value—$17.50 plus premium of 20%

P/E ratio . . . .

Less—

Book value of assets of acquired company . . . .

Increased value of tangible assets (less future tax cost) . . . .

Amount assignable to increased value of physical assets and to intangibles on a 10% present value computation basis . . . .

*See previous page.

NOTE: Acquirer has refused to accept 10% return valuation basis contending that this factor should be at least 11%. The effect would be to include more than 9 years of forward pricing of future earnings.

BREAKDOWN ANALYSIS OF MARKET PRICE OF STOCK OF COMPANY BEING CONSIDERED FOR ACQUISITION BASED ON 12% COMPOUNDED ANNUAL GROWTH IN EARNINGS THAT WAS USED AS BASIS OF NEGOTIATION

Value of Present and Future Earnings Included in Present Price of Stock at Date of Acquistion		Breakdown of Cost of Acquisition Based on 10 Million Shares at $21 Per Share Representing			
			Cost of Prospective Future Growth Consisting of		
Amount	Percent of Total Price	Existing Productive Assets	Productivity Growth 29.2%*	Future Retained Earnings 70.8%*	Total Consideration for Acquisition
(7)	(8)	(9)	(10)	(11)	(12)
			In Thousands		
$10.80	51.4%	$108,000	$ —	$ —	$108,000
1.18	5.6	—	3,446	8,354	11,800
1.16	5.6	—	3.387	8,213	11,600
1.20	5.7	—	3,504	8,496	12,000
1.22	5.8	—	3,562	8,638	12,200
1.24	5.9	—	3,621	8,779	12,400
1.29	6.2	—	3,767	9,133	12,900
1.33	6.3	—	3,884	9,416	13,300
1.32	6.3	—	3,854	9,346	13,200
.26	1.2	—	759	1,841	2,600
$21.00	100.0%	$108,000	$29,784	$72,216	$210,000
19.4					
....		(80,000)	—	—	(80,000)
....		(25,000)	—	—	(25,000)
....		$ 3,000	$29,784	$72,216	$105,000

149

Thus, the so-called "difference" under Opinion No. 16 consisted of the following component items:

Intangibles—properly and affirmatively determined as relating to present property serving present customers.		$ 3,000,000
Payment to selling stockholders for future growth—		
Productivity growth. . .	$29,784,000	
Retained income from future operations. . .	72,216,000	102,000,000
Total "difference" under Opinion No. 16-Par. 68..		$105,000,000

Thus, instead of an "unspecified difference" this analysis identifies the several components, and proper accounting can now be applied to the specific components making up that "difference," which previously had to be blindly accounted for.

Proper accounting for components of group purchase cost

The accounting for each of the components can now be accomplished according to the nature of those components:

(1) Intangibles on present net assets serving present customers amount to $3 million, and evidence exists that the present property and present earnings will continue indefinitely. The value of the intangibles continues into the future the same as land values. As such, it is not subject to amortization. If present earning capacity is lost, the entire amount of intangibles should be written off, but it does not represent a quantity of services, material or assets that decreases in volume as operations occur and, therefore, is not properly subject to periodic or partial write-off.

(2) Productivity and retained earnings growth:

The amounts in these categories are the distributions to selling stockholders of future growth of the acquired company prior to their being earned. The nearest analogy to these components is a payout of future capital growth—an earnout that is included in the calculated price of stock in advance (see prior pages).

The period of this forward pricing of future growth agreed to in the negotiation, if a part of the final agreement, would be included in the group cost as defined by Opinion No. 16, Par. 68. In the acquisition/merger example, the present value of future growth is for nine years based on a 12% per annum compounded. As long as this growth rate continues and nine years of forward pricing in the market value of stock is equitable, no reduction of net income by amortization, or otherwise, of this amount is proper on the books of the acquirer insofar as public stockholders of the acquiring entity are concerned. To make such an amortization would be a representation that earned income had been reduced, but the facts are that no reduction has occurred because of this item. To represent that earnings have been reduced by such forward pricing would be a gross misrepresentation of earning capacity of the company and, thus, cause damages to every public stockholder. Nonetheless, the degree of forward pricing in the market price of a stock is a stockholder function and not a corporate function.

The inclusion of this amount in the "group" purchase cost also does not affect the future growth that actually occurs. The amount of that growth when earned will in fact be transferred to retained earnings. Such actual earnings will be less, or greater, than the amount contemplated at acquisition. Whatever amount the actual earnings is, it will be offset by the amount distributed in the purchase price to previous stockholders in the sale of their stock at the time of the acquisition/merger. That distribution does not affect the amount earned from later operations but affects only those to whom the earnings were distributed.

The new owners possess the earning power demonstrated by future operations, and this earning power, whatever it is, will continue to be reflected in the market price of the acquirer's stock in the marketplace. This will be done by whatever forward market pricing is deemed equitable by those public investors in the merged or combined operation as a whole. The acquiring company should not reduce that actual earning power by a market exchange value of stock that happened to exist at the acquisition/merger date. To do so would seriously mislead the new stockholders as to what earning capacity they possess.

The forward pricing that the acquiring stockholders agreed to as a basis for merging the acquired company operations into the pricing of their own stock (even though paid for in cash) should preferably not be retained on the balance sheet of the acquirer. To do so would simply place the public investors' valuation of stock at one specific date in the market on the balance sheet. This forward pricing of growth, if continued in the market price, justifies retention on the balance sheet rather than amortization to income as long as it exists. Nonetheless, since it is a function of the stockholders' appraisal of value and not a corporate operating asset, a write-off to retained earnings would be the preferable accounting to public stockholders. The only collateral the acquiring company has put at risk by including the forward pricing of future earnings of the acquired company in the combination price is its own retained earnings (surplus). Consequently, the amount of all forward pricing of earnings in an acquisition "group cost" should be deducted from retained earnings by the acquiring corporation. The amount so deducted or written off will be restored, or offset, by actual operations of that entity

through transfer of actual income to retained earnings.

In the meantime, the market price of the stock of the acquiring company (regardless of the medium used for acquisition) will adjust to reflect actual operating results as reflected by income determined for the combined company. The adjusted price will include a longer or shorter forward pricing of future earnings, regardless of what might have been the stock market investor judgment at the time of the actual acquisition.

In summary, that part of "group cost" representing the present value of future earnings is nothing more than an earnout contingency. Proper accounting for this component of "group cost" that will not mislead and damage public stockholders requires that this forward pricing of growth be offset against the acquirer's capital account.

Why blame the SEC or the New York Stock Exchange for conditions preceding Opinions No. 16 and 17

Much has been said of the guides that controlled accounting for merger/acquisition prior to the issuance of Opinions No. 16 and 17. The SEC, in particular, has been criticized for allowing deterioration in the prerequisite rules for pooling governing merger/acquisition accounting prior to October 1970. Those who make such criticisms should take stock of these so-called prerequisite rules, particularly those concerning size comparisons and the partial pooling of companies acquired. The reasons for the so-called deterioration on both counts was the artificiality of those prerequisite rules.

Criticism on identical bases is now properly leveled at Opinions No. 16 and 17. The rules preceding Opinions No. 16 and 17 deteriorated because they too were artificial and discriminatory. The relative size rule required the small businessman to accept the damage resulting from disallowing pooling for him but permitted big companies to escape similar damage. Such a rule was the antithesis of fairness. Since when is there a tight accounting principle for small business and a more liberal one for big business?

The SEC is a government representative for all persons, not just the influential or big —and it acted properly in allowing pooling for big and little acquisitions alike. This relative size rule could not stand impartial inquiry, and the SEC rightly permitted it to deteriorate.

For the same reasons, the SEC must refuse to enforce the numerous artificial requirements of Opinions No. 16 and 17. These rules reimpose accounting that is even more discriminatory against both the public investor (who does not work on financial street) and the small businessman and greatly damages both.

Blame for the failure of Opinion No. 16 to identify and prescribe proper accounting for the transactions referred to in those Opinions must rest wholly on the public accounting profession. The SEC can only be charged with failure to demand that the principles adopted treat all interested parties equitably and, therefore, that no accounting be permitted that is based on "differences" unidentified. Amounts that cannot be identified as to what they are in fact should be charged off immediately against earnings or surplus. Any other accounting permitted is unsupportable.

The public accountant can seek, but cannot hope to secure, absolution from the SEC for accounting rules that should be supportable on the profession's own responsibility, but that, in fact, have no bases capable of factual documentation. How, then, can the SEC allow retention in the balance sheet of an asset—a "difference"— that the certifying accountant has not identified? Reliance on rules professionally declared, or even on rules prescribed by regulation, does not provide the independent public accountant with either comfort or valid defense. Blind use of such rules is dangerous as well as unprofessional. Judge Friendly of the USCA, 2nd District, *United States v. Simon, et al.,* endorsed the principle that reliance on rules professionally declared is not an effective defense of any public accountant unless the transaction, in fact, is described and accounted for according to its determinable identity.

The public accountant should not accept a "difference" as a balance sheet asset or an amortization of such an unacceptable asset against income without prior approval of a court of the reasonableness of such a procedure to the public investor. Until then Opinions No. 16 and 17 give misleading guidance to the public accounting profession, the Securities and Exchange Commission, and the New York Stock Exchange.

No benefits flow to public stockholders from one-year earnings forecasts

Before the Financial Executives Institute,
Milwaukee, Wisconsin,
December 12, 1972

The investor should be provided with data that show how a particular price-earnings ratio results from a valuation of present earnings and from a valuation of future growth prospects.

Issues

THE ISSUES CONCERNING the proposition of providing "earnings forecasts" should be defined so that all questions involved in financial forecasts can be analyzed intelligently.

They appear to be:

(a) Do investors want forecasts?

The answer to this question is obvious. The name of the game in buying stock is appraising the unknown future of the company involved. Fear of the unknown is as real on the stock market as it is in any other walk of life. Investors want financial forecasts to eliminate this unknown if possible.

(b) Can "earnings forecasts" be made?

The answer to this question is that "opinions" on forecasts can be given. All opinions are only as good as the reasoning used in arriving at them and as the competence of those expressing the opinion in obtaining and using relevant data. The reliability of such opinions will vary from zero to, theoretically, 100%.

If such opinions are the consequence of using divining rod techniques, honesty requires disclosure of this derivation.

(c) Who can provide the most reliable opinion on earnings forecasts?

The answer to this question must be—whatever authority can be and is the most informed on the particular entity's future operations and the multitude of pertinent conditions affecting that future.

(d) What authority is usually the most informed and, therefore, the best authority to forecast earnings?

The management of the entity involved, if competent. This in no way implies that responsible and prudent management will not regard its own opinions, if it has any on the unknown factors of the future, as being too speculative and too misleading to permit public investors to act upon them. Only management can make that determination.

(e) Should such "earnings forecasts" be required to be made by management by regulatory decree?

This is a very complicated question that involves legal ramifications. Certainly, known facts can be extracted by legal procedures from almost anyone. The real question is whether the law can require a person to "reach an opinion" on future earnings of an entity. If so, this is tantamount to requiring a "Russian confession" from management unless the regulatory decree also permits an honest statement of fact, a statement that may be, "no reliable opinion."

(f) Should such management earnings forecasts, if given, be gift wrapped with a "belief-opinion" of a certified public accountant expressing concurrence as to reasonableness of assumptions and makeup of the forecast?

The answer to this question, in the writer's opinion, is "no." To the extent independent auditors can assist any company in the arithmetic and form of such forecasts, they will do so—just as they now do in the preparation of any report. But such arithmetic assistance does not constitute any substantive addition to the presentation to the public investor. The use of a public accountant's standing and image as a fact finder to give an aura of credibility to a lay belief-opinion perpetrates an unforgivable hoax on the public investor. The responsibility for the misleading results of such a hoax falls on that accountant who permits this gross misuse of his services and on the regulatory authority that sanctions or requires the CPA belief-opinion to be delivered to the investors. Any public accountant who allows himself to arrive at an "opinion on reasonableness of assumptions" for earnings forecasts of any entity thereby becomes one of the authors of such a prediction and thereby forfeits his status as an "independent auditor" to express an opinion on the actual results for that entity for the period covered by the forecast.

Expansion of these brief questions and answers is necessary to evaluate fully the reality of their impact.

Do investors want forecasts?

In nearly every activity in life every one of us would like to have forecasts of one type or another. The *Britannica* tells us, futurism became a fact in 1909 for the purpose of demolishing the past and glorifying the present, to exalt speed, power, violence and the beauty of machinery. It held that, since all things are in perpetual movement and subject to continual transformation, form has no final state or fixed position and that space is nonexistent except as a void in which form moves. It states, futurists represent this state of flux either by arbitrarily disintegrating form and making a synthetic pattern of its movements or by inventing linear equivalents for the forces that direct its movement.

The modern idea of making earnings forecasts involves the process of inventing synthetic patterns of real forces. It is a process that attempts to give respectability to a corporate medicine man, prestidigitator, soothsayer, or what have you. The arguments advanced for a requirement to make earnings forecasts could only be entertained by those who are detached from the reality of the forces that control operating success, the forces that are reflected in the actual earnings per share for the public investor.

Forecasts have been prepared in numerous situations in which facts and conditions, based upon specific corporate actions to be presently undertaken, were clearly demonstrable. Such forecasts have stated the analyzed results of such actions based upon opinions of knowledgeable competent engineers who were experienced in programming that operation and who could be held accountable for their prudence. The financing of the formation of Tennessee Gas Transmission Company (now TENNECO) included such a forecast in its registration statement in 1945, No. 2-5699.

One reason the Securities and Exchange Commission was organized was to anchor the public investor to a full disclosure of specific known facts. The investor could then relate those realities to the risks he was undertaking, on his own initiative or on advisory judgment, as to the future in his decision to buy, sell, or hold securities.

Prior to 1929, the utility magnates and others had worked stock values up to high levels by including future growth possibilities in the market price to the point that market prices were completely overburdened with future values which had only a small relationship to the present values. In mid-1929 Middle West Utilities System stock sold at 48 times earnings, a multiple that included the then present value of more than 50 years' future growth of companies that are today blue-chip companies. Yet, the change in attitude in forecasting the future destroyed that company in five years.

Today, we have come full circle to conditions somewhat comparable to the period prior to 1929. The vulnerability of stock market prices is in direct relation to the extent of inclusion of the forward values of future growth in present stock prices. Market prices get so overweighted with future values that prices fall from their own weight, even though the future values do mature. How often is it said that the future values are great, but can the investor stand the adversities to be overcome on the road

to reach them? It is only natural in times of temporary economic turndown that all investors reappraise downward the merit of including long-term future growth in present prices. The downward reappraisal accounts for the decline in market prices. It results not from a change in investment merits but from the fear of the unknown, 5, 10, 15, and 20 or more years hence.

It would be extremely helpful if some quick measurement of future growth could be created that would help all investors, but to tantalize investors with earnings forecasts for one year, forecasts that everyone disowns, is nothing but baiting the gambling hook—the forecast is just a small morsel of what their gamble is.

Publicized earnings forecasts of a year or so in the future have been advanced in some quarters as being a method by which public investors can measure future values. This viewpoint is valid only at first blush because:

First, very, very few market value appraisals include future growth values limited to only one or even two years.

Second, investors do not yet have the procedural tools by which to judge future earnings forecasts and convert them into present market values. These tools remain undeveloped even though they can be and are far more important to future market price appraisals than the small token of conjecture about the future contained in one year's earnings forecast.

Third, required forecasting of corporate earnings for one year will be a major disservice to investors because it will actually destroy the most important management tool available to maximize actual earnings.

One- or even two-year earnings forecasts will serve the stock market gambler but fail the long-term investor

The headlong conclusion that a forecast of earnings for the next year or even for two years will benefit the public stockholders is a myth. First, any knowledgeable investor should know that a one-year forecast is of little value at best, even when reliable, in evaluating the present market price of shares. It can only supply the toe in the water before the plunge. Earnings forecasts, therefore, have their greatest value to public investors as an indication of the growth factor. Yet, one year's growth factor is almost useless in measuring prospective growth many years into the future. In addition, the one-year growth factor to be confirmed by a forecast will generally be between 5% to 25% per annum. This measurement of the residual added over actual operations of the last year is what is sought, but this residual carries a 100% risk of error of the forecast. This residual also carries 100% of optimism; it carries more than 100% of the preparers' disclaimer.

In other words, a "growth factor" computed from the imaginative predictions of the whole operation forms the basis of earnings forecasts, and this "growth factor" has leveraged into it 100% of every risk arising from error on the whole operation. Furthermore, many acknowledge that a 10% error in a forecast would be a margin regarded as quite accurate. Thus, even realization of a forecast within a quite accurate range could wipe out the one important ingredient sought from the forecast, i.e., growth factor.

The lowest P/E ratios, and, therefore, the lowest market prices of stock are applicable to probable-zero-growth companies. History and financial economists have demonstrated most conclusively that a probable-zero-growth flow of reasonably reliable earnings has a computed worth of not more than a 10% return basis and, therefore, a value of 10 times earnings. Financial economists usually state that this value is on the low side.

Therefore, the need of the long-term public investor is not for the forecast of a single year, or even two years' earnings, but a reliable basis on which to approxi-

mate growth over a period of several years, even 10, 15, 20, or more years in the future. The one- or two-year forecast has minimal use for this purpose. However, the one year's earnings forecast does serve the gimmick salesman and the one-year gambler, the "in and outer," because he will gamble on the conservatism or optimism of management, a gamble that the long-term public investor should not take. In other words, earnings forecasts saddle public investors with one more risk rather than helping them with those they already have.

If the objective of the SEC and the accounting profession is to serve the gamblers by making a pretense of serving long-term investors with so-called earnings forecasts, all they will do is add explosiveness to the marketplace. This will induce long-term investors to become "in and outers," or just "outers," in order to protect themselves from the added risks imposed by the earnings forecasts.

The Dow-Jones average P/E ratio is now 17. This means that, at most, 59% of the present market price of stocks represents the value attributed to the present earnings flow, at a minimum valuation of 10% return ($10 \div 17$). Conversely, forward pricing of anticipated growth in earnings productivity represents at least 41% of the present market price ($7 \div 17$). This average, 41% of present market, representing future growth is allocable to the next two years as follows, depending upon the variation in the rate of growth:

Compound Annual Growth Rate	Present Price of 17x Includes Present Value of Future Years' Growth for	Portion of Present Market Price Attributable to Growth of	
		1st Year	2nd Year
5%	26 years	3%	3%
6	17 "	3	3
7	13 "	4	4
8	10 "	4	4
9	9 "	5	5
10	8 "	6	6
12	6 "	6	6
14-15-16	5 "	6	12
18-20	4 "	12	12
25	3 "	12	18

1st and 2nd year P/E ratio increase ÷ 17— see P/R ratio table on a subsequent page.

Thus, it is readily apparent that an earnings forecast for one year is of assistance to public investors in appraising from 3% to 6% of the present market price for most stocks.

Furthermore, one-year earnings forecasts may be of significant help only when growth rates are represented to the public investor to be 15% or more per annum, and then only if the public investor is made cognizant of the growth rate duration implicit in the specific market price he pays.

Consequently, it would be misleading, if not fraudulent, to the public investor to emphasize one year's earnings forecast as being basically important to the price the public investor pays for his stock. When one subtracts the negative consequences of disclaimers and the misleading and fraudulent characteristics of forecasts from the value to the public investors of earnings forecasts, the minuses are so great that it is hard to believe that regulatory naiveté could permit their serious consideration. One could understand the push to require earnings forecasts if they were urged by brokers who wanted a sales gimmick directly comparable to those used in the pre-Insull and Hopson days of 1927-1929. But to impose by regulatory fiat what experience in those days taught us to dismiss out-of-hand is rather unbelieveable.

Requiring one-year forecast will destroy usefulness of operating tools used to produce actual corporate earnings

The "forecast" or "budget" system is probably the most essential internal communication tool existing for management operating success. The words "forecast" and "budget" have always been ill-defined because management and field operators have understood their meaning irrespective of the degree of sophisticated descriptions. Nonetheless, in all cases the forecast or budget of operations consists of a game plan to maximize sales goals plus a budget game plan to minimize operating costs. The net

balance of these budgets represents the earnings goal that management strives to achieve.

However, management, like a football coach, is constantly giving the quarterback plays to use to reach the projected goal during the period of operations. Management and the coach know that every game plan is subject to fumbles, mistakes and interceptions, so that game plans must include play-to-play and month-to-month flexibility.

Basic to every management operating forecast or budget are built-in goals that have little probability of being reflected on the scoreboard irrespective of the gamesmanship of management in an effort to meet its expectations. Corporate management cannot be expected to publicize these game plans, in terms of earnings per share forecasts, for public investors to rely on for pricing securities in the stock market. To do so would seriously mislead the public investor into accepting expectations that at the time of the forecast are rank speculations. If management makes such game plan forecasts public and the plans do not materialize, the public stockholder has been led to a loss.

Experience shows that this result will practically always prevail, because the operating budget, or forecast, must include built-in optimism to achieve maximum success. A good management will not allow a safe goal to be established because such a goal is an invitation to operating personnel for mediocre performance with consequent low returns to stockholders. This system of performance incentives is built into each operating plan and every competent auditor is aware of it.

On the other hand, if management discounts the projected game plan (forecast-budget) based upon its informed judgment and actuarial experience, and provides the public with the discounted projections, investors will later charge management with withholding in-house insider information if it is revealed that the internal game plan has been greater than public predictions. This would be true particularly if management fully implements a successful game plan and achieves its goals. More important, however, is the disservice management does to existing public investors by publicly discounting in-house operational game plans. In effect, management then tells the company's whole operating organization that it believes the planned goals will not be achieved. Once that is done, stockholders can rest assured that less than a full effort will be expended toward success.

Thus, any attempt to saddle management with a requirement to publish a specific forecast of earnings will result in the existing stockholders having every opportunity of loss, and no opportunity of gain. We need to consider carefully whether earnings forecasts now being promoted as being a service to public investors will not instead destroy an existing protection of the public investor, contrary to the purposes and intent of the Securities Acts of Congress.

Public accountants are not qualified to corroborate one-year forecasts

The public accountant merits his position in society as a certified public accountant by reason of his expertise in analysis of and accounting for factual transactions and his knowledge of the means to verify such transactions. He is charged with responsibility to maintain "independence" and to avoid involvement with a client or his operations or the development of operating strategies. He can have no "conflict of interest" and no built-in self-interest in the terms or final results of any transaction.

Some contend that, since he must review estimates of future bad debts, plant depreciation lives and amortization periods for deferred charges, etc., an overall forecast of operations is merely a further use of such talents. Such a superficial conclusion could only be advanced by the inexperienced or by theoreticians who do not know how

actual auditing is performed. Every long-term estimation used by corporate management to assign costs to an expired single year is always subject to the direct or comparable test of actual past experience as a basis of verification by the public accountant. No bases for such verification of revenues, sales or costs can be made in the subjective assumptions used in earnings forecasts.

Some have also contended that requiring earnings forecast corroboration by the auditor is a new service that the SEC can require for the benefit of the public investor. It is not. Corroboration of forecasts by the public accountant was considered by the SEC over 27 years ago and found to be misleading to investors. In 1945 the SEC found such corroboration by public accountants, even when possessing a high probability of achievement, as providing no independent public accounting service to the public and rejected its use. In 1945 Tennessee Gas Transmission Company (predecessor of TENNECO) registered securities, and forecasted estimates of income for the next year appeared in the registration statement with the following comments about and by the auditors.

"ESTIMATES OF INCOME FOR 1945 (And Related Adjusted Statements, With Comments Relating To Subsequent Years)

"The tabulation below including the notes thereto, and the statements under the subcaption 'Certain Factors Affecting Years Subsequent to 1945,' have been prepared by the Company. As to the accounting matters involved therein (including matters involving Federal income taxes), they have been reviewed by and are stated in reliance upon the accompanying opinion of Arthur Andersen & Co., accountants and auditors, as experts. As to the assumptions or estimates (explained in the notes) of sales volumes, operating revenues and operating expenses, they have been reviewed by and are stated in reliance upon the opinion of Ford, Bacon & Davis, Inc., independent engineers, as experts."

"The letter of opinion of Messrs. Arthur Andersen & Co. with respect to the accounting matters involved in the information given under this caption follows:

"We have reviewed the accounting matters involved in the preparation of the tabulation and the related explanatory notes and comments shown under the foregoing section entitled 'Estimates of Income for 1945.' In connection therewith, we have examined the balance sheet of the Tennessee Gas and Transmission Company at February 28, 1945 and the statements of income for the periods prior to that date, have reviewed the entries that would be required upon the consummation of the proposed refinancing and have checked the basis and computation of the estimated provisions for the year 1945 for depreciation, Federal income and excess profits taxes, interest and other deductions. With respect to the assumptions or estimates of sales volumes, operating revenues and operating expenses (used in arriving at net operating revenue before depreciation and Federal income taxes) which are not subject to audit examination, we have relied upon the report and opinion of Ford, Bacon & Davis, Inc., independent engineers.

"On the foregoing basis, in our opinion, the accounting determinations involved in the preparation of the tabulation and explanatory notes and comments under the title of 'Estimates of Income for 1945,' have been made in accordance with generally accepted accounting principles.

ARTHUR ANDERSEN & CO."

Houston, Texas,
April 11, 1945.

When the independent public accountants' role in providing the above letter of opinion was analyzed, it was found that the letter did not require the public accountant to use his expertise in vertification of facts, a standard prerequisite to issuance of a public accountant's opinion. Therefore, the conclusion was that the letter was an improper use of his opinion. In the final registration statement, the reference to independent public accountants as well as their opinion was deleted. Thus, the present efforts to revive auditors' belief-opinions on forecasts is an attempt to breathe life into a corpse buried 27 years ago.

An analysis of misuse of public accountants' opinions in actual forecasts of earnings

A discussion in generalities of the auditors' role in preparing forecasts is secondary to a discussion of an actual presentation. An actual copy of a forecast made for use in England with the opinion by the certified public accountants is attached for analysis. (Appendix)

The following are comments on that specific presentation:

(a) In the opening sentence of the opinion of the accountants (line 20), they state they have prepared "Statements of Projected Income and Cash Flow." Preparation by public accountants of these statements makes them at least one of the issuers of the projections. It is well established that public accountants may not prepare books and records for a company without disqualifying themselves as independent public accountants. (SEC Accounting Release #126)

(b) The "company" is used to corroborate the information (line 4) to the public accountants, rather than the other way around, and then both company and auditors take refuge under the shelter of an overall disclaimer stating neither one "undertakes any legal responsibility for deviation from the projections which may occur or for the accuracy thereof." This raises the basic question, of what service under such conditions does the information provide to the public investor?

(c) In the third paragraph (line 9), the company states that it presently believes that, if prevailing financial conditions continue and it achieves the projected cash flow, the cash deficit in 1971-1972-1973 could be met on acceptable commercial terms, but no provision is made for costs thereof nor are figures provided to indicate what the qualifying "if" means. Such qualifications are necessary in any forecast, but they make the projection a booby trap for an investor who may use it.

(d) In lines 28-80 the public accountants "front" for the company and legal counsel by reciting pertinent sections of agreements to which the auditors add not a whit of substance. The data should be supplied without disclaimer of responsibility by the issuer, presumably the company. The public accountants, not being lawyers, make a secondhand presentation in which they, by introduction, state that certain facts were pointed out to them by company and legal counsel instead of company and legal counsel affirmatively presenting these facts directly to the investor. They are "facts" for which the company and legal counsel should take full responsibility directly to the investor and they should not be sheltered by auditors' disclaimer.

(e) In lines 81 to 125, the auditors proceed to establish premises of the projection by "consulting" an individual concerning his knowledge of the various agreements and his experience and background in the industry. The auditors quote him as stating "it is not possible to project the future revenues" and then this authority proceeds to provide assumptions that he believes are "reasonable for use in connection with the preparation of projections." The auditors state parenthetically that they did not attempt to verify these assump-

tions, thus leading the reader to believe they could be verified. In one place where the auditors could use their expertise, they fail the investor. Nevertheless the auditors proceed to list assumptions of projected expenses and revenues which the "supplier" has just been quoted as stating "are not possible to project."

(f) Following the above list of qualified assumptions that the auditors in no way stated were verified, the auditors proceed to list their own bookkeeping assumptions (lines 126-161) that are not even qualified as being procedures the company will follow. Therefore, again the auditors act in the role of issuers of the forecast.

(g) The auditors' closing paragraph (lines 162-170) states the "accompanying statements of projected income and cash flow for the five years . . . have been prepared using the aforesaid information supplied to us and the assumptions indicated."

Then comes the auditors' belief-opinion (lines 164-168) reading:

"We believe that the assumptions and the methodology employed constitute reasonable bases for the preparation of the statements of projected income and cash flow for five years ending June 30, 1974."

If there is any regard for the investor whatsoever, an auditor expressing such a "belief-opinion" must be qualified in every aspect of the company's operation (which they did not state they were) or be naive or irresponsible. If such a "belief" is a layman's belief, rather than a professional's belief-opinion, it must fall in the latter two classifications. No independent or certified public accountant that understands his own qualifications and limitations would publicly express a lay belief-opinion that could only mislead investors. If he does so, at best he is functioning as a notary public. His legal liability under such conditions would be incalculable, but that is only because the misleading consequences result from his own negligence if he has knowledge of his own improper conduct. If he is qualified to express such a belief-opinion on an informed basis, the opinion should be preceded by a recitation of the qualifications he possesses to do so, and these qualifications are not those of a trained certified public accountant.

No example could illustrate more aptly an application of the SEC Chairman's admonition that substance must be recognized over form. The auditors' belief in this instance is, in this writer's opinion, all form and of no substance to the investor.

The protective disclaimer of the auditors in the last sentence (lines 168-170) does not cleanse those actions taken improperly in the first place.

The attest function is not achieved by elimination of premises, assumptions and forecasts from auditors' "belief-opinion"

It is often advanced that in the United States the premises and assumptions of the forecast would be required to be issued under the company's authority—a Russian confession requirement—and gift wrapped by an auditor's belief-opinion. Assuming such a requirement could be made of management, no authority existing can require responsible public accountants to bless the reasonableness of the multitude of asumptions made by management, and such a blessing would be required for the public accountant to give a "belief-opinion."

Assume, for instance, that one client assumes "x" number of units of a product are to be demanded by the public. These products will range from tons of steel to billions of birth control pills; each company will then estimate its allocable market share from the estimated public demand for the product. A second client in the same industry goes through the same process, but assumes "2x" units of public demand for the same product. Both are supported by logic and calculation and both would have to be deemed reasonable of belief by the accountant and, thus, both would receive his blessing. Is that accountant's "belief" worth the paper it is written on insofar as the public investor is concerned?

Consider:

(a) CPA training provides no basis different from that of a layman's to support a "belief" of reasonableness of premises and assumptions in forecasts or that the premises and assumptions are fit for public investor consumption.

(b) If a firm of CPAs assesses the competence of its personnel and concludes that they have the industry statistical and operating knowledge to give substance to its "belief of reasonableness of premises and assumption of a management forecast," it should qualify itself on a recitation of that competence and remove the CPA reference from its name if honesty to the investor prevails.

(c) The last paragraph of a belief-opinion defining the basic characteristics of a projection should specifically not disclaim any responsibility by an issuer of that "belief" for error caused by lack of applicable industry operational competence or lack of use of all data available to the issuer of the belief, whether the data came from another client's confidential files or from the obligation of the issuer to do his own industry research in depth to qualify himself. He must also be accountable to justify inconsistencies among the premises and assumptions professed to be reasonable bases as among companies. Thus, he must do all those things that are necessary to become a joint issuer of the projection because that is what he is.

The dictionary defines "belief" as being a synonym of "opinion." The use by CPAs of "belief" instead of "opinion" in expressing the quality of projections provides evidence that a mere change in form is intended to create a different degree of meaning, even though the new form is no different in substance. This is deception.

The use of disclaimers to remove any and all responsibility for projections from management and the auditor corroborator nullifies the usefulness of the projection. The presentation of such so-called forecasts to the public stockholders for use in making investment decisions is patently misleading when management and auditor are allowed to undercut the substance of the forecast with disclaimers of responsibility. This leaves the investor standing alone in the use of the forecast as though he could supply substantive judgment of merit where the issuer could not.

These boiler plate disclaimers recall the early days of the Securities and Exchange Commission when public accountants sought indemnification from registrants for any losses in connection with their opinions in registration statements. The SEC denied the auditor this indemnification on the basis that, if indemnified, the auditor would fail to take proper precaution for the presentation of data given, and the cost of his errors would fall on the investors, the ones to be protected and served by the auditor. Permitting disclaimers to exempt an issuer-auditor of responsibility for substantive data in earnings forecasts creates an identical result.

An earnings forecast should not be gilded with credibility by association with an auditor's opinion when that opinion disclaims responsibility to the public investor for lack of substance by telling him that all that glitters is not gold.

Expression of subjective belief on forecasts by CPAs impairs independence; can company use same CPA as independent auditor?

The jeopardy to a CPA's independence as an auditor for a company after he has expressed a subjective opinion on its forecasts is a factual matter and cannot be disposed of by the opinion of the auditor, by the profession and/or by the SEC in a blanket or specific action. In Accounting Series Release #126, the SEC, in cooperation with the profession, laid down strict rules on maintenance of the independent status of an auditor from his client in order for the accountant to qualify as "independent" as required by law.

When an auditor expresses his subjective opinion that the conditions and transactions assumed in the forecast of future operations are reasonable, he is as much involved in and attached to any attainment of the forecast as management itself. Any stockholder must presume the auditor has a bias to have those results achieved, just as management does. The auditor and the management are then connected, and the auditor cannot have "independence" from that company for the period of that forecast.

This does not mean that the auditor's independence cannot survive his joint sponsorship of a forecast with management just as an auditor's independence can very well survive his stock ownership in a client. But, both positions are untenable for the public to accept because a presumptive bias exists. In the public mind the presumptive bias assumes factual status. The issue turns on the sound reasoning of the SEC when it stated, "Managerial responsibility begins when the accountant becomes, or appears to become, so identified with the client's management as to be indistinguishable from it."

When a public accountant keeps records for a client, the SEC holds that, by preparing basic accounting records, the auditor places himself in a position where he would be reviewing his own recordkeeping. He could, therefore, appear to third parties to lack the objectivity and impartiality with respect to that client that an independent audit requires. The same result follows with greater probability when the auditor expresses any subjective opinion on the results (actual or forecast) of operations. That is why public accountants stick to presenting facts and let readers interpret them and make their own subjective conclusions.

The SEC rightfully states, "The question of independence is one of fact, to be determined in the light of all the pertinent circumstances in a particular case." In this writer's opinion, when the public accountant issues a subjective opinion on forecasting future operations where no objective standards exist by which he can verify the data, the public accountant places himself in the same shoes as management. When it becomes necessary to make an independent audit of actual conditions, neither can be independent, be free of every bond that exists between a prediction of conditions and the actual conditions when they occur. Persons who take part in such predictions cannot then be later accepted by the public as being independent to examine actual results. Independence must be presumed to be absent here just as it is in a bankruptcy situation when the prebankruptcy auditor must be changed in order to break the bond between the prebankruptcy auditor and his previous opinions.

Since the SEC cannot resolve this point of independence in advance for itself, for the auditor or for the company, the risk and burden resulting from loss of independence of the auditor falls, first, entirely on the company and, second, on the auditor if he has represented himself as "independent" when he knew he lacked the required separation from the company's operations.

This burden to the company will be activated when the independence of the auditor is challenged. Other public accountants, to protect themselves and their professional stature, must challenge the independence of any of their colleagues, under the Securities Act of 1933, who issue a belief-opinion on a forecast and thereafter during the period covered by the forecast also give an independent auditor's opinion based on actual conditions. To make such a challenge, the other auditors must purchase securities offered by the company issuing the forecast and sue when the market price falls below the issue price on the grounds the offer and sale were illegal because of lack of an independent auditor's opinion. The suit will provide a test case for judicial review to preserve the stature of the public accounting profession, individual public accountants, and accounting firms.

Thus, the problem cannot be dismissed by an opinion of the SEC or by a consensus view among professional public accountants. It must stand the inquiry of a court determination.

*No benefits flow to
public stockholders from
one-year earnings forecasts*

What flows from one-year earnings forecasts? The results can be summarized:

(a) One-year forecasts give questionable credence at best, but probably misinformation, to only a nominal portion of the market price public investors are interested in.

(b) One-year forecasts by management will destroy operating tools and thereby inflict losses on the investors without any benefits accruing to them.

(c) Public accountants' "belief-opinions" attached to earnings forecasts simply gild the forecasts and supply no substance to them.

(d) Public accountants cannot avoid a conflict of interests while supplying "belief-opinions" on forecasts and simultaneously acting as independent auditors.

(e) Loss of public accountants' "independence" imposes heavy responsibility on corporations and, therefore, on investors. Only court action can resolve the issue.

*The SEC search for
forecasting data to facilitate
investors' evaluations of stock market
prices has substance*

While a one-year forecast of earnings provides data (even though unreliable) on one year's future earnings growth of a company, in most cases this growth accounts for a very small percentage of the total market price of the average share of stock. The SEC, brokers and public accountants have been woefully negligent in providing any meaningful tools for the investor to use to determine the makeup of the price quoted, or in requiring the broker to demonstrate the probable components of the price the investor pays for his stock. Even more important is how these components compare with past actualities. This is true even though practically no authority denies that market prices of stock are based on *value of present earnings plus the present value of future earnings growth.*

The SEC, brokers and accountants have not even tried to diagnose properly the components of P/E ratios of stock, even though they are emphasized more and more and are being published daily alongside per-share price for the public investor. All of us have represented P/E ratios to the public investor as being the result of the price determined by market action divided by present actual earnings. Yet, if P/E ratios were to function properly, P/E ratios would be a multiplier affirmatively determined and then applied to earnings to determine the price investors would choose to pay. In this way the investor would not pay a market price for a stock determined on a seat-of-the-pants decision. Investors do not know what paying a certain market price means in relation to growth or to the years of future investment in that growth that is included in market price. The investor is constantly being bombarded with growth factor rates, P/E ratios, present earnings rates, etc., as prerequisites to investment decisions, even though no demonstrated connection

among these factors is responsibly placed before him.

The investor can be informed on these matters, however, by requiring a broker to relate future growth assumptions to actual experienced growth as well as to the present value of that growth. When this is done, the security sales price components can be demonstrated to a buyer or a seller who can then evaluate whether he wishes to act on these terms. This is relatively easy to do. More important, however, is that such a procedure would also permit corporate management, public accountants and security salesmen to function responsibly in their own areas of expertise.

It has been well established that a minimum earnings rate that an investor expects on an equity investment that has stability but little growth prospect is 10% per annum. This is so rooted in equity evaluation that it is said this was the minimum earnings rate charged by Columbus on the goods which filled the holds of his ships. However, any minimum return can be adjusted either upward or downward if the minimum earnings rate on common equity is determined to be another percentage. But 10% affords an especially conservative rule-of-thumb rate for all uses.

However, the growth factor in earnings plays the greatest variable role in all stock market prices. Even though this growth factor is more important and is as universally used as any other investment decision factor, no one has assumed responsibility for its definition: not the SEC, not security analysts, not security salesmen, and not accountants, even though it is commonly used by each one. Nor have any of these authorities who have responsibility in this area required confirmation of actual growth in annual reports to shareholders, although public accountants have the expertise to evaluate and report on this factor.

In the case of IBM, for example, the compounded annual growth factor has been publicized as 13%, 15%, 20%, or 20.6%. An analysis of IBM earnings data shows that its experienced compounded annual growth can also be demonstrated as being 5%, depending entirely on the definition of growth. In addition, all compounded annual growth factors are computed before removing an inflation factor, approximately 3% per annum, even though the inflation factor is included in the growth by which market prices are determined. Since the one most important component of stock prices is growth rate, it is indeed surprising that such a great effort is expended on the speculation of one year's growth when that factor controls such a minor portion of stock prices.

Since the SEC is charged with protecting the investor, it has the responsibility of assuring that investors are properly informed on the growth factor in stock prices. The disservice to the public investor in not defining "compounded annual growth" so that investors can confidently use that factor cannot be rectified by any requirement to provide a complicated one-year earnings forecast that is disclaimed by everyone connected with its preparation. For IBM alone the compounded annual growth factor is variously stated as being from 5% to 20%. The error in stock market prices by using growth rates with such variability is equivalent to allowing actual reported earnings to vary from $5 to $20 per share, depending on the reporter's choice of definition.

If the actual compounded annual growth factor is defined as being profitability for three- and five-year periods, the CPA can readily certify to this factor because he can verify it in his regular audit work. The company management in turn can readily state its goal of growth for future periods, as many do, or speculation about growth can be left in the hands of brokers and security advisors and analysts. The investor should receive a report on actual growth rate, just as he does on earnings covered by

the auditors' opinion in annual reports, so that he can compare both factors with forecasts supplied to him from all sources. Speculation on growth factors and their effect on P/E ratios knows no bounds because they can be buttressed with arguments related to new markets, greater public demand, breakthroughs, foreign export opportunities, ad infinitum. However, whatever speculation is used, the expected effect on stock market prices should be fully demonstrated to the prospective buyer or seller of securities and compared with the experienced growth of the stock involved. Before this can be done, compounded annual growth must be defined.

Market prices of stock reflect both present earnings and present value of future earnings

The investor should be provided with data that show how a particular P/E ratio results from a valuation of present earnings and from a valuation of future growth prospects, to the extent the value of future growth is included in current or proposed prices. This can be demonstrated by showing that P/E ratios are entirely the consequence of computing the present value of a predicted future period of growth at a specified rate. With this information, an investor can decide for himself how much future growth he wants to pay for when he acquires a particular stock. Investors need not accept P/E ratios as though they were mystical in origin. The following illustrations of the actual component elements of actual market prices at variously specified growth rates—and their relationship to past experiences—can be applied to most going-concern stocks.

The table on the following page indicates two ways to define compounded annual growth for IBM that illustrates the removal of speculation as to past actual experience for the five-year period 1966-71:

	Productive Growth, After Eliminating Minimum Earnings of 10% on New Capital Invested During Period	Growth, Including Earnings on New Capital Obtained Through Retained Income
1971—EPS	$9.38	$9.38

Earnings on new capital added by shareholders during period—

Dec. 31, 1971— equity	$ 6.6 billion		
Dec. 31, 1965— equity	2.6 billion		
New capital	$ 4.0 billion		
Assumed minimum earnings on new capital— 10%	$400 million		
Per share (115.5 million shares)		3.46	
Balance—1971—EPS exclusive of earnings on new capital		$5.92	
1966—EPS		4.71	4.71
Compounded annual growth rate including inflation additions		4.68%	14.8%

Thus, the compound annual growth factor for IBM in the last five years is near either 5% or 15%, depending on the definition of growth. If an investor were told that the future growth that he was paying for in the market price today included those earnings applicable to his own stock that had been reinvested for him, he would raise some very interesting questions, to say the least.

Such a practice would appear to be roughly the equivalent to a bank selling a customer a savings account of $100 for $200 on the basis that the $200 price included the future growth from accumulated interest at 6% per annum.

However, using these growth factors of 5%, and alternatively 15%, for testing the present market price of IBM stock, the following components of the market price emerge:

IBM

BREAKDOWN ANALYSIS OF MARKET PRICE
BASED ON 5% COMPOUNDED ANNUAL GROWTH IN EARNINGS

Year (1)	Earnings Per Share—5% Compounded Growth (2)	Earnings Increase Each Year (3)	Value of Earnings at Date Achieved on 10% Return Basis (Earnings x 10) (4)	Percentage Representing Present Value (5)	Present Value Amount (Col. 4 x 5) (6)	Present Value Percent of Total Price (7)
Now (1971)	$ 9.38	$ —	$93.80	100.0%	$ 93.80	24.0%
Future—						
1	9.84	.46	4.60	91.0	4.20	1.1
2	10.34	.50	5.00	83.0	4.15	1.1
3	10.86	.52	5.20	75.0	3.90	
4	11.40	.54	5.40	68.0	3.67	
5	11.97	.57	5.70	62.0	3.53	
6	12.57	.60	6.00	56.0	3.36	
7	13.20	.63	6.30	51.0	3.21	
8	13.86	.66	6.60	47.0	3.10	
9	14.55	.69	6.90	42.0	2.90	
10	15.27	.72	7.20	39.0	2.81	
11	16.04	.77	7.70	35.0	2.70	
12	16.84	.80	8.00	32.0	2.56	
13	17.68	.84	8.40	29.0	2.44	
14	18.56	.88	8.80	26.0	2.28	
15	19.49	.93	9.30	24.0	2.23	
16	20.47	.98	9.80	22.0	2.16	15.9
17	21.49	1.02	10.20	20.0	2.04	
18	22.57	1.08	10.80	18.0	1.94	
19	23.70	1.13	11.30	16.0	1.78	
20	24.88	1.18	11.80	15.0	1.77	
21	26.12	1.24	12.40	14.0	1.74	
22	27.43	1.31	13.10	12.0	1.57	
23	28.80	1.37	13.70	11.0	1.51	
24	30.25	1.45	14.50	10.0	1.45	
25	31.76	1.51	15.10	9.0	1.36	
26	33.35	1.59	15.90	8.0	1.27	
27	35.02	1.67	16.70	8.0	1.34	
28	36.76	1.74	17.40	7.0	1.22	
29	38.61	1.85	18.50	6.0	1.11	
30	40.54	1.93	19.30	6.0	1.16	

Total present value of current earnings and of future growth at 5% per annum for 30 years	$164.26	42.1%
Market price unaccounted for above	225.74	57.9
Present market price per share	$390.00	100.0%
P/E ratio ($390 ÷ $9.38)	41.6	

IBM

BREAKDOWN ANALYSIS OF MARKET PRICE
BASED ON 15% COMPOUNDED ANNUAL GROWTH IN EARNINGS

Year (1)	Earnings Per Share—15% Compounded Growth (2)	Earnings Increase Each Year (3)	Value of Earnings at Date Achieved on 10% Return Basis (Earnings x 10) (4)	Percentage Representing Present Value (5)	Present Value (Col. 4 x 5) (6)	Present Value of Present and Future Earnings Included in Present Market Price of Stock — Amount (7)	Percent of Total Price (8)
Now (1971)	$ 9.38	$ —	$ 93.80	100%	$93.80	$ 93.80	24.0%
Future—							
1	10.79	1.41	14.10	91	12.83	12.83	3.3%
2	12.41	1.62	16.20	83	13.45	13.45	3.4%
3	14.26	1.85	18.50	75	13.88	13.88	
4	16.44	2.18	21.80	68	14.82	14.82	
5	18.87	2.43	24.30	62	15.07	15.07	
6	21.70	2.83	28.30	56	15.85	15.85	
7	24.95	3.25	32.50	51	16.58	16.58	
8	28.69	3.74	37.40	47	17.58	17.58	
9	33.00	4.31	43.10	42	18.10	18.10	
10	37.95	4.95	49.50	39	19.31	19.31	
11	43.64	5.69	56.90	35	19.92	19.92	69.3%
12	50.18	6.54	65.40	32	20.93	20.93	
13	57.71	7.53	75.30	29	21.84	21.84	
14	66.37	8.66	86.60	26	22.52	22.52	
15	76.32	9.95	99.50	24	23.88	23.88	
16	87.77	11.45	114.50	22	25.19	25.19	
17	100.94	13.17	131.70	20	26.34	4.45	
18	116.08	15.14	151.40	18	27.25	—	
Total						$390.00	100.0%
P/E ratio ($390 ÷ $9.38)						41.6	

It will be noted that, at a 5% growth rate, the investor includes in the present market price of his IBM stock 30 years' present value of future growth (EPS—$40.54) plus the value of the present earnings stream and he still has $225, or 57.9% of the market price unaccounted for.

With a growth rate of 15% per annum, a buyer pays the same price per share, or 24% of the market price, for the present earnings stream and the balance, 76%, for the present value of the next 16 years of growth (up to $87.77 EPS), which includes payment to the seller of all future retained earnings accruing to his stock, based on past dividend payout percentages.

Following the same procedures for Winnebago and Almadén, their growth ratios over the past few years under both definitions are:

	Productivity Growth, After Eliminating Minimum Earnings of 10% on New Capital Invested During Period	Growth, Including Earnings on New Capital Obtained Through Retained Income
Winnebago		
Year Feb. 26, 1972—EPS	$1.12	$1.12
Capital increase—		
Feb. 26, 1972— equity	$60.0 million	
Feb. 26, 1966— equity	2.5 million	
Increase	$57.5 million	
10% earnings	$5.75 million	
Per share (12.6 million shares)	.45	
Balance—1972—EPS	$ .67	
Year Feb. 26, 1967—EPS	.11	.11
Compounded annual growth including inflation additions	44%	59%
Almadén		
1971—EPS	$ .46	$ .46
Capital increase—		
Dec. 31, 1971— equity	$25.3 million	
Dec. 31, 1967— equity	14.9 million	
Increase	$10.4 million	
10% earnings	$1.04 million	
Per share (8.4 million shares)	.13	
Balance—1971—EPS	$ .33	
1968—EPS	.19	.19
Compound annual growth including inflation additions	20%	34%

The components of the present market price of both Winnebago and Almadén, assuming past growth (excluding minimum earnings on new capital), would be explained to a new investor as follows:

BREAKDOWN ANALYSIS OF MARKET PRICE

Year (1)	Earnings Per Share With Compounded Growth (2)	Earnings Increase Each Year (3)	Value of Earnings at Date Achieved on 10% Return Basis (Earnings x 10) (4)	Percentage Representing Present Value (5)	Present Value (Col. 4 x 5) (6)	Value of Present and Future Earnings Included in Present Market Price of Stock	
						Amount (7)	Percent of Total Price (8)
WINNEBAGO:							
Based on 44% actual growth (excluding new capital retained earnings)—1967-1972 (5 years)							
(Feb. 26, 1972)	$ 1.12	$ —	$11.20	100%	$11.20	$11.20	43.9%
Next—							
1	1.61	.49	4.90	91	4.46	4.46	17.5
2	2.32	.71	7.10	83	5.89	5.89	23.1
3	3.34	1.02	10.20	75	7.65	3.95	15.5
				Present market price—per share		$25.50	100.0%
				P/E ratio		23	
ALMADÉN:							
Based on 20% actual growth (excluding new capital retained earnings)—1968-1971 (3 years)							
Year (1971)	$ .46	$ —	$ 4.60	100%	$ 4.60	$ 4.60	15.3%
Next—							
1	.55	.09	.90	91	.82	.82	2.7
2	.66	.11	1.10	83	.91	.91	3.1
3	.79	.13	1.30	75	.98	.98	
4	.95	.16	1.60	68	1.09	1.09	
5	1.14	.19	1.90	62	1.18	1.18	
6	1.37	.23	2.30	56	1.29	1.29	
7	1.65	.28	2.80	51	1.43	1.43	
8	1.98	.33	3.30	47	1.55	1.55	
9	2.37	.39	3.90	42	1.64	1.64	
10	2.85	.48	4.80	39	1.87	1.87	78.9
11	3.42	.57	5.70	35	2.00	2.00	
12	4.10	.68	6.80	32	2.18	2.18	
13	4.92	.82	8.20	29	2.38	2.38	
14	5.90	.98	9.80	26	2.55	2.55	
15	7.08	1.18	11.80	24	2.83	2.83	
16	8.50	1.42	14.20	22	3.12	.70	
17	10.20	1.70	17.00	20	3.40	—	
				Present market price		$30.00	100.0%
				P/E ratio		65	

170

P/E ratio tables may be compiled to show an investor the components he pays for in a stock price more scientifically than has been done herein for illustrative purposes. The fixed 10% rule-of-thumb measurement of earnings required on constant no-growth profit flow can be adjusted upward to any percentage wanted. It is difficult to visualize a downward evaluation (excluding inflation), however, as long as debt rates are in the 7% to 8% range.

An illustration of a P/E ratio table comparable to a compound interest table would appear like the table shown on page 172.

From such a table (accurately prepared, based on specifically defined terms), an investor can focus his sights on P/E ratios resulting from specific years of future growth at specific rates.

A P/E ratio of 17 (Dow-Jones average) for a stock with an anticipated compounded annual growth of 5% would include the present value of that growth for the next 26 years, with a 10% compounded annual growth, for the next 8 years, etc. If an investor decided he is willing to pay a price for stock that includes five years of anticipated future growth of 8% per annum, he should buy at a price equal to 13½ times earnings.

Stock market prices, as illustrated on previous pages, on which P/E ratios are based include a component representing future growth and a component applicable to present earnings. From these analyses, it is readily apparent that many stocks are priced today at amounts that include future growth for periods that bridge customary market turndowns.

It is also readily apparent that, when economic turndowns occur, the forward inclusion of growth in present prices is shortened. When such turndowns occur, the forward pricing period is bound to be regarded as too great, thus accounting for substantially lower market prices.

The forward pricing element included in current market prices is so great a proportion of the total price that the public investor needs disclosure of it and help in understanding it if he is to be factually protected as contemplated by the Securities Acts. Except in instances of very high growth rates contemplated over short periods of time, generally applicable to new companies and new developments, an earnings forecast for one year has dubious value and results in undue concentration on a factor of small importance.

What the SEC, management and public accountant should do to assist the public investor in forecasting where he is most vulnerable

The SEC's desire to assist the public investor in the forecasting that he must do and for which he, the investor, is solely responsible should not and cannot be cast aside. But to assist him with data, even if given on *good authority* at great cost, that provides him assistance on only a small portion of the total purchase price of his stock, is like giving a thirsty man a single drop of water. The SEC, corporate managements, public accountants and particularly the financial analysts should combine their talents to provide help to the public investor where he needs it most. The information they should disclose should help the investor understand how much growth he is paying for and the basis on which he is paying for it. Each entity can play the following vital roles in this important quest:

(a) The SEC is the only authority that can define compounded annual growth so that people who deal with public investors use the term in a consistent manner. In defining compounded annual growth, the SEC should give careful attention to measurement of the inflation factor and to the practice of including the value of a stockholder's own earnings retained, to obtain additional capital as a growth element.

171

P/E RATIO TABLE—BASED ON CONTINUOUS FLOW OF EQUITY EARNINGS VALUED AT 10% PER ANNUM

Applicable P/E Ratio for an Excepted Annual Compounded Growth Rate* of

Number of Future Years' Growth Buyer Is Willing to Pay for in One Share of Stock (1)	1% (2)	2% (3)	3% (5)	4% (5)	5% (6)	6% (7)	7% (8)	8% (9)	9% (10)	10% (11)	12% (12)	14% (13)	15% (14)	16% (15)	18% (16)	20% (17)	25% (18)
1	10.1	10.2	10.3	10.4	10.5	10.5	10.6	10.7	10.8	11	11	11	11	11	12	12	12
2	10.2	10.3	10.5	10.7	10.9	11.0	11.2	11.5	11.7	12	12	13	13	13	13	14	15●
3	10.2	10.5	10.7	11.0	11.3	11.6	11.7	12.2	12.5	13	13	14	14	15	15	16●	18●
4	10.3	10.6	11.0	11.3	11.7	12.0	12.4	12.8	13.2	14	14	15	16	16●	17●	18●	21
5	10.3	10.8	11.2	11.7	12.1	12.5	13.0	13.5	14.0	15	16	17●	17●	18●	19	21	25
6	10.4	10.9	11.4	11.9	12.4	13.0	13.6	14.2	14.8	15	17●	18	19	20	22	24	29
7	10.5	11.0	11.6	12.2	12.8	13.4	14.1	14.8	15.6	16	18	20	21	22	24	27	34
8	10.5	11.1	11.8	12.4	13.1	13.8	14.6	15.5	16.3	17●	19	22	23	24	27	30	40
9	10.6	11.2	11.9	12.6	13.4	14.2	15.1	16.1	17.1●	18	21	23	25	26	30	34	46
10	10.6	11.3	12.1	12.8	13.7	14.6	15.7	16.7	17.8	19	22	25	27	29	33	38	53
11	10.7	11.3	12.2	13.0	14.0	15.0	16.1●	17.3●	18.6	20	23	27	29	31	36	42	61
12	10.7	11.4	12.4	13.2	14.3	15.3	16.6	17.9	19.3	21	24	29	31	34	40	47	71
13	10.8	11.4	12.5	13.4	14.6	15.7	17.1●	18.5	20.0	22	26	31	33	37	43	52	81
14	10.8	11.5	12.6	13.6	14.8	16.0	17.5	19.1	20.7	23	27	33	36	39	47	58	93
15	10.8	11.6	12.7	13.8	15.0	16.4	17.9	19.6	21.5	24	29	35	38	42	52	64	107
16	10.8	11.6	12.8	13.9	15.3	16.7	18.4	20.2	22.2	25	30	37	41	46	57	70	122
17	10.8	11.7	12.9	14.1	15.5	17.0●	18.8	20.7	22.9	25	31	39	44	49	62	78	140
18	10.9	11.7	13.0	14.2	15.7	17.3	19.2	21.3	23.6	26	33	42	47	53	67	86	160
19	10.9	11.8	13.0	14.4	15.9	17.6	19.6	21.8	24.3	27	34	44	50	55	73	94	182
20	10.9	11.8	13.1	14.5	16.1	17.8	19.9	22.3	25.0	28	36	46	53	59	79	104	208
21	10.9	11.9	13.2	14.6	16.3	18.1	20.3	22.8	25.7	29	38	49	56	64	86	115	239
22	10.9	11.9	13.3	14.7	16.4	18.4	20.6	23.3	26.3	30	39	52	60	68	93	126	271
23	11.0	11.9	13.3	14.8	16.6	18.6	21.0	23.8	27.0	31	41	55	63	73	100	138	308
24	11.0	12.0	13.4	14.9	16.7	18.8	21.3	24.2	27.6	32	42	57	67	78	108	151	351
25	11.0	12.0	13.4	15.0	16.9	19.1	21.6	24.7	28.3	33	44	60	71	83	117	165	398
26	11.0	12.0	13.5	15.1	17.0●	19.3	21.9	25.1	28.9	34	46	63	75	88	126	181	451
27	11.0	12.0	13.5	15.2	17.2	19.5	22.3	25.6	29.6	35	48	67	80	94	137	199	517
28	11.0	12.1	13.6	15.3	17.3	19.7	22.6	26.1	30.2	35	49	70	84	100	148	218	590
29	11.0	12.1	13.6	15.3	17.4	19.9	22.9	26.5	30.9	36	51	74	89	107	161	241	680
30	11.0	12.1	13.7	15.4	17.6	20.1	23.2	27.0	31.6	37	53	78	95	114	174	265	777

*Excluding a deduction for inflation which has in the past averaged 3% per annum. In order for a stock to maintain dollar value at date of purchase, a growth rate of 3% is required to break even.

●17 times Dow-Jones average P/E ratio—November 1972.

(b) Managements should be required to provide, and public accountants should be required to verify, along with EPS, the growth factor (as defined by SEC) for the last five- and two-year periods so that an investor has a starting point with which to ask brokers to reconcile their projected growth rates.

(c) Managements can then state in their reports the annual growth rate sought and planned for in relation to their experienced growth rate.

(d) Brokers and analysts (1) can speculate on any different future growth rate that they may deem to be in the cards, providing they compare such speculation with the actual growth rate as appearing in annual reports and that prophesied by management, (2) can demonstrate how many years of future growth at present value they recommend be included in the current market price of stock, and why, and

(3) can indicate the resulting P/E ratio.

Each entity thus properly uses its own expertise to help the public investor and to state clearly wherein the public investor is taking his own risks. Suitable forms could be prepared for a broker to advise every investor of the components of the purchase price at which he has elected to buy or sell. Tables for this purpose could be at every person's fingertips.

With such opportunities to communicate honestly and fairly with the public investor, why spend time and effort producing an earnings forecast for which no one will claim paternity and which everyone must disclaim? Why assist an investor on a negligible part of the money he puts at risk? Instead, with less effort and more clarity and simplicity, the investor can be assisted handsomely with data about the price of growth, the factor that means major *gain* or *loss* to him.

"PROJECTED INCOME AND CASH FLOW   1

Set out below is a copy of a report dated April 28, 1970, from Certified   2
Public Accountants to the directors of the Company   3

The Company believes that the information supplied to Certified Public   4
Accountants referred to below has been compiled on a proper basis but   5
neither the Company nor Certified Public Accountants undertakes any legal   6
responsibility for deviation from the projections which may occur or for the   7
accuracy thereof.   8

The Company presently believes that, if prevailing financial conditions   9
continue and if the Company achieves the projected income and cash flow,   10
the cash flow deficit which would arise on the basis of those projections in   11
the Company's fiscal years ending June 30, 1971, 1972 and 1973 could   12
be met on acceptable commercial terms by a public offering of shares or   13
other securities or from bank loans. No provision has been made in the   14
projections for such offering or loans or the related expenses or interest   15
however and there can be no assurance at this time that the funds required   16
will be available to the Company.   17

The Board of Directors,   18
The First Artists Production Company, Ltd.:   19

In accordance with your instructions, we have prepared Statements   20
of Projected Income and Cash Flow for The First Artists Production   21
Company, Ltd. (the 'Company') for the five years ending June 30, 1974   22
(Exhibits A and B appended hereto).   23

The aforementioned statements were prepared in connection with a   24
proposed sale of the Company's Subordinated Notes and shares of Capital   25
Stock, which are not being offered in the United States, its territories or   26
possessions or to nationals or residents thereof, or in Canada.   27

In preparing and furnishing the Statements of Projected Income and   28
Cash Flow, we have been informed by the Company and its legal counsel   29
of the pertinent sections of the various agreements among the Company and   30
Paul Newman, Sidney Poitier, Barbra Streisand, Creative Management   31

32 Associates, Inc., National General Pictures Corporation and certain other
33 parties from which we have extracted the following relevant information:

34 (1) Initial capitalisation of the Company consisted of the sale of
35   430,000 shares of Class A Stock for $215,000.

36 (2) Each of the three Artists (Paul Newman, Sidney Poitier and
37   Barbra Streisand), through his or her own production entity or
38   company (the 'Producer'), has entered into a Production Agree-
39   ment with the Company pursuant to which the Producer has
40   undertaken to produce and deliver to the Company, no later than
41   December 15, 1976, three feature-length motion pictures starring
42   the Artist in the principal role. Barbra Streisand and Paul Newman
43   must deliver their first pictures by December 15, 1973; Sidney
44   Poitier's first picture must be delivered by December 15, 1974.
45   The maximum budgeted cost of each picture under the Production
46   Agreement may not exceed $3,000,000 except that a musical
47   production may be budgeted at no more than $5,000,000. Each
48   picture will be financed by advances from the Company to the
49   Producer, secured by all the Producer's rights in and to the picture,
50   and will be evidenced by the Producer's interest-bearing demand
51   note.

52 (3) The distributor of the motion pictures will be National General
53   Pictures Corporation ('National General'), which upon delivery
54   of a picture will advance to the Company an amount equal to
55   two-thirds of the budgeted cost of the picture, but not exceeding
56      $2,000,000 (or $3,333,333 if the picture is a musical production).
57   Assuming the picture is completed within its budgeted cost, the
58   allocation of gross revenues will principally be:

59   (a) National General will receive an aggregate distribution fee,
60   which will vary according to source of receipts from 10 per-
61   cent to 35 percent;

62   (b) A portion of the distribution fee, ranging from 2½ percent
63   to 10 percent, will be allocated to the Company;

64   (c) The Producer will then be entitled to receive 10 percent of
65   the gross revenue;

(*d*) National General will recoup its distribution expenses;   66

(*e*) National General will be entitled to $1,000,000 against its   67
advance;   68

(*f*) The Company will recoup up to $1,000,000 of its advance   69
in the same ratio that its net advance (after subtracting   70
National General's advance) bears to National General's   71
advance; and   72

(*g*) The amount remaining of advances by National General and   73
the Company shall be recouped *pari passu,* as in (*e*) and (*f*)   74
above. The remaining amounts, the net receipts, are to be   75
divided one-third each to the Company, the Producer and   76
National General.   77

(4) The Producer of each picture will be permitted to expend prior to   78
commencement of principal photography of up to $250,000 per   79
picture for 'pre-production' costs.   80

We have consulted with Mr. Freddie Fields, President of Creative   81
Management Associates, Inc., which company is a stockholder of the   82
Company, concerning his knowledge of the various agreements and his   83
experience and background in the motion picture industry. Mr. Fields has   84
advised that it is not possible to project the future revenues to be derived   85
from a motion picture, but based upon his experience, his knowledge of the   86
prior pictures in which the Artists have starred and his familiarity with the   87
affairs and proposed business operations of the Company, he has furnished   88
us the following assumptions (the validity or underlying computation of   89
which we have not attempted to verify) which he believes are reasonable   90
for use in connection with the preparation of the Statements of Projected   91
Income and Cash Flow: 92

(1) In line with maintaining cost controls and limiting expenses, and   93
assuming that the Company does not establish a substantial   94
corporate organisation, the operating costs of the Company should   95

96 be approximately $150,000 for the year commencing July 1, 1970
97 and approximately $200,000 per year thereafter.

98 (2) The estimated production schedule for the first six of the nine
99 motion pictures contemplated by the Company, and the estimated
100 worldwide theatrical gross revenues to be derived therefrom, should
101 be as follows:

102 103 Picture	Date of			103 Estimated	Estimated worldwide
104 No. Commence-				completed	theatrical
105 ment	Completion	Release		cost	gross revenue
106 1 Nov. 1, 1970	Aug. 1, 1971	Nov. 1, 1971		$3,000,000	$12,500,000
107 2 Jan. 1, 1971	Oct. 1, 1971	Feb. 1, 1972		3,000,000	12,500,000
108 3 Apr. 1, 1971	Jan. 1, 1972	Apr. 1, 1972		3,000,000	12,500,000
109 4 Jan. 1, 1972	Oct. 1, 1972	Feb. 1, 1973		5,000,000	20,000,000
110 5 Jan. 1, 1972	Oct. 1, 1972	Feb. 1, 1973		3,000,000	12,500,000
111 6 Apr. 1, 1972	Jan. 1, 1973	Apr. 1, 1973		3,000,000	12,500,000

112 (3) The estimated flow of revenues for each of such motion pictures
113 should be as follows:

114 Period	Percentage
115 During first six months of release	40
116 During second six months of release	30
117 During third six months of release	15
118 During fourth six months of release	10
119 During fifth six months of release	5

120 (4) The estimated average share of the worldwide distribution fee
121 applicable to each such motion picture should be 25 percent to
122 National General and 9½ percent to the Company.

123 (5) The distribution expenses of National General should approximate
124 $1,000,000 for a $3,000,000 picture and $1,500,000 for a
125 $5,000,000 picture.

126 We have made the following assumptions in the preparation of the
127 Statements:

128 (1) For purposes of computing the picture amortization for the Com-
129 pany, it is assumed that the income flow will be even on a monthly

basis during each of the six-month periods and both the Company's 130
participation in gross revenues and profit participation bear amorti- 131
zation expense. Income from television and other sources has not 132
been taken into consideration and the Company's entire picture 133
investment is amortized from theatrical income. 134

(2) National General will remit to the Company the amounts shown as 135
due on its monthly reports approximately ninety days after render- 136
ing such reports. 137

(3) Any fees received by the Company for services rendered to each 138
production will be offset by costs of a similar amount and, there- 139
fore, will not result in any income to the Company. 140

(4) No interest expense has been computed on amounts of bank 141
borrowings that will be necessary to complete the production 142
schedule, and no interest income or loss has been considered on 143
the advances made for each production. 144

(5) The Company will receive on May 15, 1970 approximately 145
$3,000,000 from the proceeds of the proposed sale of Subordinated 146
Notes and Capital Stock. The Notes will bear interest from 147
May 15, 1970 at the rate of 7 percent per annum payable 148
annually. Should the net proceeds from the aforementioned sale be 149
less than $3,000,000, it is assumed that such deficiency will be 150
offset from the amounts available from the initial capitalization sale. 151
The Company will exercise its option to add interest to principal 152
and interest will be paid (or will accrue) on such accrued interest. 153
The Company will apply to the *pro rata* repayment of each Note 154
an amount equal to 20 percent of the net income of the Company 155
after provision for taxes as determined in accordance with generally 156
accepted accounting principles, plus amounts taken in each year 157
for amortization and depreciation of motion pictures (but not in 158
excess of net revenues derived therefrom after deduction of partici- 159
pations therein) less any increases during each year in the invest- 160
ment of the Company and its consolidated subsidiaries in inventory. 161

162   The accompanying Statements of Projected Income and Cash Flow for
163   the five years ending June 30, 1974 have been prepared using the afore-
164   mentioned information supplied to us and the assumptions indicated. We
165   believe that the assumptions and the methodology employed constitute reason-
166   able bases for the preparation of the Statements of Projected Income and
167   Cash Flow for The First Artists Production Company, Ltd. for the five years
168   ending June 30, 1974. However, because any forecast of future events is
169   necessarily subject to uncertainties, we cannot represent these projections
170   as specific results which will actually be achieved.

171   CERTIFIED PUBLIC ACCOUNTANTS
172   New York, N.Y.
173   April 28, 1970.

THE FIRST ARTISTS PRODUCTION COMPANY, LTD.   174

Exhibit A   175

STATEMENT OF PROJECTED INCOME   176

FIVE YEARS ENDING JUNE 30, 1974   177

| | Year ending June 30 | | | | | | 178 |
	1970	1971	1972	1973	1974		179
Share of film rentals.....................	$ —	$ —	$2,230,700	$7,576,275	$8,625,475		180
Costs and expenses:—							181
Amortization of motion picture invest-							182
ments	—	—	704,500	2,412,900	2,767,400		183
Operating costs	215,000	150,000	200,000	200,000	200,000		184
	215,000	150,000	904,500	2,612,900	2,967,400		185
Projected income (loss) before							186
interest and income taxes......	(215,000)	(150,000)	1,326,200	4,963,375	5,658,075		187
Interest expense accrued on 7 percent							188
Subordinated Notes	26,250	211,838	226,666	242,533	151,305		189
Projected income (loss) before							190
income taxes	(241,250)	(361,838)	1,099,534	4,720,842	5,506,770		191
Provision for (recovery of) income taxes...	(125,450)	(188,156)	571,758	2,454,838	2,863,520		192
Projected net income (loss)......	$(115,800)	$(173,682)	$ 527,776	$2,266,004	$2,643,250		193

This statement has been prepared on the basis of information as de-   194
scribed in the accompanying report dated April 28, 1970. Because any   195
forecast of future events is necessarily subject to uncertainties, the Company   196
and Certified Public Accountants cannot represent these projections as   197
specific results which will actually be achieved.   198

199   **THE FIRST ARTISTS PRODUCTION COMPANY, LTD.**

200   *Exhibit B*

201   STATEMENT OF PROJECTED CASH FLOW

202   FIVE YEARS ENDING JUNE 30, 1974

		Year ending June 30			
	1970	1971	1972	1973	1974
205 Source of funds:—					
206 Initial capitalization	$ 215,000	$ —	$ —	$ —	$ —
207/208 Private placement of 7 percent Subordinated Notes	3,000,000	—	—	—	—
209 Share of film rentals	—	—	1,191,350	6,593,163	9,146,450
210/211 National General reimbursement of two-thirds of negative costs	—	—	6,000,000	7,300,000	—
212	3,215,000	—	7,191,350	13,893,163	9,146,450
213 Application of funds:—					
214 Operating expenses	215,000	150,000	200,000	200,000	200,000
215 Income taxes	—	—	258,152	2,454,838	2,863,520
216 Investment in motion pictures—					
217 Preproduction cost	—	750,000	750,000	—	—
218 Production cost	—	5,150,000	9,100,000	4,250,000	—
219/220/221 Total application of funds before 7 percent Subordinated Notes sinking fund payments	215,000	6,050,000	10,308,152	6,904,838	3,063,520
222/223/224 Projected net increase (decrease) in cash before 7 percent Subordinated Notes sinking fund payment	3,000,000	(6,050,000)	(3,116,802)	6,988,325	6,082,930
225/226 7 percent Subordinated Notes sinking fund payments, applied to:—					
227 Interest	—	—	—	707,287	151,305
228 Principal	—	—	—	838,500	930,825
229	—	—	—	1,545,787	1,082,130
230 Projected net increase (decrease) in cash	3,000,000	(6,050,000)	(3,116,802)	5,442,538	5,000,800
231/232 Cash balance (deficit) at beginning of year	—	3,000,000	(3,050,000)	(6,166,802)	(724,264)
233 Cash balance (deficit) at end of year ..	$ 3,000,000	$(3,050,000)	$(6,166,802)	$ (724,264)	$ 4,276,536

234   This Statement has been prepared on the basis of information as de-
235 scribed in the accompanying report dated April 28, 1970. Because any
236 forecast of future events is necessarily subject to uncertainties, the Company
237 and Certified Public Accountants cannot represent these projections as
238 specific results which will actually be achieved.

MISCELLANEOUS 239

U.K. Exchange Control 240

All necessary consents under the United Kingdom Exchange Control 241
Act, 1947 have been given for the issue in London of the Notes and the 242
60,000 European Shares offered for sale by the Company. 243

Over-the-counter market 244

L. M. Rosenthal & Company S.A. intends to arrange to have an 245
over-the-counter market maintained in Europe for the Notes and the 246
European Shares. 247

Taxation—U.S. 248

Interest and dividends paid by the Company to persons who are non- 249
resident aliens as to the United States or to foreign corporations will be 250
subject to United States withholding taxes if the recipient does not engage 251
in trade or business in the United States. The basic rate of such taxes is 252
30 percent but lower rates apply in some cases where the United States 253
is party to a tax treaty with the country in which the recipient is a resident. 254
For example, where certain conditions are satisfied: (i) the United States 255
withholding rate on dividends paid to a United Kingdom resident or a Swiss 256
resident is 15 percent; (ii) the United States does not withhold any tax 257
on interest paid to a United Kingdom resident; and (iii) the United States 258
withholds at the rate of 5 percent on interest paid to a Swiss resident. 259

Gain on sale of shares of the Company's Capital Stock will not be 260
subject to United States capital gains taxes provided that the seller is a 261
non-resident alien or a foreign corporation, not engaged in business in the 262
United States, and (i) the sale takes place outside of the United States or 263
(ii) the seller is not present in the United States for periods aggregating 264
183 days during the year of the sale. 265

Under the United States Federal estate tax law, both shares and debt 266
instruments of a domestic corporation are deemed property within the 267
United States and thus may be subject to tax. However, this rule sometimes 268
is modified by treaty—e.g., debt instruments owned by a decedent domiciled 269

270 in the United Kingdom and held outside the United States are not subject
271 to United States estate taxes even if issued by a United States corporation.
272 Also, where shares or debt instruments of a United States corporation are
273 owned and held by a bona fide foreign corporation, a deceased shareholder
274 of the foreign corporation is not required to include such property in his
275 United States taxable estate by reason of his indirect ownership.

276   The Company has agreed with each of the Artists and with CMA to
277 make an election under Section 341 (*f*) of the U.S. Internal Revenue Code.
278 The purpose of such an election would be to ensure that gain on sales of
279 the Company's shares by the Artists and by CMA would be taxable under
280 U.S. law at capital gains rates and not at the higher rates applicable to
281 ordinary income. The election is not expected to have any adverse effect
282 on the U.S. tax position of the Company itself or on the U.S. tax position
283 of shareholders of the Company who are not citizens or residents of the
284 United States.

285 *Taxation—general*

286   It is for each purchaser of Notes or European Shares to inform himself
287 about the taxation consequences to him of acquiring and holding the same.

288 *Accountants' consent*

289   Certified Public Accountants have given and have not withdrawn their
290 written consent to the inclusion of their above-quoted report dated April 28,
291 1970 in this Explanatory Memorandum in the form and context in which
292 it is included.

293 *Delivery*

294   Definitive Notes (or, in the event of their not being available, scrip
295 certificates exchangeable therefor) and share certificates will be ready for
296 delivery at Arbuthnot Latham & Co. Limited, 37, Queen Street, London,
297 E.C.4, on or about May 5, 1970."

LEONARD SPACEK:
A Man's Contribution to His Profession

A Paper by Gordon I. Umaki,
for an Accounting Research Class,
Bowling Green (Ohio) State University,
February 6, 1972

I. INTRODUCTION

The so-called professions—medicine, law, dentistry—have enjoyed a special status in our society because of the public's deep-seated respect for the services rendered by members of those professions. While public accounting possesses most of the characteristics of the professions, including a technical, specialized body of knowledge, a professional society, a code of ethics, restrictions to entrance based upon competence, it has failed to achieve the public's respect for status as a profession. One only hears reference to the public accounting *profession* by the profession itself. This failure in large measure has been due to a lack of contact between the general public and the public accountant, but the failure cannot be wholly attributable to this factor. The primary factor is the public's lack of confidence in the public accountant's ability or desire to produce financial statements which are fair and unbiased presentations of the entities reported upon. The lack of uniformity and comparability of reporting between entities, the complexity of the presentations, and the reporting of misleading values all serve to confuse not only the general public, but also financial analysts and accountants themselves. It is little wonder that the general public has not had the respect that the profession has had for itself.

There have been few individuals in the profession who have had the ability, prestige, courage, or desire to attempt such a monolithic task as reforming the ills of the accounting profession and none have been completely successful. This paper will attempt to analyze the efforts of one such man, Leonard Spacek, to encourage progress in the development of accounting's potential contribution to society. While Spacek has not been successful in achieving some of the specific reforms he has recommended, he has been quite successful in forcing the profession, first, to recognize that a problem exists and, second, to initiate measures designed to remedy the problem. Following a brief biographical sketch, the paper will discuss in detail, in Part II, Spacek's role as a catalyst in the profession's theory development; Part III, his major contributions of original thought. The paper will conclude with Part IV, a presentation of Spacek's philosophy of accounting, and Part V, an overall assessment of Spacek's contribution.

Biographical sketch

Leonard Spacek was born in Cedar Rapids, Iowa in 1907, the second son of a poor farmer. He worked at odd jobs to supplement the family's meager income and at seventeen he took a job in the accounting department of the Iowa Electric Light and Power Co. During his four years with the company, he became interested in the work of the company's independent auditors, Arthur Andersen & Co., and in 1928 at the age of twenty-one and without a college degree, he joined Arthur Andersen. Six years later he became a manager and at the age of thirty-two was made a partner.

Upon the death of the founder, Arthur Andersen, in 1947, he was elected managing partner of the firm at the age of thirty-nine and did not relinquish the position until 1963 when he became Chairman of the firm to relieve him of operational duties and allow him more time to devote himself to reform in the profession.[1]

Spacek's prestigious position as head of the second largest public accounting firm in the country[2] provided him with an opportunity to make his views known on a wide scale and an assurance that his views would be taken seriously. Between 1956 and 1971, he made more than 200 speeches before influential professional, academic, and business groups across the country. He also served on the Accounting Principles Board (APB) from its inception in 1959 until 1963.

II. ROLE AS A CATALYST IN THE DEVELOPMENT OF ACCOUNTING PRINCIPLES

Spacek's principal achievement has been his role as a catalyst in prodding the profession to action. He has convincingly argued that the profession must adopt a consistent and cohesive body of principles on the basis of reason and not expediency or general acceptance. He argues that professional practice is replete with examples of conflicting theory and misleading presentations which can only serve to diminish the user's respect for accounting presentations and accounting's service to the public.

Spacek's criticism of the profession can be categorized as follows: A) profession's failure to define the objectives of accounting; B) profession's failure to develop guidelines or principles which are based upon logic and reasoned consideration; C) criticism of specific practices; and, D) failure of the APB as an authoritative body. Each of these criticisms and an opinion as to the validity of the arguments will be discussed in the following sections.

II. A. *Failure to define objectives*

Spacek argues that all accounting theory and practice should be founded upon, and logically consistent with, the objectives of accounting. His reasoning and conclusion seem to be obvious and should hardly require argument and yet the AICPA until recently (1971) with the formation of the Trueblood Commission has never been actively concerned with definition of the objectives of its art.

While he was a member of the Accounting Principles Board, Spacek stated:

"The differences in views now arise from the omission of a controlling point which this Board [APB] has been unable or unwilling to understand —namely, agreement on the premise or objective of all accounting postulates and principles.[3] (1961)

"Everyone is willing to talk about accounting principles and to agree that they should meet the objectives of accounting. But no one has come forth with a statement effectively supported by logic and sound reasoning as to what the objectives of accounting really are; actually, no one knows. It is obvious that the accounting profession can get nowhere until we know our destination and our purpose."[4] (1962)

It is indeed a sad but true commentary that for five centuries since the development of double-entry accounting the profession has not been able to define its purpose. Hopefully, the Trueblood Commission will be successful in its charge, although the ob-

---

[1] Arthur Andersen & Co., *The First Fifty Years: 1913-1963* (Chicago: Arthur Andersen & Co., 1963), pp. 55-58.

[2] Arthur Louis, "A Fat Maverick Stirs Up the Accounting Profession," *Fortune,* LXXXII (December 1970), p. 98.

[3] Leonard Spacek, "Views of Leonard Spacek on 'Differences of Opinion Arising from Research Projects'," *A Search for Fairness* (Chicago: Arthur Andersen & Co., 1969), p. 515.

[4] Spacek, "The Accounting Football," *ibid.,* p. 89.

stacles are formidable judging from the profession's past inertia.

It is Spacek's contention that the overriding objective of accounting is the presentation of financial information which is "fair" to all segments of the users of the information. The presentations must be "fair" to management, investors, creditors, labor, consumers, and governmental agencies and should not be biased to favor the interests of any segment to the detriment of another segment.

Of course, the basic criticism of Spacek's "fairness" objective is that it is subjective and cannot be readily defined. Spacek admits this.[5] He himself does not offer a specific definition for "fairness," for apparently he realizes that no single person could define what constitutes "fairness" and that the concept of "fairness" must be the product of the views of society as a whole and subject to change as the views of society change. Thus, Spacek considers the subjective and undefinable nature of "fairness" as an asset in that the concept of "fairness" is determined by society, not by accountants themselves and is flexible with the changes in society. This is implied in his statement of the definition of professional accounting:

> "[Professional accounting] is the process of analyzing and evaluating a multitude of transactions with the objective of testing the ·truthfulness of statements of accountability. These tests are conducted according to the moral and legal standards of fairness as set by the public. The accountant does not .set standards of accountability. [He] interprets them into principles of recording business transactions which are recorded according to the standards of conduct set by the public."[6] (1956)

However, the views of society with respect to "fairness" must be determined, in order for the "fairness" objective to be a viable one. He leaves this vital function to his proposed accounting court which will be discussed in a later section.

II. B. Failure to develop principles based on logic

Spacek's second major criticism of the accounting profession is closely related to its failure to define objectives. Since the profession does not specifically know its objectives, the so-called principles of accounting have not developed as a cohesive body of theory, but rather as a patchwork of tradition and expedience. Says Spacek:

> "The so-called accounting principles followed in preparing accounting reports to the public constitute a hodgepodge of intrenched traditional practices. They have few, if any, objective standards and they have grown up and gained authority largely by precedent and tradition, while purposes for which the reports are now used have made obsolete the reason for the original adoption of the principles."[7] (1959)

In addition, Spacek argues that the test of an accounting principle lies not in its general acceptance *per se,* as the AICPA would seem to advocate, but in its reasoning and logic:

> "It is not as important that an accounting principle is· accepted as it is to state *why* it is accepted. If our firm · accepts a so-called accounting principle or practice we cannot support, just because other firms accept it, then you might ask each of the other firms why they accept it; you would find that their answers in turn would be because we and other firms had accepted it.

---

[5] Spacek, "Presentation on Accounting Principles," *ibid.,* p. 202.

[6] Spacek, "The Elusive Truth of Business Profits," *ibid.,* p. 10.

[7] Spacek, "Business Success Requires an Understanding of Unsolved Problems of Accounting," *ibid.,* p. 129.

Does this make it an accepted principle of accounting?[8] (1961)

" 'Acceptance' is not the standard of proper accounting; the test is 'why' the accounting is accepted."[9] (1962)

As a result of the profession's failure to define its objectives and then to rigorously test accounting principles on the basis of sound reasoning in the light of the objectives, the profession, Spacek argues, has allowed, even promoted, the use of alternative accounting methods for recording and reporting the same transaction. Thus, financial statement presentations based upon alternative reporting practices are not comparable. Conversions to make them comparable, if the reader is aware of the lack of comparability, can be difficult or impossible from the information given. Spacek contends that readers have the right to assume that "the correct method of recording a transaction was followed and that corresponding transactions are handled the same way by all companies."[10] He is thus of the opinion that, for a given set of circumstances, there is only one method of reporting a transaction.

Further, he contends that the public accountant, in attesting to the fairness of the financial statements, should be required to state in his opinion not only that the statements are presented in accordance with generally accepted accounting principles, but also that the statements were prepared in accordance with the generally accepted accounting principles *considered appropriate under the circumstances.*[11] He believes that this modification of the audit opinion would aid in reducing the number of alternative accounting practices used by placing the burden on the auditor to be able to justify the appropriateness of the accounting methods.

It is clear that Spacek does not advocate complete uniformity, i.e., only one way of recording a transaction regardless of circumstances. He does, however, believe that the accounting method chosen among acceptable alternatives should be based upon logic and fairness of presentation rather than upon the effects on income and that the auditor should be prepared to demonstrate the appropriateness of the method to which he attests.

II. C. Criticism of specific practices

Spacek has been critical of a variety of existing accounting practices, the major ones being (1) failure to recognize the effect of changing price levels, (2) failure to require recognition of all long-term, non-cancelable leases, (3) failure to require provision for deferred Federal income taxes, and (4) failure to require allocation of the investment tax credit. Discussion of these criticisms will be limited to a brief review of the Spacek position, for the arguments do not appear to be original but they do give insight into his philosophy.

II. C.(1) Price-level accounting

Failure of the profession to recognize the effects of price-level changes on the financial statements is regarded by Spacek as one of the greatest deficiencies in reporting to the public and has been the topic of many Spacek speeches. His argument for price-level accounting is essentially the same as that found in the literature (e.g., Henry Sweeney, "Stabilized Accounting")—purchasing power gains and losses are just as real to the investor and the stockholder as a fire loss, operating loss, etc., and as such should be reported on the balance sheet:

"Most business enterprises have had real deterioration in the value of their net current position in terms of purchasing power, even though inventory

---

[8] Spacek, "Accounting Principles are Practical, Not Theoretical," *ibid.,* p. 176.

[9] Spacek, "The Accounting Football," *ibid.,* p. 195.

[10] Spacek, "The Need for an Accounting Court," *ibid.,* p. 30.

[11] *Ibid.,* p. 33.

profits have occurred at times. All cash and other current assets that are affected adversely by inflation result in losses that accountants refuse to recognize. . . . In addition, with relatively few exceptions, we continue in our accounts to provide depreciation on the basis of cost which represents prior years' dollars. . . . The understatement of depreciation results in a material overstatement of profits for most corporations that have substantial amounts of property."[12] (1958)

Spacek would, thus, reflect the change in the purchasing power of the dollar directly in the accounts and not as a supplementary statement to historical cost statements. While APB Statement No. 3 issued June 1969 acknowledges the usefulness of price-level adjusted statements, the Statement does not require price-level presentations and only describes such presentations as supplemental to historical cost presentations.[13]

II. C.(2) Accounting for leases

As far back as 1956, Spacek criticized the profession for its failure to recognize long-term, noncancelable leases as liabilities on the books of the lessee and to be shown on the balance sheet at the discounted present value of the contracted future payments.[14] Spacek was a member of the APB when the Board issued Opinion No. 5 on reporting for lessees, but he was the lone dissenter to the Opinion. The Board was of the opinion (except for Spacek) that long-term, noncancelable leases should be presented as a liability only when the lease contract was in substance a purchase, viz., which met the criteria for a purchase set by the Board. Spacek argues that all long-term, noncancelable leases whether or not a transfer of title is involved should be capitalized at the discounted present value since all such leases represent legal liabilities which have a claim to assets before the claims of shareholders are

satisfied.[15] He argues that lease contracts represent as much an obligation as do long-term payables. Spacek's point is well taken. There is no justifiable reason not to consider all contractual obligations as liabilities on the balance sheet. Simply because a transfer of title to the property is not involved does not make the lessee any less obligated to pay the lessor under the terms of contract. It is still a valid, legal liability and should be reported as such on the balance sheet rather than relegated to footnote status. Of course, a corresponding asset would also be presented representing the lessee's right to use of the property.

II. C.(3) Accounting for deferred Federal income taxes

Spacek has frequently commented upon accounting for the difference between the actual tax liability and the amount provided for as tax expense on the income statement. Prior to the issuance of APB Opinion No. 11, which supported his position, he argued that the profession should require the allocation of Federal income taxes, i.e., that the tax expense should be related to income before taxes and not to the amount of the tax liability. He bases his argument on the assumption that the reduction in the current tax liability due to the privilege granted by law (such as accelerated depreciation for tax purposes but straight line for books) is merely a deferment of the payment for taxes to the government; the reduction is not permanent and will have to be paid in the future.[16] Consequently, the deferred tax is simply a liability and

---

[12] Spacek, "Phantom Profits as Seen by an Accountant," *ibid.,* pp. 100-101.

[13] *APB Accounting Principles: Original Pronouncements as of August 1, 1969,* Volume 2 (Chicago: American Institute of Certified Public Accountants, 1969), p. 9013.

[14] Spacek, "Accounting Has Failed to Prevent Major Misrepresentations," *op. cit.,* p. 7.

[15] *APB Accounting Principles: Original Pronouncements as of August 1, 1969, op. cit.,* p. 6525.

[16] Spacek, "Accounting Is Being Challenged," *op. cit.,* p. 415.

proper matching of expenses to revenues would require that the tax expense for financial statement purposes be related to the pretax income shown on the financial statement. Spacek's view is in essential agreement with the APB view except that he might argue in favor of the liability method rather than the deferral method.

II. C.(4) Accounting for the investment tax credit

The APB's handling of the investment tax credit was an extreme disappointment to Spacek. He served on the Board when both Opinions Nos. 2 and 4 were issued and he fully assented to APB Opinion No. 2 which required the allocation of the investment credit over the life of the asset. The Securities and Exchange Commission (SEC), however, did not agree with the Board and filed Accounting Series Release No. 96 which permitted use of either the method required by Opinion No. 2 or taking the entire credit into income in the year of the asset acquisition.[17] Spacek's dissent to Opinion No. 4, which amended Opinion No. 2 by permitting the use of either method, is worthy of note:

> "He [Spacek] believes this Opinion illustrates the accounting profession's complete failure in its responsibility to establish accounting principles that will provide reliable financial statements that are comparable among companies and industries, for use of the public in making personal investment decisions. He states there is no justification for sanctioning two contradictory practices to accommodate the SEC and other regulatory bodies and some CPAs who have approved reporting the investment credit as, in effect, profit from acquisition rather than from use of the property."[18] (1964)

A third amending opinion regarding the investment credit was in process recently and the speculation was that it would again require allocation of the credit over the life

of the asset acquired. However, this proposed opinion comes into conflict with a Congressional bill, since passed, which requires the SEC to forbid the AICPA from forcing the use of the allocation method.[19] Consideration of the amendment has thus been dropped. Nonetheless, the APB seems to support the Spacek position that allocation should be required.

II. D. Failure of the APB as an authoritative body

Spacek's service on the APB from its inception in 1959 has not prevented him from being extremely critical of the Board as an operating body. He attributes failure of the Board to two reasons: (1) structural deficiencies in the APB, and (2) effects of the Federal regulatory agencies.

II. D.(1) Structural deficiencies in the APB

It is apparent that Spacek, during his tenure on the Board, became frustrated by the Board's inability to develop a consistent, logical body of theory, and he attributes much of the reason for the Board's failure to its structure and mechanism. He has four basic criticisms of the Board's present structure and mechanism: (1) the Board is not independent; (2) lack of an appeal or interpretation mechanism; (3) lack of documentation from which decisions are made; and (4) lack of detail presentation as to why the decision produces fair results.

Spacek's criticism that the APB is not independent is not a new one for him. Even before the formation of the APB, in noting the deficiencies of the Committee on Accounting Procedure, predecessor of the APB, Spacek stated:

> "[The Committee on Accounting Procedure's] members consist primarily

[17] APB Accounting Principles: Original Pronouncements as of August 1, 1969, op. cit., p. 6517.

[18] Ibid., p. 6519.

[19] According to Professor Willard Galliart, Bowling Green State University, History of Accounting Thought, Fall Quarter, 1971.

of practicing members of the profession who, in most cases, should be disqualified from sitting in judgment because they are interested parties. In most cases, practitioners have already made decisions on the point in question for their own client."[20] (1956)

Spacek argues that members of the Board, himself included, cannot be independent unless they completely sever all their previous ties with firms, clients, corporations, or industries. Spacek is undoubtedly correct in this matter. Only by maintaining a full-time Board adequately compensated can the Board make decisions independent (so far as possible) of their past decisions as practicing accountants and independent of the pressures from current and potential clients.

Spacek's second criticism of the structure of the APB is its lack of an adequate procedure for interpretation of the principles set by the Board. Recently, the AICPA has begun issuing interpretations to its more complex Opinions. An interpretation of Opinion No. 15 on earnings per share issued September 1971, covers a full 120 pages and represents an attempt on the part of the AICPA to remedy the deficiency observed by Spacek. Even so, the interpretations are issued at the AICPA's discretion and no set procedure is established for obtaining an interpretation to an Opinion.

Thirdly, Spacek has criticized the lack of documentation of the arguments and facts considered by the Board in issuing an Opinion. He argues (1) that all interested parties within and outside of the membership should file written briefs, held for public record, stating their positions and arguments, and (2) that the Board should only consider the written briefs in coming to a decision.[21] These briefs would indicate the consideration of views by the Board and reduce the possibility of unwritten influence from outside sources.

Spacek's fourth criticism of the APB's

current mechanism and the one he regards as its greatest deficiency is its failure to state in detail the reasoning behind its decisions[22]—why the alternative chosen produces results which are fair. Of course, this failure is directly attributable to the APB's inability to specify the objectives of reporting, which has been discussed previously.

II. D.(2) Effects of the Federal regulatory agencies

Among the problems caused by the failure of the accounting profession to define a structural basis for accounting, according to Spacek, are some of the practices required for reporting purposes by the regulatory agencies such as the Securities and Exchange Commission (SEC) and the Interstate Commerce Commission (ICC). Spacek makes it clear that he does not blame the agencies for the practices they require, for the agencies were not given the leadership they required at the time the reporting practices were decided.[23] The results, Spacek contends, are inconsistent, illogical practices required by the agencies which, because of the passage of time and the regulatory agency structure, are difficult to change, thus retarding the development of accounting principles. Spacek's criticism of some of the practices required by the SEC and the ICC is worthy of note.

Securities and Exchange Commission While the SEC has the power to prescribe all reporting practices to the accounting profession through its power over the reporting of listed corporations and has essentially been benevolent to the profession in assuming a passive role, Spacek contends

---

[20] Spacek, "The Elusive Truth of Business Profits," *op. cit.*, p. 20.

[21] Spacek, "Accounting is Being Challenged," *ibid.*, p. 407.

[22] Spacek, "The Outlook for Eventual Agreement on Accounting Principles," *ibid.*, p. 431.

[23] Spacek, "A Suggested Solution to the Principles Dilemma," *ibid.*, p. 277.

that the SEC's rejection of price-level reporting has acted as a brake on the AICPA's acceptance and requirement of price-level presentations.[24] Spacek acknowledges that the primary share of the blame for failure to accept price-level accounting lies with the accounting profession but, nonetheless, the APB has been and remains intimidated by the opinion of the SEC and will probably never require such statements until the SEC allows them for financial reporting purposes.

In addition, Spacek argues that the SEC, in issuing ASR No. 96, its opinion on APB Opinion No. 2 on the investment credit, "thwarted the efforts of the accounting profession to maintain high-quality standards of accounting in reports to the public."[25]

Interstate Commerce Commission

The ICC reporting requirements represent the most flagrant example of requiring illogical accounting practices at odds with "generally accepted accounting principles." Spacek has persistently criticized the reporting practices prescribed by the ICC for railroads. The ICC requires that railroads charge the cost of replacing rails, ties, roadbeds with like materials directly to expense, even if the useful life of these items extends beyond the current period. Only betterments are capitalized. Thus the railroads have values for track, ties, and roadbeds in their fixed assets accounts from the 1800's, long after these assets have been replaced, and for which no depreciation is reported.[26] Also, by choosing to replace or not to replace worn ties and rails, the railroads have been able to manipulate reported income. In bad years, no ties or rails are replaced, thus boosting income for the period.

Spacek concludes that the Federal agencies are not so much concerned with fair reporting to the public as to protect their individual objectives—the SEC rejects price-level adjustments because of its tendency to revalue asset values upwards, a practice preceding the 1929 crash; the ICC is tradition-bound to its historical position on replacement accounting. Secondly, Spacek

notes that the agencies may be influenced by political and industrial pressure in their decisions. The SEC, for example, could have been influenced by political pressures in rejecting the APB's position regarding the investment credit. Flow-through accounting of the investment credit, the method eliminated by the APB opinion, stimulates income immediately and consequently (1) makes financial reports to the public appear rosier, thus stimulating stock market optimism, and (2) provides stimulus to management to make more investment purchases than under the allocation method required in APB Opinion No. 2. Thus, fair reporting to the public, in Spacek's view, is not the overriding criteria for the Federal regulatory agencies.

In addition, Spacek notes that attempting to secure changes in agency policies or appealing agency decisions is difficult, for only a fraction of the policies of the various agencies are in writing. Rather the agencies specify accounting procedures via individual cases which are not made public.[27] Secondly, appeal of an agency decision to the courts can only be made by the injured party, thus precluding appeal by public accountants.[28] Thirdly, the agencies are presumed by the courts to have expertise in the area administered and have generally refrained from reversing an agency decision unless obviously arbitrary.[29]

III. ORIGINAL CONTRIBUTIONS TO ACCOUNTING THOUGHT

The deficiencies that Spacek sees in the profession and its rule-making body are real for the most part, and he makes a good case for his positions. However, criticism

---

[24] Spacek, "Phantom Profits as Seen by an Accountant," *ibid.*, p. 99.

[25] Spacek, "The Status of 'Generally Accepted Accounting Principles' and Their Meaning to the Public and to the Profession," *ibid.*, p. 527.

[26] Spacek, "Professional Accountants and Their Public Responsibility," *ibid.*, p. 23.

[27] Spacek, "Establishing Accounting Principles," *ibid.*, p. 563.

[28] *Ibid.*

[29] *Ibid.*

per se does not contribute to the development of the profession. He has hoped that his criticism would (1) force the profession to recognize its deficiencies, and (2) provide the impetus to the profession to seek and modify accounting practices in order to provide better service to the public. Spacek has also stated his own recommendations for change. In Part III, Spacek's original contributions to accounting thought will be described and discussed: (A) proposal for the Accounting Court of Accounting Appeals, and (B) accounting for goodwill.

III. A.   The Accounting Court

Spacek's proposal for the establishment of the Accounting Court of Accounting Appeals, which he first formally proposed before the 1957 Convention of the American Accounting Association,[30] stands as a significant contribution to the development of accounting theory. While understandably repugnant to most members of the conservative accounting profession and its rule-making body, then the Committee on Accounting Procedure and now the Accounting Principles Board, the idea and formulation of the Accounting Court was the product of serious consideration of the problems in the profession and the difficulty in obtaining change. The problems Spacek considered have been mentioned briefly in this paper: (1) failure of the accounting profession to develop a sound theoretical structure; (2) failure to eliminate practices which are logically inconsistent with the theoretical structure determined; (3) failure of the Accounting Principles Board as an authoritative body; and (4) detrimental aspects of Federal regulatory agencies in the development of accounting principles.

III. A.(1)   History of the proposed Accounting Court

Spacek first proposed the Accounting Court as an alternative to the Committee on Accounting Procedure (CAP) which he argued (a) had no authority over the profession since no accountant was required to follow its conclusions, (b) was not independent since members did not sever prior employment ties, (c) had not developed "standards of accountability," and (d) did not obtain sufficient documented facts and argument from interested sources in order to make a sound decision.[31]

In December 1957, four months after Spacek's criticism of the CAP and proposal for the Accounting Court, the American Institute formed a committee, which included Leonard Spacek, to determine how accounting principles were to be determined and how adherence to the principles should be secured.[32] The Committee, reporting its results in September 1958, recommended that the Accounting Principles Board be established with a research staff to serve it. Spacek had hopes that the APB would be able to accomplish its objectives, as his service on the Board indicates, but the Board's failure became more and more apparent and, after the Board's reversal of Opinion No. 2 due to SEC pressure, in Opinion No. 4 (1964), and the Board's position on the recognition of leases in Opinion No. 5 (1964) in which he was the lone dissenter, Spacek fell back on his proposal for the establishment of an Accounting Court of Appeals. In 1965, Arthur Andersen & Co., reflecting the views of Spacek, published "Establishing Accounting Principles—A Crisis in Decision-Making," a formal proposal in Congressional bill form for the establishment of the Accounting Court of Accounting Appeals as a separate agency of the executive branch of the Federal government, similar to the United States Tax Court.

---

[30] Spacek, "The Need for an Accounting Court," *ibid.,* p. 27.
[31] Spacek, "The Elusive Truth of Business Profits," *ibid.,* pp. 14-15.
[32] "Report to Council of AICPA of the Special Committee on Research Program," September, 1958 as reproduced in Appendix B in *A Search for Fairness* by Leonard Spacek, *ibid.,* p. 491.

III. A.(2) Structure and jurisdiction of the Court

Spacek conceives of the Court as a legal body whose five judges are appointed by the President and which has "both appellate and limited original jurisdiction" over the Federal regulatory agencies, which already have power to determine accounting principles.[33] Thus, the Court would be obligated only by the "standards" of accounting rules set by the bill in making its decisions but otherwise would have the power to determine accounting rules exemplifying the "standards" set. These "standards" are as follows: (1) accounting rules applicable to financial statements filed with the Federal regulatory agencies "shall be practicable and designed to furnish the agency with such information and data as may reasonably be required by it;"[34] and (2) accounting rules applicable to financial statements for general circulation or listing with the exchanges "shall be in accordance with sound accounting principles and shall be such as will result in financial statements or information which are fairly presented for the use of, and can be relied upon by, such persons."[35]

While the "standards" are broad and the Court's powers in determining rules are sweeping, Spacek attempts to placate anticipated charges that the establishment of the Court would lead to additional governmental control over accounting: "The draft of the Bill would not grant to the Court any jurisdiction over accounting matters which the various agencies do not already have."[36] He also attempts to convince members of the influential APB and members of the AICPA of the continued importance of those organizations:

"The Court would not eliminate the need for, or nullify the efforts of, the APB. Far from taking away from accountants and their professional organization any rights and responsibilities which they now have, the Court could give them additional stature.

Where the agencies frequently are now able to establish accounting practices without a public hearing, and sometimes on an informal basis, the Court would afford accountants with a public forum in which to advance and support their professional reasoning."[37] (1965)

He thus persuasively argues that the Court would give equal weight to the views of professional accountants where now the agencies dominate and appeal is difficult or impossible. He sees the function of the Court as:

"(1) Providing an effective means by which accounting rules prescribed by the various regulatory bodies involved could be reviewed on the record and affirmed, modified, or reversed by a single tribunal, and (2) [permitting] such tribunal, in its discretion, to institute accounting rule-making where an agency improperly refuses to do so. In this way, it would be possible to balance and harmonize the specific requirements of each agency within a unified, consistent pattern of accounting principles and practices."[38] (1965)

As for the procedural mechanism, Spacek's Court would hear at its discretion appeals of agency decisions by any person or corporation subject to the administration of the agencies as well as by those stating opinions of the fairness of financial presentations. The Court would also hear and decide upon petitions for original rule making. In both cases the Court proceedings would be public and fully documented. The reasons for the Court's decisions based

---

[33] Arthur Andersen & Co., "Establishing Accounting Principles—A Crisis in Decision-Making" (Chicago: Arthur Andersen & Co., 1965) as reproduced in *A Search for Fairness* by Leonard Spacek, *ibid.*, p. 571.
[34] *Ibid.*, p. 572.
[35] *Ibid.*
[36] *Ibid.*, p. 573.
[37] *Ibid.*
[38] *Ibid.*

upon fairness to all parties would be clearly indicated.[39]

III. A.(3) Criticism of the Accounting Court proposal

Spacek's proposal has been criticized for two reasons. First, unlike the United States Supreme Court, the Accounting Court would be empowered to carry out all three functions of government—legislative, judicial, and executive—under its jurisdictional powers in the accounting sphere.[40] Critics claim that the Accounting Court would, in effect, legislate the laws of accounting, interpret the laws, and execute the enforcement of the laws—functions which Congress in formulating the Constitution was careful to separate. The criticism that the Accounting Court would both legislate and sit in judgment is a valid one. However, the alternatives are limited. The accounting profession and interested parties have not been able to agree on the fundamental propositions or objectives of accounting. While most accountants would agree that the financial statements must be fair to all interested users, as a group, they have not been able to agree upon the standards which, if diligently followed, would produce the desired fair results. By reducing the number of participants to five, Spacek forces the definition of standards of reporting. Spacek's Court, thus, stands on the competence and independence of the men selected to serve as judges. Spacek's solution, while not ideal, may be the only one in the light of the profession's previous failures. The criticism that the Court would perform the executory function, in addition to the judicial and legislative, does not seem any more justified than the same charge against the United States Supreme Court. Both would sit in judgment of appeals brought before them.

A second criticism of the Accounting Court voiced by Hendriksen is that the tie with the government may lead to "governmental control of the accounting profession with greater rigidity in the interpretation of accounting principles and procedures."[41] Hendriksen, thus, argues that, while a Court of Appeals should be established, it should be a professional body sitting in judgment and interpretation of principles determined by the APB, and not a body with legal power.[42] Spacek's original proposal for the Court in 1957 was of a similar nature, i.e., the Court would be a professional body only.[43] But his views changed when it became apparent that the APB could not function as an authoritative body due to its lack of independence, its cumbersome structural inadequacies, the inertia of the profession in general, and the interference from the regulatory agencies. Thus, he modified his Court to have sweeping powers over the profession and the agencies based upon the simple yet undefinable standard of fairness.

III. A.(4) Summary

Spacek believes that the Accounting Court represents the best alternative in which (1) to develop a consistent, cohesive body of accounting theory across company, industry, and agency lines, (2) to provide a mechanism for appeal and interpretation, (3) to provide a mechanism for the modification and development of new theory, and (4) to provide a means for assuring that financial statements are fair and unbiased to all users.

III. B. Accounting for goodwill

Spacek's second original contribution to accounting thought is his proposal regarding accounting for goodwill. Accounting for

---

[39] *Ibid.,* p. 571.

[40] Professor Willard Galliart, *op. cit.*

[41] Eldon S. Hendriksen, "Toward Greater Comparability through Uniformity of Accounting Principles," *Financial Accounting Theory II: Issues and Controversies,* ed. Thomas F. Keller and Stephen A. Zeff (New York; McGraw-Hill, 1969), p. 170.

[42] *Ibid.,* p. 171.

[43] Spacek, "The Need for an Accounting Court," *op. cit.,* p. 37.

goodwill is an important concept, for the validity of the purchase method of accounting for acquisitions and mergers is founded upon accounting for goodwill. It was precisely for this reason that Accounting Research Study No. 10: "Accounting for Goodwill," by George R. Catlett and Norman O. Olson, was undertaken.[44] The study, published in 1968, caused a considerable uproar in the profession since the authors, both partners in Arthur Andersen & Co., not very surprisingly, endorsed the view of Leonard Spacek, who four years before had presented his position.

III. B.(1) *Criticism of current practice*

Spacek's position is that goodwill, as presently conceived, should not be presented on the balance sheet as an asset. He defines goodwill as:

". . . the present value placed on anticipated future earnings in excess of a reasonable return on the producing assets. Thus, it is the cost to the buyer of earnings over and above the cost of the assets required to produce the earnings."[45]

Present accounting practice records goodwill as an asset which is valued at the excess of the cost of an acquisition over the fair market value of the identifiable assets acquired. Thus, a company acquired for cash through the purchase of stock having a total market value of $100,000 and having identifiable assets with a fair market value of $80,000, would be recorded on the books of the acquired company with $20,000 of goodwill in addition to the value of the assets acquired.

Spacek argues that the balance sheet should show only what he calls "producing assets" less liabilities which are offset by a corresponding amount of stockholder's equity. He defines "producing assets" as those assets, tangible and intangible, which are capable of producing earnings.[46] He contends that the excess of the cost of the acquisition over the fair value of the pro-

ducing assets, which has been labeled goodwill, is not a "producing asset" but merely represents the difference between the public's composite opinion of the value of the corporation and the value of the producing assets.[47] This mere mathematical difference does not produce earnings. Insertion of this element labeled goodwill in the balance sheet, adds the element of investor opinion to a balance sheet which itself may serve to inflate investor opinion of the company. A company, for example, showing a large goodwill value may be erroneously valued more highly than a firm showing no goodwill in the balance sheet even though the latter firm shows other net assets and earning power on a par with the former company. In addition, Spacek argues, the goodwill value presented misleads the user since the value only represents a portion—the purchased goodwill recognized on acquisitions—of the total goodwill which may actually be enjoyed by the consolidated entity.[48]

In addition, Spacek argues that the amortization of goodwill against earnings over an arbitrary period (such as required by APB Opinion No. 17) is misleading to investors since it would lead the unsophisticated user to believe that the goodwill for the entity is actually on the wane when the goodwill of the entity may actually be increasing. The amortization also creates a distortion of income, for the amortization is "in no way related to operations and yet it decreases income in each year of the amortization period."[49]

---

[44]George R. Catlett and Norman Olson, "Accounting for Goodwill" (New York: AICPA, 1968), p. xv.

[45] Spacek, "The Treatment of Goodwill in the Balance Sheet," *op. cit.,* p. 297.

[46] "Letters Discussing the Spacek Proposal," *Financial Accounting Theory II: Issues and Controversies, op. cit.,* p. 341.

[47] *Ibid.*

[48] Spacek, "The Treatment of Goodwill in the Balance Sheet," *op. cit.,* p. 301.

[49] Leonard Spacek, "The Merger Accounting Dilemma—Proposed Solutions," *Financial Executive,* XXXVIII (February 1970), p. 50.

196

III. B.(2) Proposed solution

Spacek's solution to the problem of ac-·counting for goodwill is the immediate charge-off of the excess cost to retained earnings and if necessary to paid-in capital. In Spacek's opinion, the immediate reduction in owner's equity reflects what has actually taken place; a reduction in the stockholders' equity to the value representing the stockholders' interest in its producing assets.[50] The amount of the reduction, i.e., the amount of the excess cost written off, represents advanced distribution of stockholder equity to the stockholders of the acquired entity in anticipation of future excess earnings of the acquired company.[51]

The validity of Spacek's argument lies in what should be presented in the balance sheet and income statement. Spacek argues that (1) the balance sheet should equate producing assets less liabilities with stockholders equity, and (2) the value for goodwill is based upon investor speculation of the actual goodwill value for the company, i.e., its ability to make future excess profit, thus involving circular reasoning and inflating balance sheet values—goodwill and stockholders' equity. The income statement in Spacek's view should only be charged with the costs of producing the income[52] and not the arbitrary allocation to expense of a dubious asset value unrelated to the production of earnings.

III. B.(3) Discussion

Spacek's view, while in conflict with APB Opinion No. 17, which requires that goodwill be carried as an asset and amortized systematically over a period of not more than forty years, has been supported not only by the Catlett and Olson research study but also by Chambers. Chambers contends that the "goodwill of a going concern runs to the constituents, not to the firm" and as such, any amount paid for goodwill to the former owners is their gain and "its effect is in no way to increase the adaptability of the firm."[53] Thus, Chambers

concludes that goodwill should not be recognized as an asset by the consolidated entity but as a reduction in the "amount of the residual equity from the price paid to the current cash equivalent of the new firm's assets and liabilities."

The essential difference between the Spacek view and the view expressed in Opinion No. 17, it seems to the writer, is a difference in the objectives each sees for accounting. The AICPA traditionally has favored accounting for invested cost and allocating such costs to the periods of benefit to determine income. Spacek takes the view that financial statements must be fairly presented so that users will have an indication of the performance and financial position of the firm. Recording goodwill as an asset and amortizing it over an arbitrary period simply misleads the user. Spacek argues that the user should be presented with a picture of (1) the producing assets, both tangible and intangible, (2) liabilities, (3) stockholders' equity in the net producing assets, and (4) a meaningful income figure. From these four items the user should be able to estimate the goodwill value—the ability of the firm to earn a return in excess of a normal rate.

IV. THE SPACEK PHILOSOPHY

Leonard Spacek's philosophy of accounting is sprinkled throughout his many speeches and articles over the years. It is based on concepts of ethics and public service and encompasses not only the business sphere but also our economic system and, even broader, our democratic form of government. The essence of the Spacek philosophy is contained in the following quote:

---

[50] "Letters Discussing the Spacek Proposal," *op. cit.,* p. 345.
[51] Catlett and Olson, *op. cit.,* p. 90.
[52] "Letters Discussing the Spacek Proposal," *op. cit.,* p. 337.
[53] Raymond J. Chambers, *Accounting Evaluation and Economic Behavior* (Englewood Cliffs, N. J.: Prentice-Hall, 1966), p. 211.

"We in the accounting profession constitute one of the most important contributors to the decision-making process in the democratic system in this country. Our work in all of its aspects establishes the source and the basis for disposition of the life blood (economics) to all segments of the people in this country. In the simplest sense, we are the scorekeepers in the game of producing goods and services and the distribution of their value among the various segments of our economy."[54] (1960)

The role of accounting, according to Spacek, is to report the financial transactions affecting economic entities so that the allocation of economic resources based on the presentations is fair to all segments of society. In order to achieve this end, Spacek believes accounting must be completely unbiased to each segment and must present the economic facts in a truthful and meaningful manner.[55]

Spacek's philosophy has led him to a user orientation. What constitutes "fairness" to each segment? What are the segments? How can he best achieve progress toward fairness? Here Spacek turns to his Accounting Court:

"I have found only one small body among all segments of society that was interested in the meaning of the word "fairness" with respect to financial accounting to the various segments of the people. That is the higher courts of our land. And why? Because it is the only spot where the views of all segments are heard and their rights determined—not on the basis of some undemonstrated contradictory set of so-called accepted principles of accounting, but on the basis of the reasoning on which accounting principles should be, but are not, based—that is, the reasoning as to why they are fair or unfair."[56] (1960)

As if to prove Spacek's point, a few years later in the Continental Vending case (1968) the auditors were found guilty of the criminal charge of gross negligence in spite of the fact that eight eminently qualified accountants testified in behalf of the defendants that the financial statements were prepared in accordance with "generally accepted accounting principles." The jury was simply charged to make their decision on the basis of whether the statements were "fairly presented." It is clear now that the courts will not allow accountants the shield of "generally accepted accounting principles." To a certain extent Spacek's concept of fairness has been forced upon the profession by the courts.

Spacek's own concept of "fairness" to user segments has directed him away from historical cost presentations toward current cost of price-level adjusted statements. Fairness to users would require reporting asset values at current values rather than at historical cost values which are irrelevant to current and future investment decisions. Thus, Spacek says:

"The change in price levels, coupled with deficiencies in accounting whereby costs are not properly capitalized, make carrying amounts for many assets in financial statements misleading and useless. The carrying amounts are far removed from current realities and present-day values."[57] (1970)

Although Spacek advocates recognition of current costs in the accounts through the use of price-level indices,[58] he would not go so far to consider income the change

[54] Spacek, "To Whom is the Profession Responsible and for What?" *A Search for Fairness, op. cit.,* p. 150.

[55] Spacek, "Accounting Is Being Challenged—Do We Have the Solution?" *ibid.,* p. 408.

[56] Spacek, "To Whom is the Profession Responsible and for What?" *ibid.,* p. 153.

[57] Spacek, "The Merger Accounting Dilemma—Proposed Solutions," *Financial Executive, op. cit.,* p. 42.

[58] *Ibid.*

in total value of the firm from year to year. Spacek is tied to the cost allocation principle although he would allocate current cost values to periods rather than historical cost:

"The real reason for charging depreciation to operations is to determine the true net income after a full provision for the fair value of the capital consumed in creating that income. The present practice of providing depreciation based upon cost is a rule that is rigid and meaningless as measured against the objective sought."[59] (1958)

Spacek's philosophy has been the force and impetus of his determination to reform the accounting profession. Throughout his speeches and articles he emphasizes the need for accounting to increase its service to the public through fairness in reporting.

V. A MAN'S CONTRIBUTION TO HIS PROFESSION

It is difficult to assess the effect that Spacek has had on the accounting profession and the development of accounting principles. No doubt he has had a significant effect even though his major original proposals—the Accounting Court and accounting for goodwill—have not been accepted by the profession. Formation of the APB soon after his controversial proposal for the Accounting Court may be an indicative effect. Formation of the Trueblood and Wheat Commissions to determine the objectives of accounting and how to determine accounting principles, respectively, may also be indicative effects. The Board's recent production of draft proposals for new opinions may also reflect Spacek's influence.

It is my opinion that Leonard Spacek has made a significant contribution to the development of accounting theory. At the very least, he has forced the profession to recognize its deficiencies and has started the profession moving from inertia. It may be that the profession will one day look back and recognize the leadership and foresight of a man, Leonard Spacek, and his contribution to his profession.

---

[59] Spacek, "Can We Define Generally Accepted Accounting Principles?" *ibid.*, p. 90.

BIBLIOGRAPHY

APB Opinion No. 2: "Accounting for the Investment Credit." New York: AICPA, 1962.

APB Opinion No. 4: "Accounting for the Investment Credit." (Amending No. 2). New York: AICPA, 1964.

APB Opinion No. 5: "Reporting of Leases in Financial Statements of Lessee." New York: AICPA, 1964.

APB Opinion No. 7: "Accounting for Leases in Financial Statements of Lessors." New York: AICPA, 1966.

APB Opinion No. 15: "Earnings per Share." New York: AICPA, 1969.

APB Opinion No. 16: "Business Combinations." New York: AICPA, 1970.

APB Opinion No. 17: "Intangible Assets." New York: AICPA, 1970.

APB Opinion No. 20: "Accounting Changes." New York: AICPA, 1971.

Accounting Research Division (AICPA). ARS No. 6: "Reporting the Financial Effects of Price Level Changes." New York: AICPA, 1963.

"Another Blast at Accounting Principles." Editorial, *Journal of Accountancy*, CXVIII (November 1964), pp. 39-40.

Arthur Andersen & Co. *Accounting for Income Taxes*. Chicago: Arthur Andersen & Co., 1961.

Arthur Andersen & Co. *Accounting for Leases*. Chicago: Arthur Andersen & Co., 1962.

Arthur Andersen & Co. *Accounting and Reporting Problems of the Accounting Profession*. Chicago: Arthur Andersen & Co., 1962.

Arthur Andersen & Co. *Establishing Accounting Principles—A Crisis in Decision Making*. Chicago: Arthur Andersen & Co., 1965.

Arthur Andersen & Co. *The First Fifty Years: 1913-1963*. Chicago: Arthur Andersen & Co., 1963.

Bedford, Norton M. "Goodwill," *Handbook of Modern Accounting Theory*. Edited by Sidney Davidson, New York: McGraw-Hill, 1970. pp. 19-1 to 19-24.

Black, Homer A. *ARS No. 9: Interperiod Allocation of Corporate Income Taxes*. New York: AICPA, 1966.

Catlett, George R. and Olson, Norman O. *ARS No. 1: Accounting for Goodwill*. New York: AICPA, 1968.

Chambers, Raymond J. *Accounting, Evaluation and Economic Behavior*. Englewood Cliffs, N. J.: Prentice-Hall, 1966, pp. 209-212.

"Comments of Leonard Spacek," *Accounting Research Study No. 1*. New York: AICPA, 1961, pp. 56-57.

"Comments of Leonard Spacek," *Accounting Research Study No. 3*. New York: AICPA, 1962, pp. 77-79.

"Comments of Leonard Spacek," *Accounting Research Study No. 10:* New York: AICPA, 1968, pp. 155-161.

Dunn, Keith W. Letter to the Editor, *Journal of Accountancy*, CVII (April, 1959), pp. 18, 20, 22.

Eiteman, Dean S. "Critical Problems in Accounting for Goodwill," *Journal of Accountancy*, Vol. 131 (March, 1971), pp. 46-50.

Grady, Paul. *ARS No. 7: Inventory of Generally Accepted Accounting Principles*. New York: AICPA, 1965.

Harmon, David Perry. "Pooling of Interests—A Case Study," *Financial Analyst's Journal*, XXIV (March-April 1968) pp. 82-88.

Hendriksen, Eldon S. *Accounting Theory*. rev. ed. Homewood, Ill.: Richard D. Irwin, Inc., 1970, pp. 432-440.

Hendriksen, Eldon S. "Toward Greater Comparability Through Uniformity of Accounting Principles," *Financial Accounting Theory II: Issues and Controversies*. Edited by Thomas F. Keller and Stephen A. Zeff. New York: McGraw-Hill, 1969, pp. 161-173.

"Letters Discussing the Spacek Proposal," *Financial Accounting Theory II: Issues and Controversies*. Edited by Thomas F. Keller and Stephen A. Zeff. New York: McGraw-Hill, 1969, pp. 336-345.

Louis, Arthur M. "The Accountants Are Changing the Rules," *Fortune,* LXXVII (June 15, 1968), pp. 177ff.

Louis, Arthur M. "A Fat Maverick Stirs Up the Accounting Profession," *Fortune,* LXXXII (December 1970), pp. 96ff.

"Maverick from the Midwest" *Business Week* (October 18, 1969), p. 128.

Moonitz, Maurice. *ARS No. 1: The Basic Postulates of Accounting.* New York: AICPA, 1961.

Myers, John H. *ARS No. 4: Reporting of Leases in Financial Statements.* New York: AICPA, 1962.

Ross, William W. Letter to the Editor, *Journal of Accountancy,* CXVIV (January 1965), p. 17.

Ross, William W. Letter to the Editor, *Journal of Accountancy,* CXX (November 1965), p. 29.

Spacek, Leonard. *A Search for Fairness in Financial Reporting to the Public.* 52 Selected Addresses and Articles, 1956-1969. Chicago: Arthur Andersen & Co., 1969.

Spacek, Leonard. "Are Accounting Principles Generally Accepted?" *Journal of Accountancy,* CXI (April 1961), pp. 41-46.

Spacek, Leonard. "Case for Income Tax Deferral," *New York Certified Public Accountant,* XVIII (April 1968), pp. 271-276.

Spacek, Leonard. Letter to the Editor, *Harvard Business Review,* XXXVII (July-August 1959), pp. 174, 178.

Spacek, Leonard. "The Merger Accounting Dilemma," *Financial Executive,* XXXVIII (February 1970), pp. 38ff.

Spacek, Leonard. "The Need for Unbiased Reporting," *NAA Bulletin,* XLIV (October 1962), pp. 3-9.

Spacek, Leonard. "Purpose and Use of Financial Statements," *The National Public Accountant,* XI (January 1966), pp. 12-3.

Spacek, Leonard. "What I Would Do if I Had to Live My Career Over Again," *The Arthur Andersen Chronicle,* XVIV (April 1959), pp. 107-115.

Sprouse, Robert T. and Moonitz, Maurice. *ARS No. 3: A Tentative Set of Broad Accounting Principles for Business Enterprises.* New York: AICPA, 1962.

Williams, Paul D. "Thirty-fifth Anniversary of Leonard Spacek," *The Arthur Andersen Chronicle,* XXIV (April 1964), pp. 23-28.

Wyatt, Arthur R. *ARS No. 5: A Critical Study of Accounting for Business Combinations.* New York: AICPA, 1963.